No Place Like Home

No Place Like Home

Women Philosophers' Struggles with Domesticity

SANDRINE BERGÈS

OXFORD
UNIVERSITY PRESS

OXFORD
UNIVERSITY PRESS

Oxford University Press is a department of the University of Oxford.
It furthers the University's objective of excellence in research, scholarship,
and education by publishing worldwide. Oxford is a registered trade mark of
Oxford University Press in the UK and in certain other countries.

Published in the United States of America by Oxford University Press
198 Madison Avenue, New York, NY 10016, United States of America.

Library of Congress Cataloging-in-Publication Data
Names: Bergès, Sandrine author
Title: No place like home: women philosophers' struggles
with domesticity / Sandrine Bergès.
Description: New York, NY : Oxford University Press, [2026] |
Includes bibliographical references and index.
Identifiers: LCCN 2025041990 (print) | LCCN 2025041991 (ebook) |
ISBN 9780197687383 hardback | ISBN 9780197687390 epub |
ISBN 9780197687413 | ISBN 9780197687406
Subjects: LCSH: Home—Philosophy | Women philosophers
Classification: LCC B105.P53 B47 2025 (print) | LCC B105.P53 (ebook)
LC record available at https://lccn.loc.gov/2025041990
LC ebook record available at https://lccn.loc.gov/2025041991

DOI: 10.1093/9780197687413.001.0001

Printed by Integrated Books International, United States of America

The manufacturer's authorized representative in the EU for product safety is
Oxford University Press España S.A. of Parque Empresarial San Fernando de Henares,
Avenida de Castilla, 2 – 28830 Madrid (www.oup.es/en or product.safety@oup.com).
OUP España S.A. also acts as importer into Spain of products made by the manufacturer.

Contents

Thinking About the Home   vii

1. A Room Somewhere   1

2. The Creation of the Spheres   17

3. The Spheres Begin to Melt   32

4. A Loom of One's Own   54

5. Of Home and Bondage   74

6. Revolutionary Matrons   94

7. New Architectures of Domestic Power   112

8. The Master's House   136

9. The Feminist at Home   156

Postface: Under the Rubble   173
Notes   177
References   187
Index   195

Thinking About the Home

Why should philosophers think about the home? The answer seems obvious: because home is central to human life and development. It keeps us alive, allows us to grow into ourselves, to develop relationships with others, and to function in the world, outside the home. Our question should really be: Why *don't* philosophers think about the home? And this book is my answer: they do, or at least women philosophers thought about the home. This is likely because, in the past, women had a closer relationship with home, often responsible for it, and confined in it. So I ask: What did these women philosophers think about the home, its work, its constraints? And though I do try to find out what we can learn from them, I will not look for a final lesson, something that we can all agree on about the meaning or value of the home. Rather, this work is about facilitating philosophical thinking about the home, from the point of view of women, whose central or chosen occupation was to think. Going into this book looking for a unified account or theory would definitely be a mistake. But if you like the idea of listening to voices from the past, women's voices, and think you can use their thoughts as a springboard for your own, then I hope you will enjoy this book.

The topic of domesticity has been on my mind for a rather long time. Twenty-two years ago, my second child was born. Fifteen years ago, he was diagnosed with autism. Because of where we lived, he ended up spending a lot more time than we'd anticipated at home, being cared for and home-schooled. He would also have to attend special education classes in various parts of town, where my husband or I would have to accompany him by bus. Between these practicalities and various other consequences of special needs education, our home life has been pretty much defined by this diagnosis. For us, home was always a place of work, a place of struggle, and (less often) a place of rest and comfort. The office, where I could work mostly undisturbed between classes and tutorials, was in many ways a place of rest. At first, my husband, Bill Wringe, and I juggled our timetables, with a great deal of help from our chair, Simon Wigley, and then we decided we could afford for the person who came to clean our home to come more often and keep our son company while we were taught. Münevver Özker, who transformed herself into a special needs carer, made life much easier for us, though I know she had a hard time some days. Home became again the place we came back to after work, and it was clean, if not calm. And then Covid-19 hit, and we lost that. I still had access to a space where I could work: our friend, Valerie Kennedy, was away in Scotland, so I walked to her flat every day to keep her cat, Ginger, company and to write. This is when I started working on this book, and focusing my thoughts and energy on that helped me deal with the trauma of everything that was going on at the time.

I would like to thank all the people who helped—knowingly or not—during the four years since I started working on this book. My husband, who, while I was writing about how men never do enough of the child care, prioritized looking after home and son so I could prioritize writing during the Covid-19 epidemic. My editor, Lucy Randall, was not only warmly encouraging, but was able to see what, in my proposal, was worth pursuing and what was not. Had it not been for her early advice, I would probably have gotten stuck half way through a bad rendition of the 'why do women do all the housework all the time' rant.

During the first two years of the pandemic, Alan Coffee, Eileen Hunt, and I set up a "Writers' Coven." We met every two weeks on zoom to discuss each other's work (and vent and gossip). They read through several versions of the proposal I sent Lucy and of my sample chapter. And they helped break through the sense of isolation we all felt at the time.

Once the Covid epidemic slowed down enough that I could travel again, I presented various parts of the book to conferences. I went to London to talk about Lucrezia Marinella's *Essortationi*, and got great feedback from Alan Coffee, Eric Schliesser, and Sarah Hutton. Then I took a paper on Cornelia Africana to the Centre for Eighteenth Century Studies at York, and to a conference in Berlin on Rewriting the History of Political Thought from the Margins, and again got very useful feedback from the audience. Then I took Lucrezia to the APA in New York and enjoyed a great discussion with my panel members, Martina Reuter and Michelle Kosch. Then I sent chapters around to friends and colleagues: Dorota Dutsch, Dan Wolt, and Carol Atack read and commented my chapter on the Greeks (hope they'll never tell how many mistakes I made in the Greek words!). Chuck Goldhaber gave me insightful comments on Sor Juana de la Cruz. Marguerite Deslauriers advised me about how to read Lucrezia Marinella, and shared her photos of the edition of the *Essortationi* she had from Biblioteca Aprosiana, in Ventimiglia.

She and I wish to acknowledge the Biblioteca Aprosiana, and the librarian, Giovanni Russo, for their help in accessing this material.

At any time, but especially during hard times, not much gets done without friends and family. So, I would like to thank those who have sustained me through the last few years, virtually and in person. My two children: they tolerated and sometimes enabled my work. My husband, Bill Wringe, who provided practical solutions to my finding places and time to work, and who read, commented, and advised me throughout. My sisters, Céline and Marianne Bergès, who are always just on the end of our messaging group; my parents, Anne-Marie Chaput and Christian Bergès; my husband's parents, Sally Barclay (whom we lost two years ago), Colin Wringe, and Gabrielle Heathcote; and my sister-in-law, Ally Wringe, all wrote and messaged weekly through Covid, keeping us tied to the people and countries we could not visit. I have many friends whose support I am grateful for, and if I forget some, I hope they won't mind. I'll just name the ones who were particularly close to us during the Covid-19 pandemic and the years that followed, when we all tried to reconstruct our social lives: Valerie Kennedy, Sibel Sayın, David and Ann-Marie Thornton, Louise Barry, Costa Costantino, and the Jonathans (Jonathan Williams and Jonathan Payton). It was noticeable that when, having lost all my capacities for normal socializing, I started going on about what I was reading or writing in a middle of a dinner conversation, they didn't try to shut me up, and they still (I hope) want to hang out with me now.

1

A Room Somewhere

Audrey Hepburn, as Eliza Doolittle in *My Fair Lady*, bursts into her first song dressed in a gaudy hat with mud on her face and tears in her coat. With a screeching cockney accent, she sings:

> All I want is a room somewhere
> Far away from the cold night air
> With one enormous chair
> Oh, wouldn't it be loverly.[1]

What Eliza, the heroine of *Pygmalion*—the George Bernhard Shaw play that inspired the musical—wants is a place of her own, where she can sit down after a day's work and where she can eat chocolate by the fire while cuddling up with a handsome man who looks after her well. Before she met with Professor Higgins, Eliza, a cockney flower girl, was living in poverty in a London slum, a room that wasn't "fit for a pig to live in" (Shaw 2004, 437). When Henry Higgins, a professor of phonetics, decided to treat her as an experiment and teach her to speak "proper English," Eliza moves into his home and gets her own, much nicer room. But the lyrics of the song suggest that she wants something more than a clean room of her own: a home with a husband, where she can "sit absobloominglutely still."

At the end of the play, Eliza has got some of what she wanted: a home above her own flower shop and a husband she has chosen for herself, the impoverished and rather silly aristocrat Freddy. She has comfort, love, and work that is much less arduous than selling flowers in the streets was. Yet, somehow, she seems to have disappointed everyone. She disappointed Professor Higgins, who managed to teach her to speak such good English she can now pass as a princess and thinks she'll be wasted on Freddy; her father, who was hoping she'd stay with Higgins and help him siphon money off him; and even her author, Shaw, who thinks that she was not ambitious enough, and that she'll soon find herself wishing she'd stayed single. What should Eliza have done? Higgins, hoping to keep Eliza to himself, wanted

No Place Like Home. Sandrine Bergès, Oxford University Press. © Oxford University Press USA 2026.
DOI: 10.1093/9780197687413.003.0001

her to continue sharing his home, to move her husband into her room on Wimpole Street, as she would a piece of furniture.² Or she could have tried to make something of herself, become independent, safe from poverty and preying men. But would that have been good enough for anyone?

Chances are it wouldn't. Eliza is not the only woman in the play portrayed as making an unusual choice. Her husband Freddy's sister, Clara, at first a pretentious and unpleasant woman, discovers literature and leaves home to join H. G. Wells's bohemian circle. Staying home, Clara's prospects were rather depressing: as an impoverished aristocrat she could not marry into her own class. So she would have spent her spinsterhood caring for aging parents. Now she is no longer respectable, but she is finding her own feet, becoming independent. Except that this is not quite good enough either. She makes mistakes of judgment and taste and she is mocked. She can be tolerated, maybe accepted, but she will never be a success. Like Eliza, she will never marry a rich man, and become a hostess in a beautiful home.

The message that stories like *Pygmalion* send is that the home, whether a woman chooses to be a homemaker or not, is never really a way to success or emancipation. Either one falls prey to tradition and accepts subordination unquestionably, or one becomes ridiculous in trying to live a life that, for a woman, society deems unnatural. This is of course a very male perspective on what a woman's place is supposed to be. And this perspective offers up contradictory edicts which—if they listen to them—place women in a double bind. They're damned if they're home, they're damned if they're not. It's likely that there are contradictions that are inherent in the very idea of "home" and not simply the product of a male perspective. But if we are serious about figuring out what is truly desirable about the home for women, and what is oppressive, it may be good to start with women's own perspectives. What does the home mean to women themselves? Is it a safe haven, or is it a cage? Does it exclude women from participating in political, professional, and social life, or is it a platform for them to grow their influence and affect social progress? Does it prevent societies from realizing gender equality by enforcing complementary roles on men and women? Or can it, instead, nurture so-called feminine qualities in young boys so that future generations may be less gendered? The questions are both urgent and fraught, as any couple, throuple, or moresome; heterosexual or queer; cis or trans, who've ever sat down to try and divide up domestic chores and child care will know.

While the World Economic Forum reckons that it will take over a hundred years to close the global gender gap, at least in some countries, women's lives are very different than it was just two generations ago.[3] Women go to university, women work outside the home.[4] The domestic lives of women—and the options for women to have any other kinds of lives—looked very different in centuries past. Still, as we'll see, voices from the past can help us think through some of the crucial questions women and families face today concerning the domestic realm. I'm hoping that bringing their perspectives to attention will help us reflect on these issues and perhaps help lessen the pressure of modern domestic life.

* * * * *

What is the home, anyway? What do we mean by domesticity? I won't try and define these terms in the analytic philosophical way of giving necessary and sufficient conditions for it. This isn't a game we have to play in order to say something meaningful about homes. And I suspect that if we did, we wouldn't find a definition that included all the things we may mean when we talk about homes. This is because there are too many different ways in which we use these words. "There's no place like home"—Dorothy's famous realization, suggests that home is a place, and usually a place where one can shelter from the outside world except for a few close family members. But it doesn't have to be. Home can be a sensory memory, which relates to one's experiences at some earlier time, but maybe not an actual building. It can be a feeling, a sense of security, the knowledge that there is somewhere you can go to lick your wounds or die. As Robert Frost writes in "The Death of the Hired Man": "Home is the place where, when you have to go there, They have to take you in."

Some places where people live do not deserve the name of "home": the "residential schools" where native American children were forcibly moved to, a prison cell where someone will end their lives, a hotel room, a spot under a bridge to lay a cardboard box, a refugee camp, and many other types of habitation where people are forced to spend large parts of their lives.

Domesticity, likewise, can mean many things. It can refer to a "sweet domestic scene," of a kitten playing with a child, or an elderly couple falling asleep together watching a movie after a day of caring for grandchildren. It can be a place of sexual intimacy, where people can engage in sexual intercourse with their chosen partners. Or it can refer to the work done by a poorly paid immigrant man or woman, cleaning toilets in rich people's houses. There is no real sense that the words refer to something specific.

When things are hard or impossible to define, when we can't find an actual set of sufficient and necessary conditions that help us decide what things are and aren't definitely the thing we are trying to define, philosophers sometimes appeal to the concept of family resemblance. One concept this works particularly well with is art. We all know what art is, and despite arguments about whether some particular things ("Comedian"—a banana duct-taped to a wall) or types of things (AI art) are art, people tend to recognize that something is meant to be art, and not, say, medicinal supplies or food. But things we recognize as art tend not to have enough in common to warrant a definition. What do George Romero's zombie film trilogy, Louise Bourgeois's giant spider sculpture, "Maman," and a Greek vase depicting an episode of the Troyan war have in common? How can they possibly belong to the same category? One reason we might say they do is that they share a family resemblance. In this case, they are very distant cousins. The movies and the vase both tell a story, albeit in very different ways. The vase and the sculpture both engage our attention through their plasticity: shape, material, and color. The sculpture and the movies perhaps don't have much in common (except insofar that their subject matter inspires horror, but that is specific to these works, or, in the case of the movies, to the genre they belong to, not to their artistic nature as such). But we can tell they are related because they are both related to the vase. This is how family resemblance works. Three siblings may share a number of family features among them, such as a nose, a coloring, but not in a systematic way. The firstborn may have the family nose and dark hair, the middle child may have the nose and light hair, and the youngest dark hair but a different nose. If we only see the middle and youngest child together, we might not guess they are related. But as soon as we see them together with the firstborn, we know they are.

Of course, not all features count as "family traits." In the case of siblings, they tend to be inherited features, or perhaps, features that we acquire as a habit of living together as a family—certain ways of talking, or posture. But dress, for instance, is not a relevant feature. Two people who dress alike are not thereby twins (no matter what your daughter and her kindergarten friend tell you). Also some people share traits without being at all related: my own mother once told me that my nose looked like Socrates (not a memory I cherish).

Unless you go at it with a DNA testing set (and a great trust in science), it's unlikely that establishing whether two people are really family members is going to be straightforward. The same goes for family resemblances writ

large. We have to rely, in great part, on things that are not scientific, not pre-
cise, not entirely objective to make our judgments. We'll need to bear in this
mind when trying to define "home." First, if we want to talk about homes
as sharing a family resemblance, we need to specify which features are relevant to something being a home. They need to be the sort of things that only
mostly home-type things would have. But we'll also have to be wary of the
"false negatives" of those things that share a trait that most homes share, but
that are definitely not homes, like the American residential schools, perhaps.
For a start, let's look at some candidates for a resemblance. I will focus on
three features—and I hope it will become clear why these three: the domestic
space, domestic work, and domestic relationships.

Homes come in very different shapes or size, can be made of different
stuff, and can be organized in various ways. A home can be a converted van,
a castle, a tepee, an igloo, a yurt, a Roman villa, a room in a shared house,
an apartment in a high rise, a cell in a medieval convent, and a straw bed in
a cupboard by the kitchen. But homes are also be the village where we were
born, the city or country where we would prefer to live, without being a specific location in that village, city, or country.

So what do a home country or ancestral village have in common with a
converted van, a convent, a villa, or a bedsit? Why do such things come to
mind when we think of home? The answer is family resemblance. Homes
aren't just places where we live, or where we'd like to live. They aren't just
shelters, or places where we may sleep, eat, and wash. They are that, of too,
but not necessarily all of that. And they are also more. Philosopher Emanuele
Coccia, in his book *Philosophy of the Home*, wanted to understand his relation to "being at home," how he could move in and out of dwellings and
grow roots every time. His thesis is that the home, or "domestic space"—
our first of three features—is about the family, the relationships of the
people, and the objects that populate that space. But the book itself ends
up very much being about the author's own relationships with the rooms
in the home, and the discussion remains very much at the metaphysical
level. A case in point: his relationship with the bathroom. He begins to talk
about how the bathroom was where he measured his penis as a child, and
moves on to questions of gender: what it means to be a man. But while his
reflections start from his own body, they don't stoop to other prosaic topics,
activities that typically take place in the bathroom, like cleaning the toilet.
This is what I call "domestic work," the second of the three features we're
focusing on.

Is cleaning the toilet essential to what it means to "be at home"? After all, there are toilets that need to be cleaned elsewhere: public toilets, office toilets, and airport toilets. Your home can be a tent in the wilderness: toilet-free. And more generally, the work of cleaning and cooking is not necessarily domestic, it happens wherever humans need to spend any amount of time, or even where they just pass through on their way to somewhere else. So why insist that cleaning or cooking are considered essential parts of the home?

Activity is how we tend to describe human life. What we do, and who we do it with makes us who we are. This is true from Aristotle—who believed that it is through our actions that we build character, and become virtuous or vicious—to the existentialists, who thought that the choices we make are what define us. But these choices, these acts, tend to happen in the public domain. We work, we study, we vote, we volunteer, we exhibit works of art, and we publish books. All these things define us, but only until the end of the day, when, tired, we go home to rest. Even those of us who work from home—in increasing numbers since 2020—try to distinguish between the workspace and the non-workspace in their home—even if it's just clearing a corner of the kitchen table. One of the most common complaints of working adults or school children during the Covid years was about having to share their workspace with everyday going-ons. In that sense, the home is not supposed to be a place of activity, it is a shelter from the outside world, the world where we do things. Post-Covid, we often feel the need to make sure the study door is closed when we come down for dinner. We find it easier to relax if the tools of our trade are not in plain sight. At home, we like to put our feet up, to share pleasant meal with our family, perhaps a glass of wine, and we rest our head on the pillow and sleep till the morning, when we have to start doing the things we do again.

This picture is precisely what early twentieth-century social philosopher, Charlotte Perkins Gilman, thought the home ought to be: a place to go to after one has exerted oneself for the public good and our own development.

> The home should offer to the individual rest, peace, quiet, comfort, health and that degree of personal expression requisite; and those condition should be maintained by the best methods of the time. (Gilman 2002)

And again:

[. . .] home was a place to come out from and go back to; the sweetest, dearest place—for there was mother, and father, and one's own little room to sleep in; but the day hours were to go somewhere to learn and do, to work and play, to grow in (1911, 206).

This second quote is from a piece of speculative fiction, a novel about a world which has achieved gender equality, where women do the same works as men, for equal pay, and very short hours. And homes have become free of the sort of work the nineteenth-century home (and indeed most homes now) required: all cleaning, washing, and cooking is done outside, by professionals. There is no "work" done inside the home.

What can we make of this? A male philosopher writing in the twenty-first century sees the home through the same lens as a woman philosopher writing a century earlier. But his work is a piece of philosophical analysis of what he perceives homes to be. Hers is science fiction. Have homes caught up with Gilman's fiction during the century that lies between her and Coccia? Certainly not. But the idea that home is or should be primarily a place of rest, and not of work, is still firmly in place, despite the challenge of rising home-work. The fact that for centuries, women and servants have had to work hard to make the home a place where people could be fed and rest at night seems to have escaped the notice of philosophers like Coccia, and possibly more generally of inexperienced men and women who dream of setting up their homes, and pick pretty couch cushions and ornaments, with very little thought of the work that keeping this home will involve. We mustn't make that mistake. If we are to define the home, we need to think of it as a place where work happens.

Coccia, as an author, works from home. He reads, he writes, he thinks. He sends emails and does videoconferencing. Philosophers have always done that: Descartes didn't have an office in a university; he wrote from home. And nowadays, many of us work from home, selling, buying, managing, editing, and designing. But the work I refer to here is not the professional or paid work that the home's inhabitants choose or have to do to earn a living. It is the work of maintaining the home, work that has historically fallen to women, the unpaid "lady of the house," her poorly paid servants, or even enslaved women. And this work is still being done, whether or not people are doing their paid job from home.

In interview, Coccia admitted that before Covid, he only spent time at home to write, and that if he could, he would only ever sleep in hotel rooms. So perhaps his perspective on what it means to be at home is a little skewed, and perhaps he is not the best person to write about it. But he does raise the question what else we need to define the home, in the loose sense of establishing a set of family resemblances, aside from the building itself. The home, he says, is determined by who lives there together, partners, parents, siblings, or children, and the dynamics that develop between them as they share a living space. This is our third feature, "Domestic Relationships."

Coccia's thesis is not new. A home, if we derive the concept from the ancient Greek one, *oikeo*, is a household: not just a place, but the people who live there, and their relationships to each other. There are those who are in charge (typically the husband or father), those who obey and do the work (the wives, the servants, or slaves), and those who are being raised and cared for (the children). And while Coccia thinks of the home as the dwelling place of the nuclear family, homes can be a lot more open. There are of course domestic employees who clean or look after children, or au pairs whose role maybe simply to expose the family to a different language or culture. Guests can also become part of the household for a period of time. And relatives, beyond the nuclear family, sometime move in either to help with the work or to be cared for.

If we now put all of three "domestic" features together, we can see that there is not one single model for the home. Instead, we have different types of living arrangements that share some (but not all) common features among those created by the three categories we considered: place, work, and relationships. Imagine a few: the single woman living in a van, traveling for work; the foster family with a house full of children; the nuclear family; the village house with four generations living and working together; the roommates who use a household chores sharing app to divide up the work; the rich couple who pay a woman to come and clean for them every day; and more—there is not one single model for the home. But all things we call "home" or use the adjective "domestic" to describe are related, they share some features with each other, sometimes one (or more) step removed. This means we have no trouble relating to the band Pulp's Jarvis Cocker when he sings "I'm the man who stays home and does the dishes" as well as Eliza Doolittle's desire to snuggle up and eat chocolate, Orphan Annie's "Hard Knock Life," and Tom Jones' "Green, Green Grass of Home." All tell us about things that we like and don't like about the home (and notice the trend here: housework rarely makes the "pros" column).

Home then, and more generally all that is "domestic," may be defined, loosely, as a combination of these three factors: the physical domestic space; the domestic work of cooking, cleaning, and caring; and the domestic relationships with other members of the households. And these three factors are bound to affect each other: a small flat is less work to clean than a larger one, but it's also claustrophobic for its inhabitants and can harm relationships. Having a partner who likes to dominate may make life in a beautiful house unbearable. And having to spend a great part of the day cleaning, when that work isn't fairly shared, may lead to resentment and have negative effects on one's relationship with a partner or children.

I now want to turn to a particular problem with the home that concerns me here and concerned the women philosophers of the past whom we'll soon meet. That problem is that of freedom, and whether it is achievable for those who have to spend a lot of time in their homes. Because a home typically requires money—to buy, rent, or just maintain—and work—to keep everyone in it clean and fed, and perhaps happy—relationships of domination are likely to develop. The physical home is a confined space, and its upkeep requires time and effort, so that household members who are in charge of the work may end up feeling or being restricted in their freedom to move in and out of the home. On the other hand, at least one person in the household needs to be able to earn money by work they do either from home or outside of the home. If this is an all-consuming task for one person, perhaps the other is more focused on the daily demands of maintaining the household in other respects—and this role could be played by a man or a woman. (Same-sex couples will figure out the division of labor while steering free of the potential pitfalls of the traditional, fraught, male/female, professional/domestic divide.) And of course, as many households do, both members of a couple could each bear shared responsibility not only for earning but also for home upkeep and childrearing, or for caring for the pets and cooking meals. Permutations abound. So there is no inherent reason why the conflation of domestic needs and financial ones for the household's survival should result in domination of women by men. There is no reason why both types of work can't be shared, or regarded as equally valuable by all parties, and rewarded with equal access to freedom and relaxation. And this is what many families are now moving toward, if they haven't already achieved it. But we know that this is very much work in progress, and that historically, home hasn't been a place of equality, in particular gender equality, but one of domination. For women philosophers in the past, this meant that if they wanted to think about freedom, it made sense to start by thinking about the home. Charity, the saying goes, starts at home. So does freedom, and for those who spend most of their time confined to the home, home may be the only place they can achieve freedom.

* * * * *

However we tell it, wherever we start, the history of the home seems to be bound up with the history of women's subordination to men and of the division of the spheres, or, in other words, the story of how women became unfree. The place of women in the development of humankind, state-of-nature theories, the advent of agriculture which led to the supposed end of nomadic life, the disadvantages brought on by motherhood—all these threads are tangled together, producing a large Gordian knot, the sight of which leads us to nod wisely and say that yes, all this was inevitable, what a shame.

The premise that women were domestically bound as soon as fixed abodes came into being is highly questionable but rarely questioned. Certainly, most of those who make that claim have no evidence that it is so, and while there is a tradition of saying this in anthropological essays which goes back at least to the nineteenth century, again, there is very little evidence for any of the claims made in support of women's early domestic bondage.[5] But the habit of saying so is hard to break. Even Simone de Beauvoir floundered:

> This world has always belonged to males, and none of the reasons given for this have ever seemed sufficient. By reviewing prehistoric and ethnographic data in the light of existentialist philosophy, we can understand how the hierarchy of the sexes came to be. We have already posited that when two human categories find themselves face-to-face, each one wants to impose its sovereignty on the other; if both hold to this claim equally, a reciprocal relationship is created, either hostile or friendly, but always tense. If one of the two has an advantage over the other, that one prevails and works to maintain the relationship by oppression. It is thus understandable that man might have had the will to dominate woman: but what advantage enabled him to accomplish this will? (2009, 96).

Beauvoir was of course following in the footsteps, not just of the nineteenth-century anthropologists, but also of the eighteenth-century state-of-nature theorists, who, with Hobbes and Rousseau at the helm, wrote an imaginary—that is, fake—history of humankind. Under the guise of building a hypothetical framework which would serve as thought experiment for the study of injustice, Rousseau decreed that human beings started off as nomadic individuals but later gathered into small villages. This, he claimed, was the point at which man discovered the full value of "his female"—not only as a provider of companionship and children, but also as someone who is good at keeping the hut clean.

> The first developments of the heart were the result of a new situation which united husbands and wives, fathers and children in one common habitation. The habit of living together gave rise to the sweetest feelings known to men, conjugal and paternal love. Each family became a small society, all the more united since reciprocal attachment and freedom were its only bonds. And it was then that the first difference was established in the ways of life of the two sexes, which up to this point had had only one. The women became more sedentary and grew accustomed to looking after the hut and the children, while the man went off to search for their common sustenance. In this way, through a slightly softer life, the two sexes began to lose something of their ferocity and vigour. But if each one separately became less ready to fight against savage beasts, on the other hand it was easier to gather together to resist them in common.[6]

The prehistoric and ethnographic data Beauvoir mentions pretty much repeat what the state-of-nature theorists of the Enlightenment were saying: it was the advent of agriculture and the settlement of family groups that came with it which brought about women's subordination. Rousseau says it, and modern science says it. Except that it doesn't anymore. It turns out that prehistoric data shows no such thing, and that the evolution of human tribes from hunter-gatherers to agricultural villages to national states is a bit of a myth.[7] Human history (and prehistory) is far more complicated and far more interesting than the simple, convenient, recycled stories would tell us, and it's impossible to pinpoint a time or a place when injustice or the oppression of a particular class set in. Injustice and oppression, including the gendered kind, it turns out, come and go as much as much as anything else. They are not necessary features of human existence.

We probably shouldn't be surprised at such debunking: Why would twenty-first-century science conveniently agree with the stories imagined by the eighteenth-century philosophers? This coincidence should have raised serious alarm bells with anyone not interested in maintaining the gendered hierarchical *status quo*. Except it didn't. We are far too ready to trust learned men or women. But it's critically important that we don't tell tall tales about why women so often end up in the kitchen instead of in political office, that we don't pretend we know the reasons and causes of oppressions, and that they are so clear as to render the situation immutable. The reasons are complex, and their histories reflect many twists and turns which show how things may have gone differently, how they did go differently sometimes, and how women themselves were actors in their destinies and not just victims of historical shifts.

This is one reason why, in this book, I take care to look at many periods, many places, and many women. There isn't one history of domesticity, one reason why we have the second shift,[8] why women who iron their husband's shirts don't get paid for it, or why parents have to negotiate much of the burden of caring for the next generation in their homes. There are many reasons, many historical prompts, and, therefore, many ways to fight back and reclaim the freedom to live and flourish outside, as well as inside, the home. And while this is no longer entirely the case—women work outside the home and are economically independent, men do more housework and childcare than they ever did—historically, it was mostly women who experienced the home as a place of work and domination. So it is perhaps no surprise that it is mostly women who have found interesting philosophical things to say about the home.

* * * * *

In this book, I will look at the home and the ways it can both prevent and enable freedom, taking the perspective of women philosophers, from antiquity to the twenty-first century, from Japan to Mexico, and Constantinople to Boston. What I hope to do is reinstate the home as a philosophical problem, worthy of inquiry. I say reinstate because now the home just doesn't feature in the sort of philosophical debate you can have at university or read in books on the history of philosophy. As things are, we would be forgiven for thinking that home and domesticity were new problems for philosophers, brought to light, maybe by Simone de Beauvoir in the *Second Sex*. But in fact, the home was only absent from (historically recorded) philosophy because the women were. Men did not, bar a few exceptions, regard the home as a source of philosophical questions. But women certainly did, and this is what I mean to show here: bringing up their perspectives on the home enables us to study that problem in all its historical richness and variety.

What I hope to show is that the home, whatever form it may take, works both as an enabler and preventer of women's freedom and flourishing, both as a springboard for their participation in political society (though often not in what we now consider the traditional form of the home) and as a source of oppression and domination, and so a place to escape from. As with most philosophical problems, domesticity can and should be investigated to work out which of the various aspects I have highlighted here should be developed and which should be quashed. The point is that we have a history of philosophical reflection on the home, we are not at sea, and we have the tools to draw our own conclusions. Some of mine will become apparent over the course of the book, but mainly, I hope to prompt readers to engage in their own philosophical reflections about the home, taking the work of women past as their springboard.

Chapter 2 looks at the women who were present at the creation of the spheres, women from Ancient Greece and Rome. These women had possibly the least freedom any woman has had since, because, aside for a few exceptions, they were confined to their homes, allowed out on special occasions, and always covered and heavily chaperoned. Chapter 2 begins with stories of Xanthippe, Socrates's wife, and a most undomestic woman, who often serves as a warning to men to train their wives better. I'll then look at texts by women philosophers who seem to accept their lack of freedom and try to understand it in terms of virtue. In Chapter 3, I introduce Anna Komnene (eleventh-century Constantinople), Christine de Pizan (fifteenth-century France), and Sei Shōnagon (tenth-century Japan). These women, in very different contexts, all found themselves having to negotiate freedom and relationships to the ruling elite without crossing the lines between the spheres—they exercised their freedom without ever really claiming it.

Women in the seventeenth century had perhaps more freedom to educate themselves than they did during most of the Middle Ages, but they were still very much limited in their lives and careers, that is, they could live at home or in a convent, serving a husband or God. But what some of them had, to some extent, was the freedom to argue back, to philosophize about why they should be free. Chapter 4 looks at how three women philosophers of that period attempted to subvert their domestic destiny either by rejecting the role they were expected to fulfill and working on philosophy or by trying to enrich their domestic lives by drawing connections between the work done to sustain life and philosophy, either at home or in a convent. I start with Venetian philosopher Lucrezia Marinella's last work, *Exhortations to Women and Others If They Please*, and I argue that she attempted to revalue domestic work, by making it an appealing proposition for women for whom intellectual pursuits were not an option. I will then turn to English philosopher Margaret Cavendish, who worked out ways in which domesticity not only supported philosophy but could also be read as a form of scientific pursuit. Last, Sor Juana Ines de la Cruz, who used the convent where she lived as a base for writing and disseminating feminist critiques of Aristotle. Joining a convent appears to have been to leave the constraints of home, but not its works. Perhaps, I conclude, what is binding about domestic work is not so much the work itself as the inevitability of its distribution within the family.

The women discussed in Chapter 4 looked for ways to participate in the progress of the Enlightenment, whether in philosophy, religion, or science, from a home or a convent, sometimes using the tools of domesticity. But in the eighteenth century, women's ambition took on a more political turn. They began to ask more pointedly how they could be free, even when they were confined to a home. Chapter 5 looks at what women who wrote in English and had ties with England thought about domestic power structures, and particularly about the compatibility of freedom and domesticity. I begin with Mary Astell's *Reflections on Marriage* and make my way to the end of the century with Mary Wollstonecraft's works, and finally, Mary Prince's *Narrative*.

Chapter 6 takes us to France, at the end of the eighteenth century. The French Revolution was a philosophical moment in history where politics and domesticity were not incompatible. This enabled women to participate in politics in several ways. Some women philosophers, Marie-Jeanne Phlipon Roland, Louise Keralio Robert, and Olympe de Gouges, wanted political influence but thought they could either exercise it from within their homes or combine a life that crossed over the two spheres, so that they could be political while fulfilling their duties as wives and mothers. The republican home was supposed to be a place of freedom and virtue, a merging of the public and the private sphere, and a place where political ideals and reforms could be born and nurtured. Yet as these women's influence became more visible, they were severely repressed. Unfortunately, they were not able to hold on to this freedom, and by the time Napoleon was emperor, they lost any foothold they had created for themselves to enable them to participate in the politics that could free them.

The progress made in Europe in the eighteenth century seems to have all but disappeared from the nineteenth century, in particular in England and North America where family life was dominated by the concept of the "angel in the house"— a woman bound to her domestic work and incapable of living a more politically active life. Chapter 7 looks at the role of the home in nineteenth-century America from the point of view of three white women social philosophers, Catharine Beecher, Angelina Grimké, and Charlotte Perkins Gilman. The debate between Beecher and Grimké vividly illustrates how feminist discourse was tied in many ways to slavery. The conservative Beecher wants women to stay home and out of the fight for abolitionism, while Grimké wants all emancipated. Beecher and Perkins Gilman also provide an interesting contrast. Both were critical of the angel in the house picture of domesticity. But Beecher thought it could be defended, provided women were given the right kind of education: she was the first to propose that domestic science be taught in schools. Perkins Gilman argued that with the best education women could not and should not be confined to domestic work. We will look at her arguments for a reform of the home and ask whether these reforms could in fact achieve social progress for all women.

Nineteenth-century African American women writers also debated domesticity—with more urgency, as having a home of their own was for many of them still an impossibility. People who had been enslaved and were now nominally free needed to settle on some domestic arrangement that did not depend entirely on the plantation. They needed a new setting for their freedom. This is what we'll talk about in Chapter 8. Frances Harper argued that acquiring domestic habits was—for both men and women, but with the responsibility resting on women—crucial to the progress in America of those who had been previously enslaved. She was joined by Anna Julia Cooper who believed that educated, domestic Black women were the key to social progress. At the same time, some Black women writers such as Harriet Jacobs and Sojourner Truth were itinerant lecturers who did not make it a priority to set up a home for their families. Freedom—their own, but also that of others— was the goal to work for. The contrast between these philosophers' various takes on the role of domesticity will give us a better grasp on what is and is not at stake in the debate on the value of the home. Is having a home essential to human flourishing and freedom, and in particular to human beings' freedom to participate in society? Or is it a way of helping some human beings (men) participate to the full by keeping others (women) working for them in the home? Are there ways for human beings to flourish and be free that don't involve a traditional domestic setup?

Chapter 9 concludes by bringing us back to Simone de Beauvoir, this time in dialogue with Betty Friedan, author of the *Feminine Mystique*. What do these two middle-class twentieth-century white women really tell us about the home and how to be free? How much can we learn from them? And where should we go from there?

2

The Creation of the Spheres

Pericles, the famed politician of the Peloponnesian wars, once gave a funeral oration to comfort the grieving Athenian population.[1] This was the first year of the war, and many had lost sons, husbands, fathers, and brothers. To each, Pericles offered a piece of wisdom to live by: parents should know that their children died happy, because they died for their city, children that their fathers or older brothers were virtuous, and that they should seek to emulate them as they grow older. To the Athenian women, he gave the following advice: they should avoid being the subject of talk—for better or for worse, that is, live their lives in the obscurity of their home and not distinguish themselves in any way: "The greatest glory of a woman belongs to she who is least spoken of among men, whether for good or for bad."[2]

Plato, in one of his dialogues, tells us that the speech in question had been written by Pericles's mistress, Aspasia, a foreign resident from the colony of Miletus.[3] How ironical that his famous pronouncement about women's discretion should be written by a woman. But Pericles remained true to his (or her) principles, by making sure she did not get the credit for his words. It is Plato who, by announcing it to the world, who breaks the rule.

One woman who seems to have failed entirely to take up Pericles's advice that women should be neither seen nor heard was Xanthippe, Socrates' younger second wife. Socrates was in his fifties when he married her, and already had two sons by another woman, Myrto. Myrto was also married to Socrates, but it's not clear whether it was before or during his marriage to Xanthippe. It is possible he was married to both at the same time, through some legal loophole that allowed men to marry more than once, if it was for the purpose of legitimizing children. In any case, we know nothing of Myrto's life, which means that she was probably deserving of what Pericles called a woman's glory, that is, she was not spoken of. This was not the case for Xanthippe. In the *Phaedo*(66b), the dialogue in which Plato paints a moving picture of Socrates on his death day, Xanthippe is portrayed as having a bit of a reputation. She is "known" to Socrates' disciples, Plato tells us—and you can feel his eyebrow rising—even to those who come from distant foreign cities.[4]

No Place Like Home. Sandrine Bergès, Oxford University Press. © Oxford University Press USA 2026.
DOI: 10.1093/9780197687413.003.0002

And no one is surprised when they hear that Socrates had her thrown out of his cell because she was making too much noise (she was crying). That's just the sort of thing that would happen when you are married to someone like Xanthippe. We find plenty of anecdotes about her in the ancient gossip literature to back this up.[5] In one story, she throws a pot of water—or was it water?!—on her husband after an argument. Socrates shrugged and said: "I knew that after her thunder, rain would come." Another story tells how she chased after Socrates in the marketplace and tore his coat off him. His friends thought she was a proper shrew and wondered why Socrates tolerated her.[6] Socrates just replied: "Because she is my wife and the mother of my children."[7]

Xanthippe had plenty of reasons to be angry and want to throw stuff at her husband.[8] Whether Socrates expected it or not, she had to run his home and bring up his children. There was no financial security as Socrates was not working, and she had to rely on handouts from his rich friends. But then she also had to cater for those same friends, when Socrates brought them home, with no notice at all. And she had to serve them whatever she could get her hands on and worry that they wondered what she did with the money they kept giving her, because the rich never really know how hard it is to make ends meet.

Xanthippe was probably, as other women have been since, the victim of her husband's ill-thought-out ideology: her life was not regulated by the sort of superficial social mores Socrates disliked, but nor was it an "examined life," as he recommended for his male acquaintances. Xanthippe might have been less angry had she been instead encouraged to follow Socrates around the marketplace, asking and answering questions. Keeping house on a budget is no easy task, even when one is well established in a particular section of society. Older husbands were expected to help younger wives learn how to do this. But Socrates had no interest in "training" Xanthippe to be a proper housewife. Scornful as he was of material comfort, why would he care for a good housekeeper? But then what was Xanthippe supposed to do with herself and their children? Could she leave the children to fend for themselves and join Socrates' followers (who were all men, and all aristocratic and educated)? And if she couldn't, or wasn't welcome, then shouldn't Socrates have helped her make her homelife easier for her, and at the same time more comfortable for himself? This is a question that Xenophon put to Socrates in his *Symposium*. If Socrates thinks that men should educate their wives to serve them better (as he had just argued), then why didn't Socrates educate

Xanthippe? Xenophon's Socrates answered that living with Xanthippe as she was—like a wild horse, untrained and intractable—would help prepare him to interact with humanity at its worse. That, he concluded, was the most valuable thing she could do for him.[9] He does not ask what he can do for her—but that was not the question put to him. On Xenophon's account, Socrates had a reason for treating his wife as he did, and that reason was entirely to do with his own well-being as a philosopher, and he was apparently willing to sacrifice Xanthippe's well-being to that. Xanthippe, like many women after her, was forced to live the applied philosophy of her husband, but without any help in implementing the principles, and under the blind assumption that the principles had to be right, and that failure would always be her fault, and her responsibility to fix.[10]

According to Pericles, women can speak but they should not be spoken of. This imposes serious limitations on respectable women's freedom of expression in Athens: whatever they say should be unremarkable enough that no one will want to repeat it. And it should not be written down in such a way that others might read it. This leads to the conundrum: if we cannot have any first-person testimony from women who had the relevant experience of being housewives in ancient Greece, how can we now have any informed discussion of what it was like to be a housewife then? Yet Classical Greece set the tone for many later writings on domesticity—it established a story of the creation of the private and public, or domestic and political spheres. Yet that story is not quite as simple as it may seem. Certainly Aristotle, in particular, has a lot to answer for when he famously argues that women are by nature incapable of political reasoning and so should stay home. But his was not the only voice that carried through to later readers. Stoic philosophers in the first and second century proposed a subtly different picture of the sphere and of the roles men and women were expected to play in them. And while there are many issues with attribution (who really wrote those texts?), we do have a series of philosophical fragments signed by neo-Pythagorean women discussing the domestic arrangements of antiquity.

Here, I'll try to gather whatever philosophical evidence we have for the confined domesticity of ancient Greek and Roman women, and recover whatever voices are there to be recovered, so as to create the richest possible picture of an ancient philosophy of home. And what the evidence shows was that the topic of the home was clearly not undervalued then by philosophers as it is now. Philosophers spent time and effort writing about household management, and how that contributed to human development. The science of the home, *oikonomia*, was then as important as its English derivative, economics, is to us now. And its influence, now obscured, lasted until at least the eighteenth century, in particular, in the works of women philosophers. It is therefore crucial to this project that we start by looking at some of the texts of antiquity that discussed the home.

Homes and Cities

There are many narratives of the creation of the domestic sphere, and of its separation from the public or political sphere. Many of them, we saw in Chapter 1, take place in hunter-gatherer societies; they are the least well-documented, the least plausible, and also the most popular.[11] But they are also tied to the Middle Ages, where European women were supposedly locked in their homes, with a chastity belt, while their husbands went to fight in the Crusades, Early Modern England, where Protestant religious sects rediscovered the value of wives as helpmeets,[12] the Industrial Revolution, Rousseau,[13] the French Revolution,[14] and the nineteenth century's "True Womanhood" movement.[15] Perhaps these were all steps in an overall movement, each consolidating the separation of women and men's worlds. Or perhaps they were fresh attempts each time, never quite succeeding but always trying to keep women in the home, and out of politics. In any case, as we saw in Chapter 1, it's likely that there is not one origin of the separation of the spheres but a myth, told and retold, hiding more complicated truths about the evolution of the relationship between men and women.[16] Some of these narratives come from philosophers who tried, at several moments in history, to delineate separate spheres for men and women. These were influential narratives which, as they supported the social *status quo*, were not openly or successfully challenged, and therefore came to tinge each following generation of philosophical views with their prejudice. More than simply stories, they offer justifications for the separation of men and women's worlds and conceptualize it so that future generations of philosophers can further develop these justifications, fit them into their own arguments. In that sense, they are more harmful than simple myths: they shape not just what we believe, but how we form our beliefs.

As some of the earliest and perhaps most influential incidence of such arguments can be found in the writings of Ancient Greek and Roman philosophers—men philosophers mostly, but at least some which are attributed to women authors—it makes sense to start here.

One, fairly well-known Ancient Greek origin of the spheres stories goes something like that: Aristotle argued that there were two main units of human association: the home and the city-state. Though the home is a natural necessity (for shelter, and for bringing up children), it is the city-state that truly enables human flourishing. Human beings, for Aristotle, are political animals. As animals they need a home for their individual survival as well as that of the species. But as political animals they need a place where they can convene to discuss justice and to find ways of instantiating it in their communal lives. Unfortunately, Aristotle tells us, not all human animals are capable of this sort of flourishing. To partake in a political life, one needs a certain degree of what he calls practical reason, the ability to put together what we know about the world, what we want for ourselves, and turn it into good decisions. Free men have this, he says, but women and slaves don't. Slaves, Aristotle say, have just enough reason to be able to obey simple instructions but they lack the deliberative element to understand them. Women have sufficient practical reason to obey their husbands in a more reflective manner, and to manage some aspects of the household, but not to do politics. So it is better for everyone if women stay home and supervise the work their husbands have ordered, while their husbands go to the Agora and debate politics.[17]

It was Aristotle who started the trend of thinking about home philosophically, as a sphere parallel to the public sphere. But many other philosophers, men and women, Stoics, Epicureans, and neo-Pythagoreans took it up. It is not clear when the home stopped mattering philosophically. But it was a good long while before philosophers stopped discussing the home, and its role in human life and development. Women philosophers, in particular—as we'll see in the coming chapters—spent time reflecting on the ideas and arguments developed by Aristotle and other philosophers of Ancient Greece and Rome and used them to develop their own.

What I propose to do here, and as I go through excerpts and treatises, is to find the sources that women used to talk about the home. And I will show that there were two main positions. The first is that the home is superficially like a small city, but essentially very different, because men and women are essentially different. The second is that the home really is a small city, and that a large city is nothing but a grouping of homes that support each other in their pursuit of survival and happiness. In the first narrative, the distinction between the spheres is strict and principled, and women's role is very limited even in the home, where she can only manage according to her husband's orders. In the second narrative, it is easier for men and women to share duties at home, and for women to have a say in political matters. The separation of the spheres is still very real, and an obstacle to women being fully political, but this is due to unbreakable social laws rather than natural ones.

Both positions, sometimes mixed, have influenced later philosophical musings on the home and the distinction of spheres of activity for men and women. Understanding that there were at least two basic positions helps us gain a clearer and deeper perspective on later philosophical developments.[18] So I'll ask you to bear with me, for a few pages, while we look at what men wrote about the home. In the final part of the chapter, I promise, we'll come back to women writing.

Aristotle

There are two major works which were, for a long time, both attributed to Aristotle and which discussed how human beings live together. The *Politics* discusses the *polis*, or city-state, and the *Economics*, discusses the *oikos*, or the household.[19] But the household features in both texts. In his *Politics*, Aristotle suggests that the household, while a necessary and natural element of human flourishing, does not reflect human essential nature in the way that the city, that is, a political association, does:

> Some people think that the qualifications of a statesman, king, house-holder, and master are the same, and that they differ, not in kind, but only in the number of their subjects. For example, the ruler over a few is called a master; over more, the manager of a household; over a still larger number, a statesman or king, as if there were no difference between a great household and a small state. [...] **But all this is a mistake, as will be evident to anyone who considers the matter according to the method which has hitherto guided us.** (*Politics* Book I, 1252a9–15, my emphasis)[20]

The household cannot be the same sort of thing as the city-state, because it is not a political association. It cannot be political association simply because there is only one member of the household qualified for public life. He is the master of his wife, children, and slaves, but cannot associate with them as equals, and therefore cannot develop a political relationship with them. In order to be political, a man needs to leave his home and go to the city, where he can meet with other free men and attend to the most important part of his nature and flourishing:

> Hence it is evident that the state is a creation of nature, and that man is by nature a political animal. (1253a1–2)

In Book I of the *Economics*, the message is subtly different. It suggests a stronger tie between the home and the city, but also that the good the home brings is part of human flourishing, rather than simply necessary for human survival:

> Now a city is an aggregate made up of households and land and property, self-sufficient with regard to a good life. This is clear from the fact that, if men cannot attain this end, the community is dissolved. (*Economics*, I, 1343a10–13)

"Aggregate" here means number, or quantity.[21] "Economic" means science of the home, "oikeo." So it is not the way in which the households are arranged together that makes them sufficient for the good life, but simply the fact that there are many. Each household is seeking the good life, and they achieve their goal either by joining together into a city or by separating again.

The difference between the two texts is significant. In the *Economics*, it is simply size that matters. If you have only your household to rely on, you might struggle to achieve self-sufficiency, you may grow your own food, but you'll be hard put to find someone who can repair shoes and fix the plumbing, and you'll have to rely on the people you live with for your entertainment—no theater or parties. So your life will be diminished, but it will still be human. The *Politics* says something quite different, that you just can't fully exercise (and develop) your humanity without a political structure. Why can't a home be a political structure? Given what Aristotle says elsewhere in the *Politics*, it is because the head of the household is a man, and he rules as a king over women, children, and slaves. And according to Aristotle, women don't have the requisite form of reason to be considered political equals, children's reasoning capacity is underdeveloped, and slaves have none. So the master of the house finds himself the sole being capable of politics, and he needs to move in circles outside the home in order to exercise this capacity.

Whatever Aristotle thinks about the value of the home, and its role in human happiness, he is very clear about one thing: the private and the public spheres should be clearly separated, and their work attributed according to gender. Only men can do politics, and women must stay in the home. In Book III of the *Economics*, he explains why it would be wrong for a man and woman to exchange responsibilities:[22]

> [The house], then, is the province over which a woman should be minded to bear an orderly rule; for it seems not fitting [*indecens*] that a man should know all that passes within the house. [...] considering that it is less un-seemly [*turpe*] for him to deal with a matter within the house than it is for her to pry into those outside its walls. It is fitting that a woman of well-ordered life should consider that her husband's uses are as laws appointed for her own life by divine will, along with the marriage state and the fortune she shares.

Aristotle establishes moral barriers to the crossing over of spheres. I leave the Latin words in the passage as they are so much more suggestive than the tamer English ones. And if the Latin text is a translation of Aristotle's Greek, then it is likely that *turpe* (in English we have "turpid") stands for *aischos*, which is a very strong condemnation of shamefulness in 4th BC Greek. So what Aristotle is saying here is that crossing over from the private to the public sphere is one of the worst things a woman can do in moral terms, and that for a man to cross over from the public to the private is also really quite disgraceful. This is momentous: Is Aristotle responsible for the fact that still some men today still don't know how to load a dishwasher or vacuum the floor?

This is when the objections come in: Aristotle never said that; no one believes anymore that he wrote the *Economics*. It's true that the authenticity of the *Economics* as a work of Aristotle's has been seriously doubted, but it's less clear where the doubt comes from.[23] It's hard not to suspect that it's the subject matter which makes people want to discount. We think of Aristotle as the father of all branches of science. Economics counts as a science, as politics does. But that's economics in the sense of wealth or production man-agement, not in its original sense of household management. The science of household management is now known in English as "home economics," a topic which until recently was taught to young women in schools. This may well have something to do with the devaluation of the topic for serious philosophers, and the falling into disrepute of Aristotle's book. Indeed, the last of the English language commentaries on Aristotle's *Economics* correspond roughly to the birth of "home economics" as a discipline taught to girls in schools in the United Kingdom and the United States.

Would it have made a difference if the text were still taught? It is worth emphasizing that while the *Economics* still contains a great deal of sexist views and arguments, it does at least take seriously the idea that the home is necessary for the good life. In Ancient Greek terms, that makes it a topic for philosophers to think about. Reading the *Economics* as an Aristotelian text may also have led to more willingness to take seriously the discussions of the home by later Greek and Roman philosophers, such as Musonius Rufus, Hierocles the Stoic, and the group of writers sometimes called the neo-Pythagoreans. These writers made claims about the home that shaped later discourses on the public and private spheres. But they were partially erased from the philosophical corpus, so their influence was very limited. This is a glance at what could have been.

The Stoics

While Aristotle is usually blamed for being the father of arguments for the oppression of women, some philosophers look to the Stoics for a better attitude to gender. One favorite is the first-century Roman Stoic philosopher Gaius Musonius Rufus.[24] Musonius sets out his view of domesticity in a series of discourses.[25] One of them argues that marriage is "community of life with a view to the procreation of children."[26] Far from using this as a formulaic dismissal of domestic question, he uses it as a way to explore what married life must be, and what its legal and moral implications are. Home, for Musonius, needs a beating heart to keep it going, and that beating heart is the relationship between husband and wife. If they fail to understand each other, to care for each other, then nothing will go right. They must keep all their property in common and share affection; otherwise, their union is doomed to failure. But does Musonius think they must also share the housework? To some extent. He thinks we should all be trained to do the work that is needed to keep us alive, regardless of gender. There are some kinds of work, he admits, that are generally better suited for men, or for women, and that is mostly to do with physical strength. So spinning and indoor work are more suitable for women, gymnastics, and outdoor work, better left to men.[27] But when it comes to the mind, men and women are on equal footing, which means that all must study philosophy.[28] But here's the hitch: the Stoics were conservative, they believed that it was proper to accept hardships, rather than challenge them.[29] So back to the learning of philosophy: women should still study it, but as they would only use it at home, they do not need to learn "technical skills and acuteness in argument," as that would be "quite superfluous."[30]

Musonius sends a very mixed message. In principle, men and women should be able to do the same jobs—whether indoors or outdoors—but there are practical restrictions. First there are laws and customs that must be respected, and secondly, there are physical differences that need to be accounted for (and if these physical differences come about because of established customs which mean that women exercise less than men, see first condition!). But unlike Aristotle, he doesn't seem to think that only men can think about justice and says that women ought to learn to do so. He also thinks of marriage as a community, one where husband and wife can in fact think and work together. So that's progress from Aristotle.

While Musonius offered a more egalitarian picture of marriage than Aristotle did, he still managed to lock women into the private sphere and restrain their activities to domestic ones. If we want to find a slightly bigger opening for women to participate in the public life, we need to turn to another Stoic, Hierocles, who wrote half a century or so after Musonius.[31]

Hierocles, like Musonius, emphasizes that the purpose of marriage is not merely procreation, but the common pursuit of the good life. Musonius says that husband and wife belong to each other body and soul and pretty much leaves it at that. Hierocles gives a more detailed account of what it means to be part of a couple. Being married, he says, is a solace in old age and illness, as it provides companionship and the sharing of burdens. A wife is a blessing because she will help her husband in all areas of his life, and where she cannot reach physically, because she is not allowed to be out in the public place, she will listen to him recount his day, and either help him resolve problems or, if that is not possible, bring him comfort and relief.

So far, this is perhaps not terribly appealing: women can't go to work outside the house, and they still have to listen to their husband go on about his day at the office. But marriage is more than just a one-way sharing of emotional burdens, Hierocles tells us. A husband and wife must also share physical burdens. Household management is "a matter of shared activities between husband and wife."

Before we rejoice at this potentially liberating statement, we should re-member that the Stoics, no matter how generous they are in their principles, are not prone to advocate change in the way human society works. So does Hierocles, like Musonius, draw back from the claim that all activities are to be shared? Yes, he does, to some extent. His treatise on *Household Management* makes the claim that household tasks ought to be divided between husband and wife according to their appropriateness. Husbands work in the field, marketplace, and city business. Wives spin wool, make break, and perform other domestic tasks.

Although Hierocles thinks that some activities are better suited to men than to women, he does not believe that the two sets of tasks ought to be strictly separated. He even goes as far as to say that husbands should receive some training in womanly duties and vice versa. He also believes that women ought to be physically strong, so that they can work in the fields if neces-sary, and that their husband should share with them business and political concerns, so that they may solve problems together and take over from them when the husband is sick or traveling.[32]

If women can help men with their business, can men take on traditionally female work, like breadmaking and spinning? Here Hierocles is quite spe-cific. Some of these tasks are indeed quite appropriate for men as they require physical strength: grinding, kneading flour, splitting wood, drawing water, moving furniture, shaking out bedding, etc. But what about more delicate work, such as spinning or embroidery? There is nothing wrong with men doing these things, says Hierocles, unless their masculinity is not secure:

> I myself would not advise any men who did not exhibit complete confi-dence in their own masculinity and restraint to touch such a thing. If, how-ever, through a life of this kind he should have rendered himself free of every absurd suspicion, what will prevent a husband from sharing in these things too with his wife?[33]

Hierocles does not advocate reforms that would affirm equality between hus-band and wife: he still believes that wives should stay mostly indoors, and men work outdoors. But his division of the spheres is not principled—it is not strictly based on physical difference between men and women (as it is for Musonius). Nor is it moral (as it is for Aristotle)—there is nothing inherently shameful, he says in men performing feminine tasks and women masculine ones. Hierocles avoids discussion of politics, interestingly. Men travel for

business, and outdoor work is agricultural. He does not, therefore, find himself in the position of having to argue that women too can (or can't) do politics. Perhaps this was less pertinent for the first-century AD Roman writers
than it was for Aristotle: but it is nonetheless worth noting that Musonius's
men are distinguished from women because they can use their philosophical
training more extensively in everyday life (perhaps simply because their everyday life experience is richer than women's), and Hierocles's men simply by
their doing more heavy-lifting and occasionally traveling for work. There is
nothing, in either Stoics, that corresponds to an ability to do politics, that is, a
well-developed practical reason that allows one to give orders. For Musonius
and Hierocles, women stayed home because that was the tradition, not because they lacked the capacity for non-domestic work.

What the Women Said

Aristotle, Musonius, and Hierocles were men writing about women. This
is especially clear in the way they discuss marriage: what kind of woman
should a man marry, and how should the man behave toward his wife. This
is a definitely male perspective, which gives us very little idea of what it was
like to be a woman thinking about the home. The corpus of texts called "neo-
or pseudo-Pythagorean," particularly those treatises and letters attributed to
women authors go some way toward providing a more feminine perspective.
These are texts written about women and for women, about how to think
about marriage and domesticity.

Some philosophers and classicists, such as Mary Ellen Waithe, Sarah
Pomeroy, or Michèle le Dœuff, when they write about the women listed
in Diogenes Laertius, or those named in other texts, insist on their historicity.[34] This is a mark of respect, a way of showing that we are taking women
philosophers as seriously as we are taking the men (many of whom we have
no real evidence for). And it's also a welcome counterpart to the sexist treatment ancient women philosophers tend to receive in literature. Women
philosophers of antiquity are often written off as myths, constructs, or
prostitutes. They become the butt of jokes, or they are simply ignored.[35]

Asserting historicity is not always straightforward. There is good evidence that the works attributed to neo-Pythagorean women, for instance,
were created later than their putative authors' lives, and that suggests to
some readers that they were fakes.[36] But not all: Stobaeus, a fifth-century

collector, put together an anthology of fragments from Greek philosophers, which included short treatises on domestic virtue, which he attributed to Perictione and Phintys, and letters of advice signed by Theano and Myia. All those names were famous and belong to women associated with Plato, in the case of Perictione, and Pythagoras, in the case of the others. Yet all these famous women had lived between the third- and the fifth-century BC, whereas the texts can be dated around the first- or second-century CE. So it is highly unlikely that Plato's mother, or Pythagoras's wife or daughter, actually wrote these texts. But that doesn't mean they were written by men. There is no reason why women writers might not use other women's names when writing pseudonymously. And there are good reasons to think that the topics they wrote about, domestic topics, would have been appealing to women writers.[37]

The consensus, among classicists, seems to be that women did not write these texts.[38] The voice of reason is often disappointing, if not downright patronizing. "Good try," the serious (male) philosopher will say, "but there was never any serious chance that a woman could have philosophized in antiquity." Resisting those sensible objections makes one seem stubborn and churlish or worse. But there is a way around it. Classicist Dorota Dutsch, who recently published a book all about the neo-Pythagorean women's texts, suggests that there is a way the texts can be empowering for women, even if we don't know who wrote them. If we succeed in proving that the authors existed, that they were who we think they were, then we have done just this. We've established the existence of a small number of women who wrote philosophy in ancient Greece. But if those texts were written, by men or women, to be read by the public as philosophy for or by women, this tells us something more. It tells us that people were interested in what women philosophers had to say, that they accepted that women could do philosophy, and that they thought the home was a suitable topic for philosophical investigation.[39]

Neo-Pythagorean domestic advice often made use of a variety of philosophical doctrines and principles. Perictione I's "On the Harmony of Women" is a Pythagorean treatise in that it places domesticity at the center of women's moral duties and argues against luxury and wearing jewelry. But it is also Platonic, in that it argues for something akin to the unity of virtues (there are four virtues, and it's impossible to have one without the others). It also suggests that women should pursue virtue and that when they gain it, they will not only benefit themselves and their household, but their cities if they come to rule. This is again Platonic, Plato being the only Greek philosopher who said women could become rulers. Finally, it is also Stoic, as it appeals to the model of cosmopolitan development in its discussion of how women become virtuous: we start with those closest to us, and then we extend our influence to those who are further and further, neighbors, co-citizens, and foreigners.[40]

Perictione I has some serious implications for women's potential political participation: they are instrumental in growing toward a more cosmopolitan political life, and they are potential rulers of cities. But not all texts attributed to neo-Pythagorean women are empowering for women. Phintys's two fragments, "On Woman's Self Restraint" 1 and 2, follow Musonius in arguing that women can and should learn philosophy, but that this will in no way affect their social boundaries: they must stay home and behave in an exemplary manner toward their husbands on pain of death.[41] Other letters are also a source of moral advice, and some offer validation of a wife's capacity for virtue. Melissa to Cleareta's letter of advice on what to wear begins by stating that Cleareta, as a young woman, wants to learn from other, older women, and that this is a good sign (239). Cleareta is on the right path, that is, she is learning to be virtuous, and beginning to care for her household. Eventually, if she carries on this way, her home will become a source of good for everyone connected to it.[42] Theano's letter to Nicostrate, advising on what to do with a cheating husband, gives a sobering look at what virtue meant for a housewife. As Perictione already suggested in *On Woman's Harmony*, a woman "must bear everything that befalls her husband, whether he is unlucky, does something wrong through ignorance or disease or drunkenness, or lives with other women." She needs to protect the marriage bed, because "everything depends on this."[43]

When Nicostrate's husband strays, Theano reminds her of this duty: "The virtue of a wife lies not in keeping close watch on her husband's affairs, but in being his companion. And companionship means tolerating his error." Nicostrate should ignore her husband's failings and instead, she should, Theano tells her: "distinguish yourself by your tactful behavior towards your husband, by care for the household, friendly behavior towards your acquaintances, and tender love for your children." In other words, she should continue extending her virtue from the home to the world, not only because that is worthwhile in itself, but because it will eventually help get back, if not her husband's love, at least his respect.[44]

Theano in a letter to Callisto this time explains that it's proper for younger women starting out as wives, to seek the help of older women. New wives are thrust into household management with very little training, so they must rely on a network of older, more experienced women to be successful. But the first step has to be to admit one's ignorance, and to pinpoint precisely what it is that we don't know and need help with. So this is in part a Socratic exercise: examine yourself and see what is lacking. But really, Theano says, the relevant education should have been meted out when they were still children. It's only because it was not that it becomes necessary to rely on the advice and experience of older women.[45]

The treatises and letters of the neo-Pythagorean corpus do not promote a particularly feminist understanding of home life. But what they do is to develop a portrait of the housewife as a focus of virtue, virtue that is acquired through philosophical practice, or at least through exchanges with philosophers—otherwise what is the point of using these famous philosophical names? And more than that, they develop the concept of the household as the center for moral development. This puts women and men on an equal footing when it comes to moral capacity. And if you squint hard enough, you can glimpse something more: the possibility that once the process of their moral development is well established, women might become a ruler of cities.

3

The Spheres Begin to Melt

We spent a whole chapter in a survey of ancient philosophical writings on the home. The authors were mostly men, and through their writings, they managed to confine women to the home, the private sphere, and make sure they only took part in "domestic" activities, but never politics, or even political philosophy. But the story doesn't stop here. In fact, it's where it begins. Women who were of a temperament to philosophize about the human experience had to find ways around their exclusion, poke holes in the spheres. And through these gaps came a few books, philosophical texts that not only went beyond their domestic experience but also reflected on it. Because I have to start somewhere, I start with the Middle Ages and I look at three women who wrote philosophical texts: Byzantine historian and philosopher Anna Komnene; late medieval philosopher, poet, and military author Christine de Pizan; and tenth-century Japanese poet, philosopher, and palace chronicler Sei Shōnagon. These women did not belong to one period or to one culture. But they had important things in common. First, the division of the spheres was non-negotiable. As women, they were supposed to stay home, and they were excluded from public life. We can now read their books, so obviously, they found a way out. But what is most interesting about them is that they succeeded in reclaiming their political identities without challenging the distinction of home and city. They found ways around, rather than through the spheres. These were not typical women, if there is such a thing. They all had strong relationships to the ruling elite. Perhaps that is why they were able to live exceptional lives in times and places when patriarchy had such a strong hold on women's choices. Without any claim to provide an account of what domestic life was like for medieval women in general, let me introduce these three women, who through their writings succeeded in working with the spheres to be both domestic and political.

What did these three women, a twelfth-century Byzantine princess, a fifteenth-century French court writer, and a tenth-century Japanese writer and lady-in-waiting have in common? All three women's domestic lives were exposed to the public to a much greater extent than would have been the

No Place Like Home. Sandrine Bergès, Oxford University Press. © Oxford University Press USA 2026.
DOI: 10.1093/9780197687413.003.0003

case for their contemporaries. Anna Komnene lived in a palace, and she entertained philosophers at home, Christine de Pizan worked from home for royal and aristocratic customers who ordered books from her, while her mother took care that everything in the home ran smoothly. Sei Shōnagon lived at close quarters with other women, all attending princely events and entertaining men secretly whenever they fancied. Yet all three were somehow still held to an ideal of feminine virtue which meant they did not belong in the public sphere. And, somehow, all three women used philosophy to negotiate the rules that tied them to the home. In doing so, they made space for women who came later to question these rules and challenge them in their own works.

Family Connections

Anna Komnene (1083–1153) introduces herself to her readers as the first child of Emperor Alexios Komnenos and of Empress Irene Doukaina. She tells us she was "born in purple." This meant born to a ruling Emperor in Constantinople, and inside the Porphyra, the reddish-purple stone chamber in the great palace reserved for imperial births.[1] Her *Alexiad* is an epic history of her father's reign, but also a philosophical-political commentary on his rule.[2] One of the most interesting part of the history are the texts where she praises the women of her family: Anna Dalassene, her paternal grandmother who administered the Empire on behalf of her son; Irene Doukaina, her mother who accompanied her husband at war; and Maria of Alania, twice empress, whose son, Konstantine Doukas, Anna was due to marry so that they could rule jointly. Maria had helped the Komnenoi brothers, Anna's father and uncle, in their military and political campaigns and the betrothal was a recognition of her role. Unfortunately, Konstantine died young, and the marriage didn't happen. And, as Alexios and Irene gave birth to a son, also born in purple, that son became the heir. This ended a line of politically powerful and influential women. Anna did not become empress but married a politically powerful man who was, like her, a scholar.

Did Anna Komnene resent not inheriting the throne so that she tried, as some believe, to take it from her brother, John Komnenos? While Anna talks of her mother, grandmother, and nearly-mother-in-law with great love admiration, she doesn't give the impression that she feels she has missed out by not becoming the next empress. The accepted narrative of Anna Komnene's life portrays her as a power-thirsty intrigant, who, at her father's death, was convinced by her mother to ask her husband, Nikephoros, to stage a coup, so the couple could reign instead of John. But Nikephoros, the story goes, refused. Anna and her mother were then forcibly exiled in a convent where they lived until they died.[3]

However, the medieval sources for these stories are very uncertain, and those who knew her and her work portray her as uninterested in leadership.[4] The *Alexiad*, which also serves as Anna's autobiography, confirms this. Anna presents herself, from childhood until old age, as a reader, a thinker, and a writer, rather than a politician. If she had in fact been exiled, it might have been in her interest to present herself as politically harmless. And she could have been both an intellectual and an activist. But while there is no strong evidence of her supposed political activity (no contemporary records of a coup she and her mother orchestrated), we know that she devoted much of her life to intellectual pursuits. It seems there always was a tendency to portray powerful or influential women as power-thirsty, desiring the crown for themselves, rather than as a means to working for the welfare of their country.[5]

Anna Komnene takes great care to present a narrative of her intellectual awakening. At the very beginning of the *Alexiad* she establishes herself as a scholar:

> I devoted the most earnest study to the Greek language . . . and was not un-
> practiced in rhetoric, and read through the treatises of Aristotle, and the
> dialogues of Plato, and fortified my mind through the Quadrivium of sci-
> ences [geometry, arithmetic, astronomy and music].[6]

It is likely that her parents encouraged her studies.[7] Anna herself tells us that it was her mother's example that first prompted her to read. As a child, she writes, she tried to imitate her mother by reading "hard" abstract texts.[8] She was determined to become a philosopher. But she recognized that her mother's examples and her ambition would not have been enough if she had not benefited also from what she called divine intervention, her nat-ural abilities, and the royal palace's library.[9] Another strong advantage she had over other women who might have had an inclination toward the intel-lectual life was her husband. Anna Komnene did not marry the heir to the throne, but she married a man who was also a scholar and had no objection to allowing her to continue her intellectual pursuits. Anna and Nicephoros set up a salon in their home and famous philosophers and mathematicians visited regularly. Once Anna moved to the convent of Kecharitomene (whether because she was forced to or out of choice) the circle continued to meet there.

Anna Komnene's circle is responsible for a set of commentaries on Aristotle's moral philosophy treatise, the *Nichomachean Ethics*. Some of the commentaries are now well known among scholars: those written by Michael of Ephesus (on books V, IX, and X) and by Eustratios of Nicea (books I and VI).[10] And although she did not write commentaries herself, Anna M. Komnene was much more than just a rich patron. According to the members of her circle, she selected the texts to comment on and the commentators. And as convener, she directed their work by chairing debates and reading drafts. Members of her circle thought she was particularly well suited for this job, as her philosophical ability was "that which makes one capable of discerning if a disposition is philosophical or not and the nobility or depravity of a soul."[11] They also testified that she herself was "habituated into virtue," that she had practiced until she acquired stable character traits conducive to virtuous action.[12] In other words, she had practiced what Aristotle's text preached: learning to be virtuous by exercising virtue. And she had made more inroads in her journey toward ethical goodness than most. The choice of *Nicomachean Ethics* as a text to comment may have been a mark of personal preference or philosophical affinities. But it was also a good marketing decision. The *Nicomachean Ethics* was quite obscure at the time so that there was a "gap in the market" for a good set of commentaries. The *Nichomachean Ethics* is now one of Aristotle's most popular books.

To the modern reader, it is not the choice of text that is curious but the choice of author. Why focus on Aristotle, though, when he so explicitly excluded women from philosophy and leadership—two domains Anna Komnene had good reasons to believe women could succeed in? It is likely that this wasn't how people read Aristotle at the time. We don't always realize that the authors we read are working against us, until someone else tells us so. Also, Aristotle's comments on women only echoed those of Thucydides and others, and were milder, in any case, than the orthodox Christian scriptures of the time.[13] In any case, the *Nicomachean Ethics* leaves space for a less sexist interpretation. Women, Aristotle says in Book VIII, can become friends, philosophical friends, even if they are not entirely taken up with the business of raising children.[14] And Anna Komnene, as a member of the imperial family, certainly was not that. So reading Aristotle could confirm her own position as a person of philosophical influence, provided she did not try to extend it to all women. As a member of the ruling elite, this probably suited her.

To her work as an editor Anna Komnene added, at the end of her life, that of an author. She wrote the *Alexiad* after the death of her husband. Nicephoros had initially been commissioned to write it but had died leaving a very incomplete draft. Anna Komnene took over and made the work her own. In her introduction, she made sure to assert herself as the author, while acknowledging her husband's contribution. Her description of her work shows that she devoted herself to that pursuit with the same energy and enthusiasm as she had in managing the Aristotle commentaries. This did not, of course, stop readers (up to the twentieth century) from arguing that she was merely putting together her husband's notes and calling the work "Nicephoros's Alexiad."[15]

So Anna Komnene, born in purple, was a philosopher and an historian, rather than a ruler or political intrigant. But given that she devoted her efforts to writing about her father, mother, and grandmother's political careers, what can we learn from her about the home and domesticity? It is clear from her writings and the context that women in Komnene's times and place were expected to be domestic. Much of what had been true of the Greek wife, or of the Roman matron, was still true for the Early Christian Byzantine woman—her domain was the home, not the public space, she was not to be heard nor seen—Byzantine women were expected to cover themselves on the rare occasions in which they left their home. But more rules had been imposed since the already strict demands of Greek and Roman antiquity: they were now bound also by the laws of Christianity, which stated both that women were the source of sin and that their only value was in trying to emulate the Virgin Mary as devoted and unquestioning mothers, wives, and daughters.[16] All of this is present in Anna Komnene's work, as she is at pains to portray herself with the right amount of modesty, daughterly duty, and feminine emotional displays.[17]

While it's questionable that Anna Komnene was exiled for attempting a coup against her brother, John Komnenos, it is true that Anna Komnene moved to a convent with her mother when her husband was on campaign. Her husband had been very supportive of her circle—an unusual attitude in a medieval Christian husband, because it meant that men who were not related to her got to spend a great deal of time in their home, in close quarters with his wife, and speaking freely with her. But while he was away from home, the meetings could not continue. Neville suggests that moving to the convent of Kecharitomene may have provided Anna with more freedom to continue working with her circle.[18] The convent was built by Anna's mother and contained several private apartments that were separate from the nuns' quarters. Anna and Irene could eat and pray with the nuns if they wanted to, but they could also keep themselves entirely to themselves. This arrangement provided Anna with the best of both worlds. Because their living quarters had their own entrance, male visitors could come in an out without disrupting the nun's routines. But because the apartments were part of the convent, their visit still had the necessary aura of chastity and modesty. Nothing untoward could be happening under the auspices of a convent. Moving to Kecharitomene did not make Anna a prisoner or a recluse. It gave a space of her own and provided a sufficient veneer of respectability that she could continue her editing work—and later write her history—unimpeded. This was not an exile—as the story goes—but a deliberate move, designed to facilitate her career as a philosopher and historian.

The power to move to a convent, especially when one could live there without having taking part in the daily activities and devotions that were the nun's lot, was a luxury medieval women were glad to have. This was tantamount to going on a luxurious retreat where everything is taken care of, and life's necessities do not need managing. While it's unlikely that Anna or her mother ever had much to do in terms of household work, they definitely had their share of duties when it came to entertaining important visitors, managing staff, and supervising their children's education. At the convent, they had nothing to do but please themselves. For Irene, that meant spending time in charitable work, and for Anna, devoting even more of her time to her intellectual pursuits.

It's quite easy to see how male interpreters may have read Anna's move as a forced exile. She was leaving her own home, the place that is supposed to be the source of comfort and power. But this perspective is easily shifted if we think that her home was a large politically significant and sensitive household. Living in a palace is a bit like living in a zoo: everything is for show, and there is very little privacy. Also, the house itself belonged to her husband, whereas the convent was her mother's and later became hers. With her children married, and her husband away for months or years at a time, it made more sense for Anna to move somewhere where she could focus on her own work. Anna was not alone in wanting to leave home in order to write. Her decision recalls that of Simone de Beauvoir, choosing to live in hotels for most of her adult years, Maya Angelou, leaving home every morning at six to work in a hotel room, or Agatha Christie spending weeks at a time writing in the Pera Palace hotel in Istanbul, just across the Golden Horn from the Kecharitomene convent. These were the best options available to women who wanted to work and needed to shake off the duties of household management.

What is also clear from the *Alexiad*, and in particular the portrayals of her mother Irene and her grandmother, Anna Dalassene, is that the home was in fact, for imperial women, tied to political duties. Imperial women were instrumental in helping decide who would succeed to the throne, and how to bring that about. A Byzantine queen's home was her castle. Both Anna Dalassene and Irene also had to take on a political role in their son or husband's absence, both acting as regent at some point in their lives.

Much of Alexios's imperial career was based on military campaigns. His wife, Irene, accompanied him—which was unusual, as women were meant to stay home, in the *gynaikeia* or women's quarters.[19] But what is perhaps more surprising is that in his absence, he gave his mother, Anna Dalassene, full control over the administration of the empire. When her granddaughter, Anna Komnene, relates this, she anticipates criticisms of her father and grandmother and makes the following apology:

> At this point the reader may well censure my father *for transferring the government of the empire to the women's quarters*, but if one knows this woman's spirits, her surpassing intelligence and energy, one's reproaches would soon turn to admiration. For my grandmother had an exceptional grasp of public affairs, with a genius for organization and government. She was capable, in fact, of managing not only the Roman empire, but every empire under the sun as well. She had vast experience and knew the nature of things, aware of how everything starts and how it ends, which things destroy others and which contradict and complement the other. She was intuitive about what needed doing, and clever at getting it done.[20]

This is a very revealing passage. Anna Dalassene is described as having all the traits one would want in an exceptional leader: practical knowledge, experience, organizational skills, but also intuitive intelligence and a deeper, philosophical understanding of the world. It would have been foolish, Anna Komnene implies, for her father not to hand over the administration of the state to such an individual. But the most interesting aspect of this text, as far as we are concerned, is the way in which the handover is described.

Anna Dalassene is not called upon to step out into the public sphere, but the government is "transferred to the women's quarter." The former would have brought into question Anna Dalassene's continuing feminine virtues, in particular, her modesty. Instead, Alexos takes the role of administrator away from the public sphere and into the private one. And that seems to have worked for over twenty years, as Anna Dalassene remained in power.

What the *Alexiad* shows, then, is that the private space did not have to remain free from political, philosophical, or other scholarly activities. These could be transferred to the home, and performed excellently, as they were by Anna Dalassene and her granddaughter, Anna Komnene. Irene, Alexos's wife, left the private sphere to accompany her husband on his military campaigns. Her daughter, when she mentions it, is "deeply apologetic."[21] This is because by doing so, she broke the first rule of womanly virtue: seclusion. She went out into the world, protected only by the thin cloth of a military (though royal) tent, and was almost certainly exposed to the eyes of strangers, including foreigners. But while it would have been impossible to acquire military experience without actually going on a campaign, state administration could just as well be practiced from the women's quarters as the men's quarters. And the same goes for philosophy—although in both Dalassene and Komnene's case, this required granting access to some nonrelated men to the women's quarters. For Anna Komnene and her grandmother, the home, and even the women's quarters, could be a place of political power and engagement and did not necessarily mean that they had to be cut off from the world's political and intellectual developments.

The home that is depicted in the *Alexiad* is a place of power and politics. For many defenders of domesticity, before and long after Komnene, the home is a place of rest, comfort, care, and respite from the outside world, and women, who never leave the home, are in charge of making it that way. Komnene agrees that a woman must stay in her home. But for her, this does not mean that women cannot occasionally engage in the work that men typically do, whether political or scholarly. All it requires is that public work be moved to the private quarters, where the women are. This would explain why women like Anna Komnene, her mother, and grandmother were so deeply resented (and accused of treachery). Moving politics or scholarly work to the women's quarters meant that fewer men had access to these particular works. While any (free, nonworking) man can step up in the Greek Agora, only a few can join a lady's salon, and even then, only if the lady herself invites them. This is what would lead Robespierre, seven centuries later, to complain about the Girondins gathering in Madame Roland's salon, and making decisions there, "behind closed doors" rather than at the assembly. This seemed unfair and undemocratic, because it excluded so many men, including some who had been elected to office. But what Komnene, as well as the women of the French revolution, understood was that exclusion is a matter of perspective. If politics happen in a place where women are in charge, then some of the men who would normally take part in debating, planning, and decision-making may be excluded—by virtue of not being invited. But if the political work happens in the usual "public" place, then all women are excluded—on principle.

The Writer and the Maiden

Anna Komnene tells us that when her father left the rule of Constantinople to his own mother, Anna Dalassene, the government was "transferred to the women's quarter". That is, the most important political activities were displaced from the public domain to the private one. Again, when Anna Komnene's husband allowed her to welcome a circle of philosophers in their home, he introduced a part of the public world into the private sphere. In both cases the point of displacing the activities was so that women could participate in them without leaving their home. But Anna Komnene and her grandmother were part of the imperial family: the world could be made to change for them. This was not so for other women, even those from well-off families, such as Christine de Pizan. If they needed to take part in activities that traditionally fell to men, they would have to leave home. But in late fourteenth- and early fifteenth-century France, women were still expected to stay very close to their homes and only leave it to move to a new husband's home, or to a convent.

Christine de Pizan (1364–1430?) was the daughter of a wealthy Italian scientist who came to the court of Charles V, in France, as his physician and astrologist. Christine was married at fifteen, and unusually, it was a love match. A year later, Charles V died, leaving Christine's father unemployed and struggling to find work. By the time he died, he had nothing to leave to his wife and daughter. Christine herself was widowed at 25 with three children. She still loved her husband. and had a hard time coping both emotionally and materially after his death. Now an impoverished widow, she found herself in a highly vulnerable situation. As a woman, she could not go to court and so was unable to claim her husband's military pension or to defend herself against lawsuits brought against her by those who wanted the pension for themselves. From a place of privilege and comfort, she now needed to find a way to support herself, her children, and her mother, all at the same time as she dealt with her own bereavement. She turned to writing, at first love poetry to console herself from the loss of her husband. As her writings became popular and started to sell, she diversified. Until her death in her mid-sixties she wrote eighteen books among which were two volumes of love poetry, a book on the art of chivalry, a critique of the *Romance of the Rose*, a history of the world (*Les Mutations de la Fortune*), two mirrors for women (*The Book of the City of Ladies* and the *Treasure of the City of Ladies*), a biography of Charles V, a political treatise (*the Body Politic*), and her last work, a poem about the exploits of Joan of Arc.

The death of a husband usually meant, for a fourteenth-century French women, a second marriage or retiring to a convent. The latter was not an option for Pizan at that point in her life, as it would have meant leaving her mother and children destitute. Nor was finding a husband a guarantee of their safety. She might not be lucky twice; her second husband could be a tyrant. So she found a third way. Her first poems had been read favorably at court. This led her to an extraordinary decision: she would make money from her writing—something that even men writers at her time did not do (as most of them derived a salary from the church, the university, or patrons).

Part of the work of a writer could be done from the home. Pizan tells us, in the *Book of the City of Ladies*, that she had her office at the top of their house, and illustrations on her books show her receiving customers there. But this does not mean that Pizan could live a confined life. A home (or convent) study was sufficient for Anna Komnene, because she did not need to sell her books for money and because she had a guaranteed audience. But in order to sell her books, Christine de Pizan had to do more than rely on word of mouth, and she needed to show herself in court and visit potential patrons. The production of her books also required stepping outside the home to visit the convents where nuns did the copying. One commentator even suggests that before she could sell her own works, Pizan herself worked as a copyist.[22]

Even if Pizan could do most of her work from home, that did not mean that she could live a traditional domestic life. The life of the late medieval French woman, we know, was quite busy, especially when there were children involved. The home had to be cleaned, the stores managed, which included ending a garden for herbs and vegetables and trips to the butchers to choose meat, the linen had to be kept clean (and perfumed with lavender), clothes clean and in good repair, and children had to be taught, especially where there was no money for tutors.[23] We know that Pizan relied on her mother for much of the work of keeping home and family together—in the *City of Ladies*, we hear her mother calling her down from her work to dinner. In that sense Pizan's household was not devoid of a wife. But it was devoid of a husband, and that meant it could not function well.

Did Pizan think that she could make do without a man if she could only manage to earn enough money to keep herself and her dependents? Not quite. We know that one of the ways her household was in trouble was through lawsuits carried out by unscrupulous lawyers who knew that, as a woman, Pizan was not allowed to go to court. The only way a woman could protect herself was to have a man acting on her behalf, one who had her interest at heart. This is an issue she tackles in the *City of Ladies*. Having put forward arguments for the conclusion that women are equal to men in reason and courage, Christine, the narrator,[24] asks why women are not allowed to enter courts of laws or even argue for their cases or adjudicate others. The answer is twofold: one, a judge or a lawyer needs more than reason to do their work; they also need to have a deep voice and a strong body. The authority of the law, in the Middle Ages, sometimes needed to be reinforced by brute strength or at least, a show of strength. Next, it is right, she says, for men and women each to play a particular role in society, and that it is men's role to work the law.

There is a lot to unpack in this argument. The second part of the answer shows Pizan's allegiance to the theory of the body politic. Derived from Aristotle, the theory states that every individual or class has a particular role to play in the survival or flourishing of the *polis*/country, and that for one person/class to step out of their role, or worse, rebel against another part, is only conducive to their, and possibly the whole's end. Aristotle, in his *Politics*, uses the metaphor of a hand attacking the head: if the hand is successful, it does not survive (12353a 18–29)! Pizan's use of the body politic argument is particularly poignant because she is writing during a very fragile period for France (and Europe). In 1328, the French king had died with no male heir and the French law would not allow a woman to take the throne, and because England *could* provide a successor, the two countries entered into what is known as the Hundred Years' War. At the time Pizan was writing, France was devastated, entire villages burned, which led to famine and rioting. The ruling king, Charles VI, suffered from severe mental illness, and there was infighting among his wife and successors so that there was no firm government. A women's rebellion, Pizan thought, would only make things worse. Now was not the time for anyone to challenge whatever order remained. So if women were assigned by tradition (or divine command) to stay out of law courts, then that was what they should do. But this entailed that a woman in need of legal action was also in need of a male presence in her household.

Aside from the need to respect order, Pizan knew there was no reason to think that women were not in fact capable of becoming lawyers or judges. The characteristics they are said to lack are merely physical and possibly not unsurmountable with a little exercise and vocal practice. Pizan certainly believed it was possible for women to outdo men in physical feats: in the *City of Ladies*, she describes the strength and battle skills of the Amazon warriors, as they defeated the Greek army (Pizan 1982, 40). *The City of Ladies* is as full of examples of women who surpassed men in every conceivable way as it is of arguments for equality of male and female capacities. Yet, Pizan does not argue that women could and should share men's roles in society equally: the very fragile state of France meant that she was essentially conservative. One thing the country did not need was another challenge to power, or another revolt. Yet, she had no problem with the idea that it was possible, on an *ad hoc* basis, for individual women to challenge their place in society and take over from less competent men. Her *City of Ladies* can be read as an injunction to the Queen regent, Isabelle de Bavière, to step in fully and restore French power. But there are other interesting examples, and I'll talk about two of them here. The first is from Pizan's own life: as a widow who has to earn her keep and protect her family, she took became, for all intent and purposes, a *pater familias*. The second is Joan of Arc—the subject of Pizan's last book—who fought the English and had the heir to the French throne crowned before she was burnt at the stake. Let's look at these in turns, as Pizan herself describes them, and see what the implications were for the home and domestic life in the early fifteenth century.

Pizan, we saw, needed a man to support and protect her household. A woman was needed to keep it running from the inside, but only a man could bring in the money needed to support it and keep away those who would attack it. Pizan had brothers but they were busy in Italy, trying to make a living for their own families. She did not wish to remarry—and that would not have necessarily resulted in the right kind of support for herself and her dependents, as a new husband may have sent her mother away and married off her daughters before their time. Christine's solution was simple: she became a man.

The story of Christine de Pizan's metamorphosis into a man is told in the first book of *The Transformations of Fortune*:

> And I who was formerly a woman, am now in fact a man (I am not lying, as my story will amply demonstrate), and, if I was formerly a woman, my current self-description is the truth. But I shall describe by means of fiction the fact of my transformation, how from being a woman, I became a man, and I want people to name this poem, once the story becomes known, *Fortune's Transformations*. (Pizan 1997, 91)

It is not unusual for Pizan to use autobiographical elements in her works. She refers to herself by name (in *Fortune*, she explains that her name is that of Jesus Christ with the letters INE added to it). This is not sufficient reason to believe, perhaps that the works are autobiographical. Indeed, as one commentator points out, although she claims in *Fortune* that she has become a man, the illustrations of the author remain the same.[25] A vignette in which the author is shown at work on the book *Fortune* (with a little dog at her feet) represents her very much as a woman, with the same blue dress and white coiffe she always wears in these representations. If the Christine of *Fortune* has become a man, in body as well as in mind, the Christine who writes the story has the same body and female-coded attire she always did.

But there are other reasons to believe that *Fortune* is a metaphor of Pizan's. Or at least, it's consistent with the ways she tells stories elsewhere. In the *Book of the City of Ladies*, the heroine, also named Christine, is found in her study working, until her mother tells her to stop soon for dinner. She then decides to take a break from serious reading and comes across a book from a minor author called Matholeus, which turns out to be a piece of horrendous sexist nonsense. Reflecting that even good books (Aristotle, Aquinas) on her shelves seem to despise women, Christine starts to feel depressed. She is shaken out of it before her depression takes hold by three ladies flying into her room from the window. They tell her to get a grip and start working at refuting these accusations against women. They use the metaphor of building a city where women can freely be all they are capable of being. Here there is no reason to suppose that the description of what it feels like to realize that respected authors think very badly of you is not in fact autobiographical. Nor is there any doubt that what follows—the three ladies flying in through the window—is meant to be read as anything but an allegory. *Fortune* can also be read as a mixture between philosophical metaphor and autobiography. There the narrator specifies that the story will be expressed through fiction—but that it is true in essence, allowing for a certain amount of biographical interpretation. So: What is the story?

The narrator—whom I shall call ChristineN and refer to as "they"[26]—starts by telling us about their family: ChristineN's father is very much like the author's own, that is, an astrologist and a physician who wishes his daughter had been a man so he could share his knowledge with them. ChristineN's mother, on the other hand, is none other than mother nature herself, which explains why they were born, despite their father's wishes, female. Their mother's power was such that she could not help but transmit her sex to her child. In every other way, ChristineN says, they were like their father.

ChristineN is then sent to serve at the home of Fortune, and Fortune eventually sends them to the home of Hymenes. Hymenes gives ChristineN a husband, whom they refer to as a master whom they have to obey, but also as someone who is in every way loveable and hard working so that ChristineN was comfortable and "well fitted out" at the court of Hymenes. Then the couple is sent by ship to the court of Fortune. There is a storm and ChristineN's husband dies. Devastated, they go to sleep, expecting to die, but Fortune comes to them, and by applying her hands on ChristineN's body, effectuates the metamorphosis:

> [Lady Fortune] touched me all over my body; she palpated and took in her hands each bodily part, I remember it well. [. . .] I awakened and things were such that, immediately and with certainty, I felt myself completely transformed. I felt my bodily parts to be stronger than before, and the great pain and lamentation which had earlier dominated me, I felt to be somewhat lessened. Then I touched myself all over my body, like one completely bewildered. Fortune had thus not hated me, she who had transformed me, for she had instantly changed the great fear and doubt in which I had been completely lost. Then I felt myself much lighter than usual and I felt that my flesh was changed and strengthened, and my voice much lowered, and my body harder and faster. However, the ring that Hymen had given me had fallen from my finger, which troubled me, as well it should have, for I loved it dearly. [. . .] I found my heart strong and bold, which surprised me, but

I felt that I had become a true man; and I was amazed by this strange adventure. (Pizan 1997, 106)[27]

As they realize what they have become, ChristineN is freed, to some extent, from the emotions that had them prostrated, and they use their new bodily strength to fix the ship with a hammer and nails, thus immediately taking up the man's role of preserving the (waterborne) home and the lives of its inhabitants. Without a man at its head, the ship was lost, so ChristineN became a man, and the ship was saved. The author Christine de Pizan, if she was not physically transformed (as witness the images of her she published at the time), did at least metaphorically become a man, for the sake of the security of her household. And while she no doubt continued to participate in some womanly activities, her mother, it seems, supported by Pizan's labor took on the role of the housewife: at least this is what is suggested in the opening page of the Book of the *City of Lady* when Christine interrupts her work because her mother is calling her down to dinner.

The home for Pizan, like a smaller version of the body politic, requires different individuals to play different roles. These are typically: the wife, who looks after the home from the inside, and the husband, who supports it by working outside. This is very much the same plan as that which the Greeks and the Roman had, the same division of labor around the walls separating the household from the city, to ensure the survival and, if possible, the flourishing of its inhabitants. But the roles are not set in stone, or rather biology. Provided she makes a good enough show of manly strength—in Pizan's case through her writings—a woman can take on the husband's part if needed. Pizan made it very clear in the *Book of the City of Lady*, and indeed in other texts, including *Fortune*, that aside from bodily differences, which in some cases (she gives examples of women warriors) can be overcome, there are no real differences between a woman and a man. Everything that a man can do, whether physically, morally, or intellectually, so can a woman (Pizan 1982, 117–118). The key is to look the part so that one is not rejected by society.

If a woman can metamorphose into a man to save her home, and if the home, or household, is a small body politic, like a city state, then we may ask whether a woman could become a man to save her country. This brings us to another fifteenth-century transgender celebrity: Joan of Arc, the teenager who fought the English, defeated them, and then accompanied the *dauphin*, Charles, to Reims where he was crowned, thus re-establishing a French king.

Joan was eventually captured by the English, tried, and burned at the stake as a heretic. One of the accusations (recorded on the court transcript) was that she dressed as a man and refused to put on the women's clothes she was given in prison.[28]

Christine de Pizan's last work *Le Ditié de Jehanne d'Arc* (1429) was a poem about Joan, the prophecies that had preceded her, and her heroic actions to save France. The mystery surrounding the questions of how a young peasant girl, who spoke *patois* and couldn't read or write, came to know how to bear arms, speak eloquently to members of the court, and direct an army is still fascinating. Pizan scholar, Karen Green (2021), suggested that part of the mystery could be solved if we consider that Christine, herself well-versed in the arts of war (she had written a book about it),[29] disappeared for a long period during the time Joan would have needed to be trained. Did Pizan decide to put her theories into practice? Did she decide that the best man to lead France to victory was in fact a woman, and help Joan become a warrior and a leader? Despite Green's work, there is not enough evidence yet to make those claims. But on any reading of the *Ditié*, it is clear that whether or not she had anything to do with Joan's exploits, Pizan thought of her as the general that France needed, the one who rescued the lands that men had lost, and she said she was braver than the bravest roman. She doesn't tell us that to make this happen, Joan had to become a man. Instead, she relies on God's power to help the "maid" carry and handle heavy weapons. So if we think of Pizan only as a chronicler of Joan's exploits, the story doesn't quite fit. Instead of having to become a man to perform the work that was needed, Joan is appointed by God, as an exception. But in practice, from her own experience, Pizan must know, even if she had nothing to do with it herself, that even God tends to operate with human help. Joan had to be trained, she had to give up womanly duties and put on a man's armor and do a man's strengthening exercises. And Joan's documented refusal to put on a dress, when it was a matter of life or death, also suggests that she had taken on a new identity as a man—a God-appointed new identity. In her case, the question of precedence arises more clearly than in Pizan's case. Pizan tells us she became a man out of necessity—while she was married, or at least while her alter-ego in Fortune was married, being a woman suited her fine. But in Joan's case, isn't it likely that a sense that she was a man, rather than a woman preceded her conviction that she could transform into an army general and lead France to victory? All this is speculation—but one thing is not. It seems quite clear that in both cases, Pizan and Joan, taking up a man's role in society was possible, but only for a woman who was willing to become a man. Structures remained the same, gender roles were unchanged, but gender itself was fluid.

Pizan's tactics for reclaiming a more active role for herself (and for Joan) is different from the Komnene and Dalassene women. Anna Komnene, her mother, and her grandmother were able to participate in public life from inside their home. The public life was brought to them, and they had some authority to influence it through their writings or direct interactions. Christine de Pizan was not in that position. She had to step outside the private sphere to earn enough to feed her family and exercise her influence. Her writings needed publicity, she needed to establish what we now call a platform, by being seen where influential people were, at court. The spheres were not any less firmly separated during Christine de Pizan's lifetime as they had been for Anna Komnene. She could not simply ignore them. What she could do was to play with the gender distribution within the spheres: from being a woman, she became a man. The structure of her home remained unchanged: her mother acted as the wife, whose job was to keep it functioning from the inside and Christine as a husband who could sustain and protect it from the outside. That Christine de Pizan did not challenge this order was a testimony to her patriotism and allegiance to the body politic theory: disturbing the order of things would risk destroying France's chance of ever reaching some sort of political equilibrium. The state had to be stable, but gender fluidity, provided it only permitted movement between two modes: male or female, was not as problematic. So Christine, a woman, could not act as a man and protect her family, but she could become a man to do so. And this is what she did.

A Gate, Wide Open

Anna Komnene and Dalassene had the public sphere brought inside their homes. Christine de Pizan and Joan of Arc became men so they could support their home (and country) from the outside. Sei Shōnagon, lady-in-waiting to a tenth-century Japanese empress, offers a different perspective on how a woman could and should navigate her home and still live life to the full.

Sei Shōnagon, also known as Kiyohara no Nagiko (Sei Shōnagon was a name given her at court, possibly referring to a male relative or husband's official post), was the daughter and granddaughter of men who had been poets and provincial magistrates. Her female relatives are absent from any available biographies. At the age of 27, married and with a son, she left home to become a lady-in-waiting for the Empress Teishi (Sadako). She stayed in this post until the age of 35. During that time, she may have traveled between home and court, or she may have divorced her husband and remarried, once or twice, or even become a Buddhist nun. Little is known of her life, expect what she wrote in the *Pillow Book*, a collection of essays, poems, anecdotes, and lists, which was published after she left court.[30]

The book is rich—even the lists can be read as philosophical reflections— and Penny Weiss, in one rare philosophical essay on Shōnagon, has argued that many of the essays and other texts provided reflections on political obligation which could usefully be contrasted with Plato's or Mill's.[31] Shōnagon's book is a prime candidate for the argument that we shouldn't limit our study of political philosophy to traditional treatises. That would, in any case, be rather hypocritical: Plato wrote dialogues, and, as Weiss points out, some of Aristotle's writings, such as the *Constitution of Athens*, are lists.[32]

Sei Shōnagon's observations don't stop at the political. There is a lot on beauty, and what concerns me here—although I believe that the home is, in fact, political—reflections on the place of the home in a woman's life. The home, she tells us at the end of the book, is where she retires to write, confident that she will be undisturbed, and that her work can remain a secret.

> I wrote these notes at home, when I had a good deal of time to myself and thought no one would notice what I was doing. Everything that I have seen and felt is included. Since much of it might appear malicious and even harmful to other people, I was careful to keep my book hidden. But now it has become public, which is the last thing I expected.[33]

We need to remember that by then, she would have served the empress for eight years, been married once or twice (or possibly more) and thus could afford a home in which she could be at peace. If she were divorced and her child grown, moreover, she had no one to please but herself and, occasionally, her visitors. Even during her vacation time from court, where she went home, either to a husband or parents, she would have had more leisure and privacy than at Court. Court life required her to be at the Empress's beck and call at all times, ready to charm, to serve and to entertain: the empress and her ladies-in-waiting lived in an enclosed area of the imperial house which meant they saw little of the outside world, but they were only separated from each other by portable screens and curtains.[34] Yet, the life of the court afforded more freedom, as she was not seen as responsible for the state and reputation of her quarters, or the people she shared them with.

Shōnagon gives us a vision of what the pros and cons of home and court are:

> I should like to live in a large, attractive house. My family would of course be staying with me, and in one of the wings I should have a friend, an elegant lady-in-waiting, from the palace, with whom I could converse. Whenever we wished we should meet to discuss recent poems and other things of interests. When my friend received a letter, we should read it together and write our answer. If someone came to pay my friend a visit, I should receive him in one of our beautifully decorated rooms, and if he was prevented from leaving by a rain storm or something of the sort, I should warmly invite him to stay. Whenever my friend went to the Palace, I should help her with her preparations and see that she had what was needed during her stay at court. For everything about well-born people delight me.
> But I suppose this dream of mine is rather absurd.[35]

Why the absurdity? Presumably because she realizes that she is trying to put two very different lives together: a family life in a traditional home, and a vicarious courtly life, with a friend almost sequestered in a separate wing, and forced to share her love letters and indeed her lovers whenever she is not at court. Sei Shōnagon would like to have her cake and eat it, the freedom of the courtly life and the comfort of domesticity. Her husband, if she had one, would of course have had both, as for him, the comforts of domestic life were what he came home to after a stint at the palace (if he were government official), or with local dignitaries (if he were a provincial official, as her father and grandfather had been). There was never any shortage of cake, to be had or kept, for well-off men.

Two more passages tell us about Shōnagon's views on domestic life, either permanent or temporary (while on leave from the palace).

> When a woman lives alone, her house should be extremely dilapidated, the mud wall should be falling to pieces, and if there is a pond, it should be overgrown with water-plants. It is not essential that the garden be covered with sage-brush; but weeds should be growing through the sand in patches, for this gives the place a poignantly desolate look.

I greatly dislike a woman's house when it is clear that she has scurried about with a knowing look on her face, arranging everything just as it should be, and when the gate is kept tightly shut.

[...] When a Court lady is on leave from the Palace, it is pleasant if she can stay with her parents. While she is there, people are always coming and going, there is a lot of noisy conversation in the back rooms, and the clatter of horses' hoofs resounds outside. Yet she is in no danger of being criticized.[36]

But leaving in one's parents' house has its inconveniences: late visitors are spied on by servants, parents worry that the gate is left open all night, and daughters are expected to go to bed rather than stay up till morning. But Sei Shōnagon pictures a different kind of arrangement, where the gates remain open all night:

What I really like is a house where no one cares about the gate either in the middle of the night or at dawn, and where one is free to meet one's visitor, whether he be an Imperial Prince or a gentleman from the Palace. In the winter one can stay awake together all night with the lattices wide open. When the time comes for him to leave, one has the pleasure of watching him playing upon his flute as he goes; if a bright moon is still hanging in the sky, it is a particular delight. After he has disappeared, one does not go to bed at once, but stays up, discussing the visitor with one's companions, and exchanging poems; then gradually one falls asleep.[37]

What really concerns Sei Shōnagon is that lovers and potential lovers should be free to come and go. Part of this is sexual freedom, but it's also about cultural life. Nighttime visitors would bring love poems as part of their courtship (if the poem is any good, the lady will reply and send her own, and the relationship will develop from there). Friends or sisters would spend time reading the poems and writing their own in response.[38] But there is still more to Shōnagon's worry. When the gate being locked, the home is closed to the outside world, to visitors, to adventure, and to change. It becomes a place of distrust and petty mindedness. A place where imagination has no part but is replaced by neatness and narrow-minded gossip. A woman—for men are not going to be locked into any home, as they must at least work—cannot be happy in a home where the gates are locked at night. If her family home is like this, she is lucky if she can leave home for part of her time to stay at her palace.

What these passages have in common with the rest of the book is a strong sense of what is aesthetically pleasing or not which goes beyond the sensory realm and into ethics. Being the kind of woman who scurries about making everything neat is not aesthetically pleasing. But this also relates more deeply to a sense of the good life. A life concerned with neatness and tidiness is not a life worth living: it is a closed life, one that excludes interesting interactions with others of the kind that will enrich us. It is closed in a very literal sense: the gate is "tightly shut." In the second text, she takes up this theme again. It is good, she says, for a woman to stay with her parents when she is away from the palace. That way she will benefit from a lively household with comings and goings and will not worry about receiving her own visitors. Yet, the parents may be mean-minded in the way that the neat woman was: they sometimes spy on visitors, ask when they are leaving, and make a fuss about closing the gate at night. What Sei Shōnagon likes is "a house where no one cares about the gate either in the middle of the night or at dawn" and where visitors come and go, discussing poetry until they fall asleep.[39]

Despite her strong words against the neat housewife, it is clear that Sei Shōnagon values homelife: home is where she has "long hours" to devote to writing, and where she might at least hope for some privacy, and the chance to keep her writings to herself until she chooses to share them. The gates of her ideal home may be open at all times, but one must at least ride to them, whereas her chambers in the palace are forever accessible to all the palace dwellers. The good life, the one she "really likes," is that where the time of day is of no concern, and details will not interfere with love, friendship, and poetry. The woman who lives alone, who does benefit from a busy household where people come and go, must at least show that she is poetically inclined, by leaving her gate open, and not caring overmuch about neatness and tidiness. The ideal home, then for Shōnagon, is in between the fully closed and the fully open: it is not a public space, but nor does it reject that space, leaving always a door or window open so that one might come into the other. Her vision is, unsurprisingly, radically different from that of the writers belonging to the Graeco-Roman or Christian tradition: defending the spheres is not the prime concern, but living a good life, filled with worthwhile interactions is. This is not to say that Shōnagon did not have to contend with spheres: she too lived in a patriarchal world, where women were more confined than men and lived separately from them. But whatever the reason, her take on what mattered and what could be done about it was not the same as either Komnene's or Pizan's. Instead of trying to modify the spheres, she talked about how to enjoy them to the full and learn to navigate the paths that led the one to the other.

4

A Loom of One's Own

Books on famous writers' work habits are always popular. We want to know how people, especially successful people, manage their working life. We want to know where and when they write, what materials and furniture they use. And because writers tend to work from home, we want to know how they manage that. Jane Austen wrote throughout the day, after early piano practice and making breakfast for her family. She sat by a window in the living room, her portable writing box set on a small tripod table. Her mother and sister sat nearby, sewing and chatting. Victor Hugo had a well-appointed study in his family apartment, Place des Vosges. In the morning, post eggs and coffee, he would put a wooden board across the door and write at his standing desk, naked (his clothes in the care of his assistant, on the other side of the door, to remove all temptation of going out), from dawn to late morning. Simone de Beauvoir spent many years sleeping in hotel rooms and writing in cafes. She would sit at her table all morning, sipping tea, occasionally stopping to talk to friends. Eventually, she became so famous that people would not leave her in peace so she decided it was time to invest in an apartment of her own. Perhaps it's to emulate Beauvoir that students often work in cafes, or perhaps that's just a nice thing to do, sitting at a table with a notebook or laptop computer, punctuating reading and writing with a latte, a friend, or a stint on social media. During Covid, when cafes were closed, students wrote in their dorm bedrooms, where the only other lifeform might have been the mold growing on leftover pizza. Some wrote in their family home, sometimes in the kitchen or living room, their workspace defined by what others needed, for their own work or to run the home. When my students would allow me a glimpse into their lives through the zoom camera, I would sometimes see a sibling running past with a toy truck, or a parent pushing a vacuum cleaner. During those long months, those of us who could constructed home offices for ourselves, little pods where we could talk to our students, while the cat prowled on the keyboard and the children banged on the door. Because—unless you're Victor Hugo—even a proper study, no matter how well furnished, gets invaded if it's at home. Invaders are children needing attention,

No Place Like Home. Sandrine Bergès, Oxford University Press. © Oxford University Press USA 2026.
DOI: 10.1093/9780197687413.003.0004

partners going about their lives, or domestic tasks nagging at us to be done ("you're not really working, shouldn't you be unloading the dishwasher/ bring in the laundry?"). There is, we found out, quite a big difference between working from home because we have to and working from home because we choose to. For someone who writes as a living, the home is often the place where they work. It's cheaper than renting office space, you don't waste time in transit so you can start early in the morning if you want to, and you have a constant supply of coffee, tea, and snacks. It's also away from the public sphere, so you don't have to worry about co-workers or students or passerby looking over your shoulder to check on your progress. But then there is the risk of being interrupted from within the home, by people who live there, or by encroaching domestic tasks. As gender inequalities are slowly erased, this is becoming a problem for some men as well as most women. Remember that BBC correspondent who read the news while his wife was crawling around the room, trying to catch his toddlers? But still, as Christine de Pizan figured out, to be a writer who works from home, it helps to be a man.

Writer Katherine Mansfield, a contemporary of Virginia Woolf, came to the same conclusion when she spent her vacation time in a country house with her partner, John Middleton Murry. This was supposed to be a writing retreat, and both were trying to get on with their work.

> The house seems to take up so much time . . . So often this week you and Gordon have been talking while I washed dishes . . . And after you have gone I walk about with a mind full of ghosts of saucepans and primus stoves . . . And you [Murry] calling, what ever I am doing, writing, "Tig, isn't there going to be tea? It's five o'clock."[1]

For Murry, the vacation home is a place where he can both work and relax. For "Tig" it's a place where she hopes to work but ends up spending most of her time feeding Murry. Their respective Wikipedia page reflects that difference: Murry is described as a prolific author, who wrote more than sixty books to Mansfield's six volumes of short stories. Yet, it is Mansfield's short stories that are remembered and were translated into twenty-five languages.

For women authors, the domestic setting is not usually conducive to study, because it doesn't provide the sort of private and quiet space needed. The women we discussed in the last chapter could participate in professional or political life (even if that professional life involved writing) by negotiating their place in the two spheres. However, finding private space to think and write, when this was not a professional activity conducted "as a man," was trickier. Sei Shōnagon waited till she had retired from the palace to write down all what had seen and thought. Anna Komnene left her home to settle with her mother in a convent, where she was able to write undisturbed. Christine de Pizan wrote from home, but only because she had, in many ways, "become a man" by earning a living and had persuaded her mother to act as her wife, taking care of domestic duties.

In the seventeenth-century Christian world, which we turn to now, very little had changed in terms of women's roles and possible life choices. There were still three available spheres of life for the reasonably well-off: court, home, or convent. The poor lived in unsanitary dwellings that offered neither safety nor comfort, of they lived as servants in other people's homes, in brothels, or in the street. Well-off women who wanted to write had to choose between the relative obscurity of the convent, the sociability of the court, or the stability of the home. Although many fought to find or make a room of their own, few managed to achieve even a fraction of the peace that their male contemporaries would, and rarely on their own terms. But one thing did come of that struggle. Women started to reflect on what the differences between the work done in the home and that done outside really amounted to. Is working a loom or embroidering a dress really less satisfying for a human being than trade, and does it require any more or any less of intellectual virtues? Can domestic work prepare one for scientific pursuits, or is it merely an impediment? Is bowing to the authority of a religious superior more freeing than obeying family members? Should Aristotle have spent more time cooking for his family, would he have been a better philosopher? The struggles of the philosophers I present in this chapter, and the ways these struggles are reflected in their philosophical writings, offer an insight into what it does and could mean to be a philosopher.

Womanly Glory and Consolation

The successful have a tendency to advise others not to try and follow in their steps. This is true of some women who succeed in making a career for themselves in a mostly male world, as writing for a public was for a long time. They advise other women not to do the same, but to stick to what nature, God, and society intended for them. So Christine de Pizan's last words in the

Book of the City of Lady advise women to marry, and not to leave or disobey their husbands, even when they are violent.[2] Lucrezia Marinella, a Venetian philosopher, appeared to do something similar at the end of her life. Having spent a lifetime writing, and arguing for women's natural intellectual superiority to men, she apparently recanted all this in a final book. She wrote that "A woman's reputation must not leave the walls of her home." This quote, attributed by the author to Gorgias of Leontini, opens the *Exhortations to Women and Others If They Please* (1645), the last book written by Lucrezia Marinella, at the age of 74. Marinella was born in Venice in the 1570s. Nothing is known about her mother, but her father was a physician who had written two medical books about women's health and well-being. She had one brother, also a physician, and she married another physician. Both her father and husband encouraged her learning and her writing, as did a colleague of her father, Lucio Scarano. She lived in seclusion, as was common at the time even in more liberated Venice, and we know very little about her personal life.[3]

By the time Marinella wrote the *Exhortations*, she was already a celebrated author who had written books about the lives of saints, romances, and a treatise in which she defended women's superiority to men, turning some of Aristotle's arguments on their heads: *The Nobility and Excellence of Women, and the Vices and Defects of Men* (1601).

The Nobility of Women had been well received, but there was a change for the worse in the intellectual atmosphere toward the end of Marinella's life. Women writers, especially those who took the view that women were not, in fact, inferior to men, were censured or denounced.[4] This might explain why her final book, the *Exhortations*, seems to recant what she had argued in the *Nobility of Women*. Women, she now claims, following Aristotle and many others, ought not to pursue an intellectual life, but should focus on the domestic arts and virtues. This is what they are naturally suited for, and what will make them, and their husbands, happiest. Did Marinella really change her mind? Several readers of the *Exhortations* reject this interpretation. One says that Marinella, reacting against the changed, hostile climate toward women, is using a rhetorical device called *Insinuatio*, whereby the author "insinuates" themselves into the mind of the reader, by making claims they will readily accept, and, once inside, carefully challenges some of those claims.[5] Others have noticed that not only does Marinella cite Gorgias of Leontini, but she also cites the texts by Plato in which Gorgias is refuted. In particular, she uses a Platonic dialogue *Meno* in which Plato rejects Gorgias' claim that women's virtue is different from men's and that it consists in taking care of the home. So we have reason to be skeptical.

It is hard to pronounce, one way or the other, on Marinella's intention. We lack the necessary context—letters, diaries, notes—to do so.[6] Still, there is no reason why we should want to read her text as a conservative U-turn. U-turns are not very conservative, for one thing, as they require a radical change of mind. One way of tackling this text is to look specifically at what Marinella has to say about domestic work. What is its value? Who is it good for? And who, exactly is being exhorted? And the first answer has to be that the *Exhortations* are addressed not just to women, but to "others if they please," meaning men also. So she extols the domestic life for all, not just women, and she recommends that everyone chooses it over the life of the intellect. In other words, what she is doing in that book is elitist—only a few men or women will truly flourish as writers, others should not even try. But it's not sexist: what she says applies to everyone, men and women. But also Marinella does something that very few writers have done before the twentieth century: she offers a revaluing of traditionally feminine work. Men too, she argues, can enjoy domestic work.

Why should we think that Marinella is recanting her old arguments for women's intellectual superiority? Because she tells us, in the very first Exhortation, that she changed her mind. She says she no longer thinks that it's important for women to be free to go in and out of the home. Previously, she tells us, she had thought that it was men's tyranny that kept women confined to the home and unable to participate in public life, whether politics or philosophy. Now thinks that this is unlikely. With more mature judgment, she says, she is confident that women's seclusion is in fact the result of "nature, divine providence and will." This follows from the fact, she says, that any condition upheld by violence is short-lasting (she cites Machiavelli) and that women have been confined to the home for a long time. As to the reason for this natural order of things, she says, it is simply the ancient argument for the division of the spheres:

> While the woman takes care of the house, the man conducts commerce and deals outside of the house, that these different tasks might result in harmonious peace and happiness. (Marinella 1645/2012, 50)

While she appeals to Aristotle to establish the division of the spheres, Marinella puts a different spin on the role and interaction of the spheres. She starts by saying, reading Aristotle in a very unorthodox way, that the home is basically a small city, and that managing the one is like managing the other. Moreover, because the city is an agglomeration of households, there is a connection between the state of the ones and that of the other. Well-run homes, she says, lead to well-run cities (53). The—un-Aristotelian—conclusion that is left unsaid is that if women run homes, and run them well, they are also responsible for cities being well-run, while men who run the city only piggyback on women's work. Perhaps the *Exhortations* are not so removed from the *Nobility of Women* after all!

Another—radical—difference between Marinella and Aristotle is that right from the beginning, she defends household crafts as objectively worth doing. Her way of establishing that is to claim that men, when they can do so without being seen, will gladly retire to the women's sphere and do embroidery to "enjoy womanly glory and consolation" (53). For Aristotle (at least the author Marinella thought of as Aristotle, the author of the *Economics*), this would be unthinkable as he believed that participating in the business of the private sphere is deeply shameful for a man.

Having established to her satisfaction that the home is the proper domain for women, but that the work they do there is essential and noble, she moves on to the part of her thesis that has struck most scholars as going back on the *Nobility*: women, she argues, should not engage in intellectual pursuits but stick with the work of managing their homes. "Let us be satisfied with our ignorance," she—rather hypocritically—tells her readers. Intellectual pursuits, she says, are dangerous, and liable to make you crazy and turn you into hermits living in poverty (79). Of course, she still believes that some people should be intellectuals, even if that means they are shunned by society and live as hermits. She talks of Saint Jerome with great admiration. And not only was he an educator of women, but he did take to the desert with his books with the company of only a snake and a lion. Presumably the greatness of his work weighed against his unconventional life. But the same might not be true of a young woman who decides to take up writing instead of doing what the work her mother tells her to do. Remember the fate of Clara, Eliza Doolittle's sister-in-law. She left home to live a life of Bohème in London. But no one liked her very much, and she was never a success. Well, Marinella would say, the life of the intellect just isn't for everyone. Nor is it useful for society as a whole. A few intellectuals are a good, maybe a necessary thing, but a surplus them is just wasteful.

Marinella is being elitist here and telling other women that they are not cut out for the life of the intellect. They just don't have what it takes, and they'd better stick to what they know they can be good at, domestic work. This is part of the story. But there is more to it than that. First, Marinella is telling men the exact same thing. In her picture of harmony, men are acquisitors and women preservers. But if the men of the household become philosophers, there will be nothing for the women to preserve, hence no harmony. Note also that many of her examples concern men, rather than women. In Exhortation 4, where she praises silence over speech, most of her examples come from statesmen or male philosophers. By then it should have become clear that she is exhorting not just women, but, as the title says very clearly, "others if they please."

While she may be guilty of elitism, Marinella does not believe that regular people should be entirely ignorant. Indeed, in Exhortation 4, after she has told women to be satisfied with their ignorance, she smuggles in a method for them—and for men—to become better thinkers, to speak mindfully and to come to know the "power of sweet reasoning." She teaches them first to distinguish between powerful arguments and those that are empty, or mere "blabbering." She then extols the virtue of silence, both for learning, and for rehearsing in one's head what one is about to say before spouting it out. She recommends the avoidance of small talk—for much the same reason that it takes up thinking and learning space. She concludes that while silence is usually better than speech, there are times and occasions when it would be wrong, unjust even, not to speak out (105–109). Her concern for the education of men and women is also present in Exhortation 8, where she tells us that children should be educated and that "for the first few years, at least, there is no reason to think that the education [of boys and girls] cannot be the same" (155).

Marinella's *Exhortations* are to men and women, to help them realize the value of domestic work. That work is valuable in itself. Even the Goddess Minerva, she says, is prouder of her textile crafts than her achievements at war. But it's also valuable for humanity, as the welfare of the city depends on homes being well-run. This, more than a call to women to give up intellectual pretensions, is a rallying cry to those who were probably not interested in becoming philosophers in the first place, to come into their powers as wielders of divine instruments (Minerva's distaff) and makers and upholders of strong cities. Marinella does not send home the women who would be philosophers as much as she empowers those who would not.

But what about the not-so-regular people who end up being philosophers? Can they be women, or must all women be unexceptional? What is notable here, are the absences. In Exhortation 2, Marinella objects to her own view that women cannot be both housekeepers and philosophers or artists:

> Many say that devoting oneself to two arts is an arduous and difficult enterprise. I say, on the contrary, that it is easy to attend to both, because ruling over your household is a pastime compared to the study of intellectual disciplines. (63)

Marinella then cites the example of Minerva, goddess of wisdom and war, and at the same time sewing and spinning. If she can manage to be the divine guardian of all these things, then surely a regular human can be a practitioner of two of them? The objection remains unaddressed: Marinella does not have anything to say against the possibility that one might excel or at least be competent at both housewifery and philosophy. But she does note that doing both carries a risk.

> [...] you cannot properly apply yourself to two tasks because inevitably, you will like one and despise the other [...]. Therefore to avoid this problem, I maintain that women should practice the art that comes naturally and is proper to them. (64)

In its context, it is fairly clear that Marinella recommends that women stick to managing their homes. But the two passages taken together give pause for thought: What if Marinella does not think that all women are essentially housewives? What if she believes that for some women, what comes most naturally is writing, not sewing? The fact that she leaves the objection in Exhortation 2 mostly unanswered and that she leaves open the possibility that some women might find philosophy more fitting an occupation than housework, brings us back to the original supposition that Exhortations is not meant to discourage women from intellectual pursuits. But for those who don't become writers or philosophers, domestic pursuits are just as valuable and should not be shunned. And this applies to both women and men. In the next section, we explore the thoughts on domesticity of a philosopher who was quite convinced that her nature was more suited for philosophy than it was for "huswifry," Margaret Cavendish.

Writing with a Distaff and Cooking in the Lab

Margaret Lucas, the youngest of eight children of a royalist family, received a very basic and careless education—she could read and write (with often interesting spelling), but she knew only one language, English, and had not been taught any of the usual domestic crafts or artistic accomplishments. As a teenager she left home in search of adventure. She joined the court of Queen Henrietta Maria of England. During the English Civil War, the Queen removed first to Oxford, and then Paris. Margaret followed her. In Paris, she met William Cavendish, Marquess (later Duke) of Newcastle. They courted for a while in secret, as the Queen wasn't keen on losing one of her ladies in waiting. But they did marry and stayed in Paris together. They hosted philosophical dinners with the likes of Thomas Hobbes (also in exile) and René Descartes (briefly back from the Netherlands on his way to Sweden). The Cavendish spent the years Cromwell was in power in exile in the Netherlands. After the Restauration, they moved back to England. Cavendish was a prolific writer of poems, plays, stories (including what we now call science fiction), and philosophy. Her husband, who'd published a bestseller on horse training, encouraged her intellectual pursuits and made sure her works were printed.

Margaret Cavendish has become one of the go-to early modern women philosophers for those wishing to diversify the (very male, very white) canon. She is particularly popular because she wrote not as other modern women philosophers often did, about women's condition, political and social rights, or education, but about science and metaphysics. She wrote poems about atoms and stories featuring scientific method, and she engaged with Hobbes and Descartes on the nature of the mind. This does not make her a more interesting or valuable philosopher than, say, Gabrielle Suchon or Mary Wollstonecraft (both concerned amongst other things, with women's education), but it does make it easier to fit her into a mostly male curriculum—hence, perhaps, (part of) her popularity.

Cavendish is also known for her rejection of the role that was meant to be hers, that of a housewife, and her many justifications why it was better for her to become a writer. This makes her a heroine of sorts for those of us who find it hard to assert our intellectual ambitions in a world that still expects us to make babies, cook meals, and clean the bathroom. Cavendish, perhaps, suffered from her childlessness, but she used this as an opportunity to do something she cared about. Rather than become a busy housewife, she wrote. In the opening pages of *Poems and Fancies*, she offers an apology for her decision to become an author: her childlessness, and the war having deprived her of a home, meant that if she did not write, she would be idle. Best to spend a little time writing and hope for forgiveness.

> IF any do read this Book of mine, pray be not too severe in your *Censures*. For first, I have no *Children* to imploy my *Care*, and *Attendance* on; And my *Lords Estate* being taken away, had nothing for *Huswifery*, or thristy *Industry* to imploy my selfe in; having no *Stock* to work on. [...] But I have nothing to spin, or order, so as I become *Idle*; I cannot say, in mine owne *House*, because I have none, but what my *Mind* is lodg'd in. Thirdly, you are to spare your severe *Censures*, I having not so many yeares of *Experience*, as will make me a *Garland* to *Crowne* my *Head*; onely I have had so much time, as to gather a little *Posie* to stick upon my *Breast*. Lastly, the time I have been writing them, hath not been very long, but since I came into *England*, being *eight Yeares* out, and *nine Months* in; and of these *nine Months*, onely some *Houres* in the *Day*, or rather in the *Night*. (1653, To the Reader).

Some, including myself, have read Cavendish's writing on avoiding domestic work as a rejection of the value of this work. This, I now realize, was a mistake. A study of the texts and the relevant secondary literature reveals a much more interesting relationship between Cavendish's thoughts on writings and her attitude toward domesticity. Not only did she value domestic skills and virtues, but she made use of them to imbue her philosophical and scientific reflections with value. This is very counter-intuitive, as we tend to think of anything associated with domesticity (i.e., women's work, women's wages, women) as less valuable than what is associated with the public sphere (business, politics, men). Yet, we know that Marinella had already done some work toward showing that the home and its work were valuable, in themselves and instrumentally, and Cavendish appeals to figures such as Homer's Penelope to show that domestic crafts are not only valuable but very much a form of creative and intellectual work (like writing).

In *Sociable Letters* (1664), the narrator explains why she (we have reason to believe this narrator is very closely based on Cavendish herself) prefers writing over domestic work, whether with textiles or food. This explanation, or apology, even, comes as the result of neighbors' criticisms: her maids are idle, and she ought to give them a better example by sitting down with them to some domestic chore or other. The narrator calls her Governess and asks her to help set something up, so she can work with her maids. The governess replies that it would be a waste of materials and time, as she has no idea what she's doing. On the other, hand, she is good at writing, so she had better stick to it, as her books do in fact provide reading material for her maids so that they can use their free time educating themselves.

> I sent for the Governess of my House, and bid her give order to have Flax and Wheels Bought, for I, with my Maids, would sit and Spin. The Governess hearing me say so, Smiled, I ask'd her the Reason, she said, she Smil'd to think what Uneven Threads I would Spin, for, said she, though Nature hath made you a Spinster in Poetry, yet Education hath not made you a Spinster in Huswifry, and you will Spoil more Flax, than Get Cloth by your Spinning, as being an Art that requires Practice to Learn it; [. . .] And after I had Mused some time, I told her, how I heard my Neighbours Condemn'd me, for letting my Servants be Idle without Employment, and that my Maids said it was my Fault, for they were willing to be Employed in Huswifry; she said, my Neighbours would find Fault, where no Fault was, and my Maids would Complain more if they were kept to Work, than when they had liberty to Play.[7]

One clear message here is that any attempt by the narrator at domestic work would result in waste. She makes that clear elsewhere in the *Sociable Letters* when she says, "I cannot Work, I mean such Work as Ladies use to pass their Time withal, and if I could, the Materials of such Work would cost more than the Work would be worth, besides all the Time and Pains bestow'd upon it" (Letter 38). This could be read as a condemnation of luxury textile and kitchen experiments in general: no one who was well-off needed to make their own thread or cloth in the seventeenth century, as it could be cheaply obtained thanks to the beginnings of mass production. On the other hand, Cavendish knew that some luxury items had to be homemade, some clothes, some tapestries. The tapestries hanging in her husband's grandmother's house, Castle Hardwick, were a testimony to artistic talent, skill, and hard work.[8] So maybe Cavendish is merely remarking that she is not very good at such things, and that her own hard work is best put to use producing books, which at least will have some value.

Cavendish is not always critical of the value of housework, or dismissive of her own skills. Her *Poems and Fancies*, written a decade before the *Sociable Letters*, draw many parallels between writing and domestic work. For instance, in the passage cited above, she tells her readers that she does not have children to take care of, or a house to manage as her husband's property had been confiscated by Cromwell. She cannot spin, as she does not have a stock of materials, and no house to store it in. But, she says, she does not want to risk being idle, so she treats her brain as her house and works there, spinning words instead of flax.

This is an attempt at self-justification, and avoiding criticisms, but it is hardly a defense of domesticity. Nor do some of the other references in the several addresses prefacing the poems constitute such a defense. To her brother-in-law, who, like her husband, clearly encouraged her writing, she says "True it is, Spinning with the Fingers is more proper to our Sexe, than studying or writing Poetry, which is the Spinning with the braine: but I [have] no skill in the Art of the first." Again, there is little there beyond the metaphorical appeal to what others think she ought to be doing instead of writing. Her notice to "noble ladies" goes further:

> Besides, *Poetry*, which is built upon *Fancy*, *Women* may claime, as a *worke* belonging most properly to themselves: for I have observ'd, that their *Braines* work usually in a *Fantasticall motion*: in their *severall*, and *various* in their many and singular choices of *Cloaths*, and *Ribbons*, and the like; in their *curious shadowing*, and *mixing of Colours*, in their *Wrought workes*, and divers sorts of they imploy their *Needle*, and many *Curious* things they make, as *Flowers, Boxes, Baskets* with *Beads, Shells, Silke*, or any thing else. (1653, Notice to Noble Ladies).

There she goes into sufficient details that one begins to sense that there is a real parallel between housework and writing. The work of creating high fashion, that is, the sort of clothes that will impress and delight aristocratic society, involves, as we know, the choosing of materials, design, a sense of what will next be fashionable, and a great deal of skill with the needle. This recalls, as Lynette Hunter and Sarah Hutton noted in the introduction to their *Women, Science and Medicine*, an observation by Bathsua Makin (1673): "To buy wool and flax, to die scarlett and purple, requires skill in natural philosophy."[9]

The epistle "To the Reader" pushes the analogy further still and shows that Cavendish has thought quite carefully about the aspects of "housewifery" she wanted to replicate in her career as a writer. In particular, she highlights the value of "thrift" or economy, which in domestic work makes the difference between a home which is sustainably managed and one where the winter months are leaner, and in writing, requires the careful picking and shaping of words and sentences:

> For *Housewifery* is a discreet *Management,* and ordering all in *Private,* and *Household Affaires,* seeing nothing *spoil'd,* or *Prosusely spent,* that every thing has its proper *Place,* and every *Servant* his proper *Work,* and every *Work* to be done in its proper *Time;* to be *Neat,* and *Cleanly,* to have their *House* quiet from all *disturbing Noise.* But *Thriftiness* is something stricter; for good *Housewifery* may be used in great *Expenses;* but *Thriftiness* signifies a *Saving,* or a getting; as to increase their *Stock,* or *Estate.* For *Thrift* weighs, and measures out all *Expence.* It is just as in *Poetry:* for good *Hus|bandry* in *Poetry,* is, when there is great store of *Fancy* well order'd, not onely in fine *Language,* but proper *Phrases,* and significant *Words.* And *Thrift* in *Poetry,* is, when there is but little *Fancy,* which is not onely spun to the last *Thread,* but the *Thread* is drawne so [thin], as it is scarce perceived. (1653, To the Reader)

Cavendish, we saw earlier, though it was best she kept out of the kitchen. Still, she thought that the kitchen played an important part of a woman's (and, it turns out, a man's) life and development. Cavendish uses mostly textile art metaphors when describing her writing process. But the kitchen arts feature heavily in her *Poems and Fancies.* This is where Cavendish begins to shape her metaphysics and philosophy of science, and where she offers an alternative to the then very popular mechanistic views of the world. The "Poems," which comprise the first section of the book, offer explanations of various phenomena in atomistic terms as well as descriptions of how atoms function and interact with each other. The first poem features Nature, as a ruler, gathering her "councell, which was Motion, Figure, matter and Life" in order to discuss the creation of the world. "Fancies" also features Nature as a leader, but this time as the ruler of her household. Nature is portrayed as carrying a set of housekeeping keys, her cabinets are explored, much as one would investigate the stores in a house. From the fourth poem of the "Fancies" section onwards, Cavendish focuses on one thing: Nature's kitchen, where everything is prepared, from "the fat of gluttons" and "roots of several vices," to hearts served up with "Sauce of Jealousie, In dishes of Carefull Industry," or tarts filled with "cherry lips" and "Sloe-Black Eyes from a Faire Virgin's Head."

According to historians familiar with English language science writing and domestic writing of the seventeenth century, the poems of the "Fancies" do more than just use recipes as metaphors for human virtues and vices. First, they demonstrate an understanding of the transmission of kitchen knowledge (Snively 2015, 24).[10] Recipes, then as now, were written in such a way that those who used them would know how to fill in the gaps. The gaps though are different: today's household cooks tend to spend less of their time in the kitchen and need to be told more, but we (typically) do not need to be told what it means to cream the butter and sugar, or that the eggs, when beaten with sugar, do not really become "white." Seventeenth-century recipes offer less detail. So if Cavendish does not say how many eggs go into Nature's breakfast in "A Possett for Nature's Breakfast," it is not because she is inexact, but because the number of eggs to be used for any dish was generally common knowledge—or depended on the size of the eggs one had. This, Snively tells us "calls attention to the importance of practical, experiential knowledge and experimentation necessary to crafting the dishes and thus reading the poems" (25). Another poem, "Nature's Cook" in which Death is shown to prepare potions in Nature's kitchen out of human diseases, demonstrates, Snively tells us, an understanding of medical complaints, and suggests that it was through kitchen knowledge that medical knowledge was not only transmitted, but also created. The kitchen, she says, was a place of experimentation for women, who not only had to work out how to create nutritious and pleasant meals while economizing resources but also had to contend with illness in the family, cure it if they could and if not nurse the sick.

Not only do the poems suggest that Cavendish knew how much actual knowledge and technique went into the daily activities of women in the kitchen, but more than that, she is drawing important parallels between cooking and science. Another commentator, Elizabeth Scott-Bauman, calls it an "innovative and interdisciplinary appropriation of scientific thought." Another way of putting it is that while in the first section of Poems and Fancies, where she lays out her atomic theory, Cavendish is writing as a scientist, in The Fancies, she is showing the reader that, as a woman, she is particularly well-suited to using scientific methods of inquiry. This is significant because women were excluded from the scientific communities that gathered at the Royal Society—even though an exception was made for Cavendish to visit on one occasion.[11] Only men (of a certain class) could be trusted to conduct scientific experiments and propose hypotheses to be tested. But even so, women were as a matter of fact involved, as kitchens served for a long time as laboratories, and later, when laboratories were purpose-built, they followed the model of the kitchen. But men never conducted their experiments alone in the kitchen. They required help from those who actually knew their way around the instruments: wives, sisters, and maids.[12] What does it mean for Cavendish? It means she is reclaiming the value of kitchen and of the women who work there. These women can read a recipe and recreate it; they can experiment with ingredients, instruments, and heat. These women, she claims, are proper scientists.

Aristotle in His Kitchen

Cavendish was not the only seventeenth-century woman philosopher to draw analogies between what went on in a kitchen and experimental philosophy. Sor Juana Inez de la Cruz (1648–1695) also thought that the kitchen had the potential to produce not only food to sustain the body but also an opportunity for the mind to make discoveries. In a text entitled "Answer by the poet" (1691), she wrote:

> Well, then, my Lady, what can I tell you, about nature's secrets as I've discovered them while cooking? I see that an egg becomes solid and fries in lard or oil, while, on the other hand, it dissolves in syrup. I see that in order to keep sugar in a liquid state it suffices to add to it a very small part of water mixed with quince or another sour fruit. I see that an egg's yoke and white have such opposite characteristics that when one or the other of them is mixed with sugar each one separately works well, but when they are combined they do not. Because I don't want to bore you with which cold facts I'm mentioning them only to give you a full account of my nature and I think this probably has made you laugh. Nevertheless, my Lady, what can we women possibly know other than kitchen philosophies? Lupercio Leonardo said it quite well: one can philosophize well while preparing dinner. When I see these trivialities I often say this: if Aristotle had cooked stews he would have written a lot more. So, continuing with my mode of cogitation, I tell you that this is constant in me that I have no need for books.

What a powerful passage. At first it seems to make light of women's scientific and philosophical explorations as "kitchen philosophies," so little more than observations of cooking processes. But what Juana says is that these observations amount to proper philosophy: "one can philosophize well while preparing dinner," she cites one male poet as having said. And the final punch is that women who philosophize in the kitchen are doing something that Aristotle failed to do, but which, had he done it, would have made him a better philosopher, or at least a more productive one. This can mean two things: one is that interesting things happen in a kitchen that Aristotle did not cover in his extensive explorations of the world and its phenomena. The second is that what is discovered in the kitchen could add depth and detail to the studies Aristotle did conduct. Both could be true. Although Aristotle may have written a book about household management, he did not explore the nature of the work that actually goes into managing a household. And he certainly did not write about cooking. So by showing us this gap in Aristotle's works, Juana is also telling other philosophers not to ignore women's universe and work. You should write about what goes on in the kitchen, she seems to say, because there too is human nature developing.[13]

Sor Juana's own kitchen observations lead us to think otherwise, however: there is much, she seems to say, that philosophers interested in the workings of the natural world could have learned from the kitchen. Aristotle does not seem to have conducted experiments, and if he did, it was probably not rigorous or systematic.[14] Had he lined up a few women of different ages, looked inside their mouths, and conducted a similar experiment with men, he would not have come up with the odd conclusion that women have fewer teeth than men.[15] He did rely on observations—so it was perhaps unfair of Bertrand Russell to suggest that Aristotle could simply have looked into his wife's mouth—but clearly, his observations were not systematic (Russell 1953, 7). But had his observations taken him to mix and separate, melt or thicken cooking ingredients, and repeat the processes every day, because food must be prepared, and also because it might be improved, Juana suggests Aristotle might have discovered the value of scientific experiments.

Independence and Tranquility

Unless one was of royal blood, and owned their own convent, as Anna Komnene and her mother did, leaving home to join a religious order was not a guaranteed escape from the arbitrary domination of others. Still there are some advantages to obeying God and his workers rather than family members. Because a nun's first allegiance was always to God, and those who dominate her are also serving that same God, a nun has, at least, a reason to protest if she is ordered to do what she deems wrong. At home, the standards are different: a girl owes obedience first to her father, a woman to her husband, and they get to decide what God wants from their female relatives. A bride of God, to some extent, can sidestep these hurdles.

By joining a convent, a woman could also hope to avoid other aspects of domestic life: marriage, running the household, bringing up children, etc. When Sor Juana Inez de la Cruz left the palace of the Vice-Roy in Mexico City to join a convent, she was putting herself out of marriage's way. But she soon discovered that there were some domestic responsibilities that a woman could not escape even in a convent.

Juana did not, according to her biographer Octavio Paz, have a religious vocation. And she did not acquire one during her twenty-seven years in the convent.[16] She did not have a taste for spending her days in prayer and seclusion and had been quite happy living a luxury life at court. This is likely why her first attempt at convent life failed. At the age of nineteen, she joined a Carmelite convent (San Jose de las Carmelitas Descalzas), one of the most severe orders.[17] Two years later, she moved to the San Jeronimo convent, an order dedicated to St. Jerome, the hermit scholar who translated the bible in the desert.

Because Juana was an illegitimate child, and had no fortune, her options for marriage were in fact quite limited. But as a very clever and attractive young woman at court, with no male relatives to protect her, she was an easy target for "seduction" or rape which would have led to her "ruin" and to being cast out from society in disgrace. So going into a convent was a way of escaping not only unwanted marriage but also possibly assault. In an autobiographical essay, *Reply to Sor Philothea* (1691), Sor Juana explains why she decided to join a convent and gives us some insight into what exactly she was running from:

> I became a nun because, although I knew that that way of life involved much that was repellent to my nature—I refer to its incidental, not its central aspects—nevertheless, given my total disinclination to marriage, it was the least unreasonable and most becoming choice I could make to assure my ardently desired salvation. To which first consideration, as most important, all the other small frivolities of my nature yielded and gave way, such as my wish to live alone, to have no fixed occupation which might curtail my freedom to study, nor the noise of a community to interfere with the tranquil stillness of my books.[18]

Sor Juana would have liked to live the life of a well-off hermit, free to read and write, without having to depend on others for her subsistence, and without having to be part of a community, demanding of her time and attention. In a convent, at least, she was not dependent on one individual: once the vows were taken, she had a roof over her head and meals for as long as she lived. She had to contend with superiors who could order her and punish her. But their superiority did not appeal to nature to justify itself—there was a religious hierarchy, and she could, to some extent, climb to the top. (Though of course, the nuns answered to men who were not only higher in the religious order but could also claim natural superiority). In a sense, Sor Juana's choice to enter a convent was a bid for autonomy. But it was not a shedding of responsibilities. A convent is not a writing retreat, or a lifelong sabbatical, all expenses paid. By joining a convent, Juana escaped a life dedicated to serving a husband and caring for children. In exchange, she accepted the duties and burdens of communal life, and she found these very difficult to cope with. She was clearly not suited for this sort of life, and any community would have interfered with her desire for peaceful writing:

> even though the exercises and shared life which a community entails were repellent to the independence and tranquility which my inclination to study needed. (210)

Sor Juana is not shy about listing the particular inconveniences of communal life. Everyone who is nearby is a disturbance, and nobody understands her need for concentration or cares for it:

> many hindrances [to studies] arising not only from my religious duties (it goes without saying that those occupy one's time most profitably and beneficially) but also from things implicit in the life of a religious community—such as when I am reading, those in a neighboring cell take it upon themselves to play music and sing. Or when I am studying and two maids quarrel and come to me to settle their dispute. Or when I am writing and a friend comes to visit, doing me a great disservice with the best of intentions, where upon I must not only put up with the bother but act grateful for the injury. This goes on all the time, because, since the times I devote to my studies are those remaining when the regular duties of the community are over, the others are also free then to come and bother me. Only those who have experienced communal religious life can know how true this is. (217)

But all those inconveniences (which she lists with what one hopes is a degree of humorous self-awareness) are better than the alternatives: marriage, or risking becoming someone's mistress and being discarded to poverty and oblivion. The choice was not, however, always obvious to Juana. As a child entertained the same ambition as Christine de Pizan: becoming a man.

> Later on, when I was six or seven years old, and already knowing how to read and write along with all the other skills that women learn such as embroidery and sewing, I heard that in Mexico City there was a University and there were Schools where people studied the sciences. As soon as I heard this I began to kill my mother by constantly and naggingly begging her to dress me in boy's clothes and to send me to live with some relatives of hers in Mexico City so that I could study by enrolling in the University.

> She refused, and she was quite right, but I assuaged my desire by reading many kinds of books belonging to my grandfather, notwithstanding the punishment and scolding intended to stop me. So, when I came to Mexico people were amazed, not so much by my intelligence as by my memory and the facts that I had acquired at an age that seemed hardly enough just to be able to learn to speak. (8)

She was also aware that her desire to study was not something that would just go away: if she could not assuage it by pretending to be a man, she had to find another solution:

> This kind of questioning happened to me about everything and it continues happening even though I have no control over it; on the contrary, usually I get angry because it tires my head.

She adds that she used to think that everyone else was as thirsty for knowledge as she was. Presumably, she learned otherwise. But she never excluded the possibility that either her nature was shared by other women or that her love of study was situational, brought about by chance when she accompanied her sister to school as a child and nurtured by her grandfather's library. As a result, she contemplated the reasons why women were not, on the whole, inclined to study. Her conclusion shows that she did have some faith in the power of female communities, as she argued that women should educate women. As things stood, if parents wanted their daughters educated, they sent them to male tutors, which often resulted in disgrace and unwanted pregnancy. Juana argued that if women were to become tutors to girls, they could develop a taste for study. In doing so, she appealed to the traditional model of women's education, the passing of skills from one generation to the other.

> All of which would be eliminated if there were older women of learning, as Saint Paul desires, and instruction was passed down from one group to another, as is the case with needlework and other traditional activities.

> For what drawback could there be to having an old woman, well-versed in letters and pious in conversation and way of life, in charge of the education of maidens? And what harm in preventing the latter from going to waste either for lack of instruction or from having it imparted to them through the dangerous medium of male masters? (232–233)

Despite her personal preference for being a reclusive writer, Juana seems to have believed in the potential of women's community, and domestic skills as a way of helping women transcend their domestic situation and become the learners they are capable of being.

The *Reply* concludes with a defense of women's education which goes through an interpretation of various biblical passages which seem to condemn it. Here Juana shows off her scholarly knowledge of the scriptures and argues that no part of the bible was intended to stop women from either learning or teaching, and that, at most, it condemned them for being too loud in church.

We seem to have come full circle. At the beginning of the chapter, Marinella was asking whether one could learn both the domestic crafts that would bring women a peaceful and pleasant life, and become an intellectual. Sor Juana proposes that the same mechanisms that enable women to learn how to embroider with their mother and sisters, or spin with their maids, Roman matron style, can also help women learn to ask philosophical questions. Marinella, who never answered her own objection that it was in fact perfectly possible to do both, would almost certainly have approved. The domestic arts may be confining when they are all one is allowed to do, but they also carry the power to teach us everything else, provided we are allowed to learn.

5

Of Home and Bondage

At the eve of the eighteenth century, in a fashionable Chelsea home, a celebrity divorcee died. She had led a colorful life, running away from a sadistic husband, abandoning their four children in his French castle, and becoming Charles II's mistress, then his daughter's. Mancini's neighbor was the philosopher Mary Astell. Astell was rather conservative, and we can imagine her behind her curtains, tutting at the laughing men and women going into Mancini's house, to drink and gamble. But Astell did more than tut: a year after Mancini died, she used her to introduce her treatise, *Reflections Upon Marriage*. Mancini was an example of how badly marriage can go for women, so Astell asked: Are women better off unmarried? Yes, probably, but then where would children come from? Should Hortense Mancini have broken her chains, and started a less dissipated life as a single woman? Astell offers a very firm "no." Marriage is not something that can be broken off by anything other than death. But women need not suffer as much as Mancini did, and Astell has a solution: should a woman be educated, the chains of domesticity will be almost bearable.

Ninety years after Mancini died, when the century begins to draw to a close, a young woman philosopher entertained a famous French aristocratic diplomat in her rooms in Store Street. She had wine, but nothing to serve it in, so she handed him a (cracked) teacup, and talked to him about female independence. After that she became known as a "philosophical sloven," a "free-thinker" with no respect for domestic life. But throughout her short life, Mary Wollstonecraft did in fact work tirelessly to rethink domesticity, and the power structures within it, trying to make the home a place of fairness, where everyone could flourish.

Whether they attempted to break their chains, soften them, or melt them down into something more useful and more just, the women philosophers of the eighteenth century were fully aware of their chains. Because they thought more about liberty, the power structures within the home had become painfully obvious to them, and in an age of revolution, it was hard to leave them unchallenged. Unfortunately, this could mean losing everything.

No Place Like Home. Sandrine Bergès, Oxford University Press. © Oxford University Press USA 2026.
DOI: 10.1093/9780197687413.003.0005

Fast forward to 1828, and another enslaved woman is brought to London. Mary Prince is neither young nor a writer. But she understands freedom and knows that it is for everyone. And in London, thanks to the English law, she can emancipate herself. But her freedom comes at a cost: once she leaves the house of her captivity, she has nowhere to go. And once free, she cannot travel back to her own family in the West Indies. Her chains broken, she is untethered, with no prospect of a home.

Once women started seeing home as a place of bondage, rather than simply defining their duties, they had to ask themselves, at least, whether they should break free. This is what the three women in this chapter wrestled with, each in their own ways, from their segment of the British eighteenth century.

Mary Astell and the Mazarin Marriage

Mary Astell (1666–1731) was born in Newcastle to coal merchant parents. Her uncle, a Cambridge graduate and alcoholic ex-clergyman, supervised her education. Losing her mother in 1788, she decided to move to London and purchased a small house for herself in London's Chelsea, where she met with other literary women who encouraged her career as a writer.

Astell didn't quite belong to the era that defended women's rights. But she was firm about one thing: women should be educated. Her first published book, *A Serious Proposal to the Ladies, Parts I and II. Wherein a Method Is Offer'd for the Improvement of Their Minds* (1694, 1697), advocated for the creation of a school for women. The school would improve their chance of a good life, whether they married or remained single. If they married, they would use their wisdom to teach their children (and husbands!). If they didn't, the school could become a refuge, convent like, where they could live a quiet life helping other women learn. The schooling would resemble the higher stage of Plato's educational program in the Republic. Women would read philosophy and contemplate moral and religious truths. But they would also learn to use a method to help them focus their untrained minds to hard metaphysical (and theological) matters. The method, inspired by the French philosopher Descartes whom Astell admired, consisted of six rules designed to encourage focus, concentration, and perseverance. Astell considered those skills to be universally useful—not just for learning, but for dealing with any problem married (or single) life might throw at a woman.[1]

The point of improving women's minds, for Astell, was not to make professional scholars of them. A conservative (and royalist) writer, Astell believed that women belonged in the home. Religion and society dictated it. But she also had a positive take on domesticity: women had a specific function in their homes. They could improve their husbands—if they needed improving, which was likely as their education was not much better than women's—and bring up children to be morally good people. And in order to improve and educate others, they needed not only a solid education before they married, but also the resources to keep on learning afterwards, so they could adapt to their role as wife and mother. That was the point of the method: teaching women to be lifelong learners.

Another benefit of education for women, according to Astell, was that it could help provide consolation in an otherwise restrictive and difficult existence. Because marriages were arranged and irrevocable, women were sometimes forced to submit to a husband who turned out to be "so much worse than a brute." When that happens, Astell says, a woman

> has need of a strong Reason, of a truly Christian and well-temper'd Spirit, of all the Assistance the best Education can give her, and ought to have some good assurance of her own Firmness and Vertue.[2]

Did Astell think that being a good wife and mother would make a woman happy no matter what sort of a husband she had? No: she was well that marriage could be oppressive, especially if to the wrong man. But she trusted that, at least sometimes, a bad marriage could be made better, or at least bearable, if a woman was educated. And if she wasn't, the remedy was to acquire an education, not to attempt to escape her domestic obligations. And escaping domestic obligations was exactly what Hortence Mancini had done, when she left her husband and children. This could have been avoided, Astell thought, if Mancini's mind had been at all trained. So Astell, looking sadly, and disapprovingly, at her famous neighbor's life, wrote a book.

When Astell wrote her second book, *Reflections Upon Marriage* (1700), Hortence Mancini, Duchess of Mazarin, had just died at the age of 53. Mancini had moved to Paradise Row, where Astell lived, a few years previously. Before that she had lived in Kensington square, and earlier, Whitehall, in an apartment in the King's residence. As his mistress, she had a generous pension. But the King died, and Mancini lost her income. She needed to downgrade. Her salon in Paradise Row was one of the most fashionable at a time when London was full of literary salons. But hers was infamous because she allowed women, as well as men, to drink and to gamble. Once her pension stopped, and she could no longer afford to host lavish evenings, her guests took to leaving cash under their plate to help with the cost of entertaining. This did nothing good to her reputation. But then, there was not much left to salvage.

Mancini was married at 15 to a very rich man, who inherited through her the wealth and title of the Cardinal of Mazarin and became even richer. In her *Memoirs*, published in 1675 when she was twenty-nine years old,[3] Mancini portrays her husband as extremely religious, mentally unstable, and with a tendency to violence. Distrustful of his young wife's fidelity, he took her away from Paris whenever the King did not require his presence there. And noting that she did not like to travel to remote parts of France, he made sure to take her with him whenever the King sent him on business. He even insisted she travel long distances on bumpy roads while she was heavily pregnant. He forbade all male visitors and conducted midnight searches to make sure she wasn't smuggling them in. And when they were not traveling, he forced his wife to spend hours every day praying. Any suggestion of sexuality made him angry, and anger made him cruel and violent. He reportedly had the front teeth of female servants removed, so they wouldn't look attractive. The Duke of Mazarin's instability was well-known, as it affected not only his wife and servants but also his extensive art collection, in part inherited from his wife's uncle. He was known for attacking and emasculating his sculptures with a hammer—either because he disapproved of sexual organs on display or because he was jealous of the admiration they'd received from one of his wife's friends. The Mazarin Adonis at the Louvres (now restored) was one of the statues he mutilated.[4]

Hortence Mancini ran away from her husband's home after seven years of an unhappy and abusive marriage. She left behind their four children— legally, they belonged to him. She survived—and indeed, for several decades, thrived—through the patronage of powerful men, including Louis XIV and Charles II, while having affairs with both men and women.

Astell's diagnosis of Mancini's life is that she sought "Consolation under Domestick troubles from the Gaieties of a Court, from Gaming and Courtship, from Rambling and odd Adventures, and the Amusements mixt Company affords." But this, Astell carries on, could only provide temporary relief, "Plaister up the Sore, but will never heal it; nay, which is worse, she makes it Fester beyond a possibility of Cure."[5] Is this unfair? Was Mancini not just choosing the life of freedom she wanted to live, and refusing to be the prisoner of a sadistic man?

It was not quite a life of freedom, of course. There was no real way out for Mancini, no escape from the need for dependence on men for her survival. She could not take up a profession or even receive an income in France—as she did from Louis XIV—without her husband being allowed to confiscate it. As a married woman in the seventeenth century, she had no right to property of her own. Nor did she have a right to her children. Had she attempted to take them with her, they would have been taken from her and brought back to their father. So Mancini could not choose to take up a quiet domestic life, away from her tyrant of her husband, where she would be a virtuous mother to her children. Nor was retiring to a convent apparently much of an option: her husband did send her to a convent, but this was another way for him to control her. And shortly after he had her released, she escaped. Mancini's only options—until her husband died—were to put up with the domestic conditions that were her lot, or to set up on her own as a courtesan and a salonière. Unfortunately for her, her husband stayed alive long enough to divorce her, so she remained poor (and disgraced).

Astell's discussion of Mancini is not completely devoid of sympathy. She does not say that Mancini just ought to have made the best of her domestic situation. She pities her for having been forced into marriage with an extremely unsuitable husband and without having been prepared for it through education. Mancini was brought up to be a party girl, not a studious one. She was trained to be successful at court, so she could find a rich husband, not to spend time alone at home. She did not have the resources to make the best of the isolation her husband enforced on her, or to attempt to reform her husband by modeling virtuous behavior. Not that this would have worked, given the sort of husband she did have. But she might, had she been of a religious disposition, found relief in the long hours of prayer he imposed on her, or enjoyed being shut up in a convent, when he sent her there. And, provided he'd let her, she could have done her best to educate her children, so that they grew up to be better humans than their father was. But that's assuming a lot from a man who was by all account determined to make his wife miserable and placing a lot of the responsibility for preventing abuse on her shoulders. And it's not even clear that Astell is making these points. What she wants to say is that marriage is hard, but for a woman who has not been trained to care for her mind, it's harder.

Astell likely knew some of the details of Mancini's life story before she moved to Paradise Row, either from the *Memoirs* or from society gossip. She certainly shows some familiarity with the state of the Mazarin marriage, and although she will not condone the wife's running away, she strongly condemns the husband's treatment of the wife:

> To be yoak'd for Life to a disagreeable Person and Temper; to have Folly and Ignorance tyrannize over Wit and Sense; to be contradicted in every thing one does or says, and bore down not by Reason but Authority; to be denied ones most innocent desires for no other cause, but the Will and Pleasure of an absolute Lord and Master, whose follies a Woman with all her Prudence cannot hide, and whose Commands she cannot but despise at the same time she obeys them, is a misery none can have a just Idea of, but those who have felt it.[6]

But even the well-documented cruelty of a husband cannot justify a woman leaving home for Astell:

> The Christian Institution of Marriage provides the best that may be for Domestick Quiet and Content, and for the Education of Children; so that if we were not under the tye of Religion, even the Good of Society and civil Duty would oblige us to what that requires at our Hands.[7]

Domesticity, Astell thinks, is a natural way for people to live with one another in mutual dependence and improve one another. An older, wiser, more patient husband may educate his wife, so that she is better able to live with him in peace and harmony. An educated wife may set the example for her husband, helping improve his character, and also educate her children, so that they may in turn have happier lives. But just as importantly, an educated woman will have the inner resources to bear an unhappy marriage, and to preserve themselves from falling into a slave-like dependency if their husband is a tyrant. An educated woman is less likely to have their spirits crushed by the constant need to obey. And this, for Astell, is key to survival, if not happiness. As Jacqueline Broad puts it, in her monograph on Astell, acquiring a tame and submissive temper is, for Astell, "to be avoided—at all costs."[8]

There is a tension in Astell that is reminiscent of what we found in the writings of Christine de Pizan between the clear assertion that women are the equal to men in all that matters (intellect, morality, religion) and that that, like men, they can be improved through education, but that at the same time, women should not challenge their place in the home, should remain under the authority of their husband without becoming subservient, and fulfill their domestic duties without protesting.

> If therefore it be a Woman's hard Fate to meet with a disagreeable Temper, and of all others the Haughty, Imperious and Self-conceited are the most so, she is as unhappy as any thing in the World can make her. When a Wife's Temper does not please, if she makes her Husband uneasie, he can find entertainments abroad, he has a hundred ways of relieving himself, but neither Prudence nor Duty will allow a Woman to fly out, her Business and Entertainment are at home, and tho' he make it ever so uneasie to her she must be content and make her best on't.[9]

Astell does provide some sort of escape from marital servitude for women in so far as she advises parents not to marry their children for profit, and men and women not to marry without friendship. A woman before she decides to marry, she says,

> had need be very sure that she does not make a Fool her Head, nor a Vicious Man her Guide and Pattern, she had best stay till she can meet with one who has the Government of his own Passions, and has duly regulated his own Desires, since he is to have such an absolute Power over hers.[10]

In other words, while there is no right or justifiable escape from domesticity, and while domesticity is the best way for human beings to live together and raise children, it is not a state that should be entered lightly. Better to stay single and participate in human development in other ways—for instance, by writing philosophy.

For Astell, marriage for women is a form of servitude. In the 1706 preface to her *Reflections Upon Marriage*, Mary Astell asks "If all men are born free, how is it that all women are born slaves?"[11] But then she goes on to argue that women are "for the most part wise enough to love their chains" and claims that a woman should "not attempt to struggle with the yoke." To a modern reader, this sounds as if she is being ironic—Why should it be wise to love one's chains? Why should a woman recognize that she is enslaved and decide she is better off that way? This doesn't sound right, especially as Astell is not the compromising kind: she claims that marriage is simply never materially advantageous to women. It is advantageous to men and children (and presumable more advantageous to those children that grow up to be men!). But what women can get out of marriage, she says, is an advantage in the next world.[12] And in order to earn this advantage, they must perform an important job well: they must educate children to be good. So they had better be equipped for the job: they must be educated.

But how far does Astell want her comparison between marriage and slavery to go? When in the *Reflections* she talks about "poor female slaves," it appears to be in order to mock the republican writers of seventeenth-century England, such as Milton, who had cried out for the freedom of aristocratic men oppressed by the King but ignored those who were truly deprived of freedom—the poor, the enslaved, and women:

> For whatever may be said against Passive-Obedience in another case, I suppose there's no Man but likes it very well in this; how much soever Arbitrary Power may be dislik'd on a Throne, not *Milton* himself wou'd cry up Liberty to poor *Female Slaves*, or plead for the Lawfulness of Resisting a Private Tyranny.[13]

While Astell thought (free) women's situation on the whole very harsh, she was skeptical of the republican slavery trope. There are many ways to be dominated, to have one's freedom restricted, and not all amount to slavery. Certainly, as a royalist, she did not believe that the King's subjects were enslaved. And women, while they are worse off than the men who represent the sole focus of republicans, are not enslaved either, and should not consider themselves so, even when they accept a husband's complete authority. They are people living under the rightful authority of another, in a situation of natural co-dependence. Women, men, and children need to live with each other in order to thrive. And for Astell, questioning the authority of men, who are in a position to provide materially for the family, over women, who—especially if they must be in charge of children—are not, is as senseless as questioning the authority of parents over children. Her conclusion states that women must accept their husband as their rulers,

> Not as an absolute Lord and Master, with an Arbitrary and Tyrannical sway, but as Reason Governs and Conducts a Man, by proposing what is Just and Fit.[14]

What Astell has to say about women and slavery can help us understand the apparent paradox in her treatment of marriage. Although marriage is often a miserable state for women, it doesn't entirely take away their freedom. They are not enslaved, but freely ruled individuals who can help their rulers and themselves by developing their wisdom and virtue. They have some control over their own faculties, and, with the help of a good education, can transform themselves, their husband, and children for the better, and contribute to the happiness of the entire family.[15] But to do so, they must be educated, and they must stay home.

Domestic Minimalism

Mary Astell thought that freedom was a bit over-rated, and that domestic peace, the improvement of others, and the promise of happiness in the afterlife were worth a lot more than trying to strike out on one's own. Mary Wollstonecraft (1759–1797), philosopher, novelist, political journalist, and travel writer, begged to differ. For her, independence was "the grand blessing of life," and anything that threatened it, such as domesticity, had to be regarded with serious suspicion.

Wollstonecraft was not, in any case, known for her dedication to domesticity. When, in the early weeks of 1792, the Marquis de Talleyrand came to visit her in her London lodgings on Store Street, Wollstonecraft served him wine in a chipped teacup. The story was told, retold, and eventually became part of the legend of Wollstonecraft—the formidable philosopher who cared nothing for social niceties (Pennell 1885, 72). One acquaintance even took it upon himself to add to the story by calling her "a philosophical sloven: her usual dress being a habit of coarse cloth, such as is now worn by milk-women, black worsted stockings, and a beaver hat, with her hair hanging lank about her shoulders."[16] If she did wear such clothing, Wollstonecraft would have cut quite an interesting figure, showing a disdain for luxury (cheap cloth and stockings) and for the arts of grooming—her hair worn down, a plain man's hat. But portraits we have of her, painted from life, show that far from being unkempt, she dressed with an elegant simplicity. And she was fashionable: in the nineties, her white dress was cut from a Parisian design.[17]

The teacup episode, it turns out, was an effect of Wollstonecraft's relative poverty at the time, rather than scorn for domesticity. At the time she entertained Talleyrand, Wollstonecraft was just starting out as a professional writer, had debts to pay and family to support, and as a result, owned very few furnishings. Although glass objects were already a consumer item, wine glasses were nonetheless expensive, and a luxury that the single professional woman, who had to move frequently because she was a lodger, not a home-owner, could perhaps not afford. In fact, she had only begun to buy her own furniture a few months before Talleyrand visited:

> In September 1791, she removed from the house she occupied in George-street, to a large and commodious apartment in Store Street, Bedford-square. She began to think that she had been too rigid, in the laws of frugality and self-denial with which she set out in her literary career; and now added to the neatness and cleanliness which she had always scru-pulously observed a certain degree of elegance, and those temperate indulgences in furniture and accommodation, from which a sound and un-corrupted taste never fails to derive pleasure.[18]

Wollstonecraft was not "slovenly" then. She was poor but also valued clean-liness and simplicity—both of which are easier to achieve if one has fewer things to take care of. Godwin's testimony tells us something more significant about Wollstonecraft's philosophical stance toward domesticity: keeping things simple was an aid to independence. Independence was central to Wollstonecraft's thought and to the plea she addressed to Talleyrand in the letter which prefaces her *Vindication of the Rights of Woman*:

> Independence I have long considered as the grand blessing of life, the basis of every virtue—and independence I will ever secure by contracting my wants, though I were to live on a barren heath.[19]

Independence, in eighteenth-century republican parlance, is also freedom from domination, the ability to live one's life without the shadow of tyr-anny darkening our every choice. And, contrary to what Astell thought, real tyrants could be in the home as well as on the throne, reducing a wife to the status of an upper servant, depending for everything on her husband's goodwill. Wollstonecraft's solution, therefore, was to argue for an in-depth reform of domestic life, parallel to the reforms (proposed by French revolu-tionary) of public life, and making sure that neither women nor men became oppressed by domesticity.

Protecting individuals from being oppressed by their domestic duties means sometimes going against their specified wishes—Why should a woman who has a stated preference for subordination to her husband over independence, and for a domestic life over a professional one, be told that she's wrong? Told that, for the sake of her daughters, she needs to change the way she sees the world and her place in it? And even if there is a right way of doing this, how should we support her in her efforts to become emancipated? Some elements of Wollstonecraft's argument foreshadow the works of twentieth-century philosophers, such as Amartya Sen, who sometimes refers to Wollstonecraft as an influence on his theory of adaptive preferences, the mechanism whereby those who are severely deprived learn to love their deprivations.[20] The theory of adaptive preferences attributes to oppressed people a form of self-deception, or false consciousness, resulting in their thinking that they are choosing to live the lives they live, and that they are satisfied with them, no matter how objectively miserable. But this theory, especially in its applications to the women of the Global South, is not without its critiques. One in particular, Serene Khader has argued that a lot of feminist interest in the global south reflects a lack of real engagement with the lives and struggles of "other" women, and a lack of recognition of both the impact of colonialism on women's lives, and of the limitations of certain feminist theorizing.

> Feminist theorists who want to write about the lives of third-world women and who endorse cross-cultural feminist interventions must be attentive to the various ways in which feminist theorizing about deprivation can function to obscure the agency of deprived people and misrepresent the causes of their deprivation.[21]

In other words, we should not assume that a woman whose life seems to us miserable is necessarily deceiving herself, and needs to be dragged into a different life, against her will if needs be, or pitied for her not recognizing how bad her life is and blamed for her failure to change it. What is needed is a deeper, less prejudiced inquiry in the life of "other" women, taking the actor herself as an authority on her life, rather than assume false consciousness; the recognition that the life of a well-off, white woman may not be the best model for understanding a woman of the global south; and that the privilege enjoyed by the white woman may in fact be part of the explanation for the others' misery as a result of past and present exploitation.

Wollstonecraft was very aware of the different lived experiences of women from different classes, having moved up and down the social ladder during her life, as well as traveled to countries where gendered customs were different, and shown a strong interest in the experience of enslaved people. Her claim, in the *Vindication of the Rights of Woman*, that her primary target audience is middle-class women is not tantamount to a claim that she cares only for the improvement of that class.[22]

The middle classes, she says, is where change must begin, because middle-class women are the best able to bring it about. But this is not where change must stop. Her final, unpublished work, *Maria or the Wrongs of Woman*, tells the story of two women, one aristocratic, and one working-class, who struggle alone, then together, to achieve the independence they crave. The story of the working-class woman, Jemima, shows that Wollstonecraft was keenly aware of and deeply concerned by the plight of lower-class women. In the novel, Wollstonecraft gives a vivid description of the variety of abuse Jemima, the illegitimate child of a servant, is victim of. Her first experience of rape comes when she is still a child:

> At sixteen, I suddenly grew tall, and something like comeliness appeared on a Sunday, when I had time to wash my face, and put on clean clothes. My master had once or twice caught hold of me in the passage; but I instinctively avoided his disgusting caresses. One day, however, when the family were at a Methodist meeting, he contrived to be alone in the house with me, and by blows—yes; blows and menaces, compelled me to submit to his ferocious desire; and to avoid my mistress's fury, I was obliged in future to comply, and skulk to my loft at his command, in spite of increasing loathing.[23]

The aristocratic Maria's abuse comes from her husband. After a reasonably happy and carefree youth, Maria makes a bad marriage, attempts to escape with her baby, but is caught by her husband. Her baby is taken from her, and she is imprisoned in an asylum. There she meets Jemima, her jailor. The two women are not immediately drawn to help each other. Wollstonecraft shows that the difference in their social class, and in the type of abuse they received, makes it difficult for them to relate to each other and trust each other. But by the end of the novel (there are several endings in note form), they have become firm friends. They work together to escape, and to find Maria's kidnapped daughter.

Although Wollstonecraft was not naïve and did not believe that all women's struggles were the same, she thought it was possible for women to assist each other in their fight for independence. One of the possible endings to the story has Maria attempting suicide and being revived in time to see that Jemima has found and brought back her daughter. Maria decides that she can live again now, for her daughter.

Maria and Jemima's experiences of domesticity until that point were unequivocally bad. Maria was decanted from her family home into that of her husband, finding out that neither home was ever truly hers legally, and that she was only ever a possession herself. Jemima was born without a home, forced to find one where she could be fed, but also abused, thrown out into the streets, and finally, bought by a man, who let her share his home. But at the end of the story, it is the prospect of living together, with no men, as mothers and friends who keep them alive.

What Wollstonecraft had to say about domesticity stood in contrast to Rousseau's then highly popular views on women's roles. Rousseau believed that when women were properly educated, that is, trained out of their "natural viciousness," they would develop domestic virtues, and that those virtues were crucial for the shaping of a nation's character. A good wife and mother, he thought, will serve as moral educator not just for her children and husband, but for her neighbors and anyone she comes into contact with.

Rousseau spells out his view of domestic virtue in his novel *The New Heloise*. The heroine, Julie, starts off as a highly intelligent and educated young woman in love with her tutor (like the original Heloise, who fell in love with her tutor Abelard). At the end of the story, she has become the virtuous wife of an older man she respects but does not love, a dedicated mother, and moral mentor to a rural community. She has undergone a sort of "Stepford Wife" transformation. She no longer reads or studies, because her mothering duties keep her too busy. Her entire being is dedicated to making others happy. *The New Heloise* was bestseller at the time and extremely popular with female readers. This is not surprising perhaps. Rousseau describes women as having sexual power, harmful, but very effective. But it's when they relinquish that, by becoming wives and mothers, that they become truly influential. They now have domestic power, and that plays an important role in shaping a virtuous world, Rousseau's vision of what a republic should be like.[24]

Despite her claim that women should be independent of men, and her strong rejection of Rousseau's claim that men and women are essentially different, with women possessing a special "feminine" power or essence, Wollstonecraft did not reject women's ties to the home. On the contrary, she believed that a woman's civic virtue was tied to her fulfilling her domesticity duties, especially those of parenting:

> The wife, in the present state of things, who is faithful to her husband, and neither suckles nor educates her children, scarcely deserves the name of a wife and has no right to that of a citizen. " [. . .] 'the care of children in their infancy is one of the grand duties annexed to the female character by nature' [. . .]" the rearing of children [. . .] has justly been insisted on as the peculiar destination of woman.[25]

Being in charge of the home and the well-being of the people in it was not only a duty, but a "grand" one, which all citizens of a republic, men and women, should in some way fulfill. And women, for biological reasons that were then inescapable (bottle feeding was not a viable option in the eighteenth century, and many orphans died through attempts at feeding them non-human milk), were mostly concerned with the care of infants.

Wollstonecraft's commitment to the flourishing of children went beyond their first two years. She decried the custom of sending boys out to boarding schools where they learned "unchaste" habits, and forcing girls to stay at home, uneducated, until they could be married off. Instead, she proposed two things. First, boys and girls should be brought up and educated together. This meant that they didn't remain a "mystery" to each other until the time came to marry, and so that they could equally benefit from the best education, and become equal, worthy of each other's love. Secondly, she thought that an education that combined home and school would be best. Being brought up in the home, not in a wetnurse's house, nor in a boarding school, would mean being in close contact with those that loved them best, their parents and siblings, and that would mean they had a better chance at a healthy emotional development. It also meant, for Wollstonecraft, that parents could supervise the moral education of their children, inculcate proper "manners" through example. So that meant having a mother that spent more time in the nursery than at the mirror, and a father that came home after work, instead of going out to drink, gamble, or visit prostitutes. At the same time, Wollstonecraft thought that children needed to be educated among peers, so they could learn to relate to each other, especially to others from different socioeconomic backgrounds and from the opposite sex. They needed to engage with other children freely, without having to impress parent or tutor, because this freedom to experiment is the best way, for Wollstonecraft to learn reasoning.

If wetnurses make for children who are unhealthy and without emotional ties to their families, boarding schools create unhealthy ties among children and problems with authority, and homeschooling shelters children from their peers and takes away from them the possibility of engaging freely in debate, thereby fully developing their rational capacities, then what is left? What is left, and what Wollstonecraft advocates, are day schools where children learn outside the home, but live with their families.

While Rousseau relegates women to the home because of what he perceives to be their nature, first, and envisages that it might have good political consequences second, Wollstonecraft is mostly concerned with the political aspect of domesticity. She agrees with Rousseau that virtue, and in particular civic virtue, is born and nurtured in the home, and that those who are responsible for the upbringing of children are also responsible for shaping the future of the republic. She does not, however, think that performance of domestic duties should come at the cost of civic rights or personal development—women should be allowed to take up any profession instead of marrying, and the state should look after them so that if they do not work, they still have financial independence. Independence, she told Talleyrand in the dedication of her *Vindication*, is "the grand blessing of life, the basis of every virtue." But women who depend on their husbands or fathers for money, who cannot buy food without a handout from a man, cannot be expected to develop any form of moral independence: they cannot think for themselves, they cannot be virtuous.

> It is vain to expect virtue from women till they are, in some degree, independent of men; nay, it is vain to expect that strength of natural affection, which would make them good wives and mothers.[26]

> [...] But, to render her really virtuous and useful, she must not, if she discharge her civil duties, want, individually, the protection of civil laws; she must not be dependent on her husband's bounty for her subsistence during his life, or support after his death—for how can a being be generous who has nothing of its own? Or virtuous, who is not free?[27]

To respond to this problem, Wollstonecraft argues that women should be financially, as well as morally and politically, independent. And if they cannot work because they are stay-at-home mothers, then the state should see to it that they have an income of their own.[28]

Wollstonecraft does not simply regard caring for children as an inevitable job that has to be shared out, as best as possible, by parents. For her, bringing up the next generation is also a way of building future equality, ensuring that with each generation, men and women will be closer in status, better able to work together to create a world that is fair and profitable for all. This explains both why she places a great deal of value on parenting—why she calls it a "grand duty"—and why she nearly always puts the welfare of the children ahead of the convenience of the parents. This is particularly true in the case of breastfeeding. A mother, she says, should feed her own child, not send them out to a wetnurse. This means that she may have to make some sacrifices—she will need to live a calmer, healthier life, spend less time at parties, and her husband will need to let go of her body as his particular property, designed for his own amusement, for a few years.

With all this emphasis on children's welfare, one might worry that Wollstonecraft ends up forcing women to put their own development and ambition hold at least till the children have left home, and that until then, they can be nothing more than mothers. Hannah Mather Crocker, an American philosopher who wrote a commentary on Wollstonecraft, had raised ten children to adulthood before she took up a career as a writer. She felt that retirement from active motherhood was "a fully ripe season to read, write, meditate and compose, if the body and mind are not enfeebled by infirmities."

Wollstonecraft, for all that she thinks the raising of children is a sacred duty, does not agree that a woman should wait till old age to engage in nondomestic pursuits. Even full-time mothering, she says, should not prevent a woman from developing other aspects of herself, and engaging in other pursuits:

> And did they pursue a plan of conduct, and not waste their time in following the fashionable vagaries of dress, the management of their household and children need not shut them out from literature, nor prevent their attaching themselves to a science, with that steady eye which strengthens the mind, or practicing one of the fine arts that cultivate the taste.[29]

Perhaps more significantly, Wollstonecraft recognized that some women had no wish to marry, or to be mothers, while others simply did not get asked.

These women should not, she argued, waste their potential, but pursue other careers that would help them flourish and make them useful citizens:

> How many women thus waste their life away the prey of discontent, who might have practiced as physicians, regulated a farm, managed a shop, and stood erect, supported by their own industry, instead of hanging their heads surcharged with the dew of sensibility, that consumes the beauty to which it at first gave lustre . . .[30]

Motherhood was an option that many women would feel compelled to choose, and that many would enjoy—but still only an option. And if they were not mothers, there was no reason, as far as Wollstonecraft was concerned, why women should not freely populate the public sphere, working in any profession they chose.[31]

Another crucial difference between Wollstonecraft's view of parenthood and domesticity and Rousseau's is that she takes particular care to emphasize that men, as well as women, must be domesticated and learn to parent:

> Till men become more attentive to the duty of a father it is vain to except women to spend that time in the nursery which they "wise in their generation" choose to spend at their glass.[32]

And:

> The conclusion which I wish to draw is obvious; make women rational creatures, and free citizens, and they will quickly become good wives and mothers; that is—if men do not neglect the duties of husbands and fathers.[33]

If men do not fulfill their own parenting duties—and these involve being home when they're not working, and actively participating in the raising of children—then women are bound to fail to fulfill theirs. Wollstonecraft saw parenting as a collaborative effort between equals on a project that mattered to all, a view she expressed clearly and beautifully in an unfinished book she wrote for her first daughter in 1797. "Lessons" reflect Wollstonecraft's idea of what a family ought to be, and perhaps of the family she briefly had with Godwin, the year before she died. In the family she describes, mother, father, and daughter are full of love and respect for each other. They care for each other when they're unwell, protect each other's workspace, and make sure there is always one parent free to interact with the little girl. So the child is taught to ask her father to play ball with her in the garden when her mother is working or has a headache. And when her father is sick, or asleep—Godwin suffered from narcolepsy—the child and her mother tiptoe and whisper or bring him chamomile tea.

Unchained and Homeless

Jemima, the working-class heroine of Wollstonecraft's novel, *Maria*, liberated herself from a life of dependent misery first through education. Learning to read meant that she could find work that did not require her to sell her body. But it was not until she left the prison where she worked with her escaped charge, Maria, that she was is truly reborn. Her final act, to find Maria's lost daughter, and bring Maria back to life, was the pinnacle of her own existence, and marked the possibility of a shared happiness. But before she met Maria, home did not feature in Jemima's life. She simply tried to stay off the streets. In that sense, her fate was not entirely unlike that of enslaved men and women, who shared the home of their enslavers, and had none other if they claimed their freedom.

Mary Prince (1788–1833) was born in slavery in Bermuda.[34] She lived with her mother until she was 12. Her father lived in a nearby plantation. At the age of 12, she was sent to work as a child-minder, then sold to a brutal owner (who also brutalized his own wife), and then to another even worse; and in 1806, she was taken to work in salt pans on Turk's Island, where she stayed for ten years before being brought back to Bermuda. Sold again in 1818, she married a free man in Antigua but was unable to make a life with him. Prince was taken to Britain in 1828 to work as a maid, launderer, and child-minder. She walked out on free soil a few months later.

Mary Prince understood early on her own status as a slave. Each time she was sold to a new planter—from the very first time when she was separated from her mother—moved from one place to another, given a different job, or in one case brought back after an attempted escape, she realized afresh her status as human property, and the outrage to the liberty she knew was owed her. Prince resisted slavery. She once escaped from a cruel planter, only to be brought back by her own father, who could see no other option for her.

Twice, she attempted to buy her own freedom, and to have someone else buy it for her, but her attempts failed, as her enslavers would not sell it to her:

> Mrs. Wood was very angry—she grew quite outrageous—she called me a black devil, and asked me who had put freedom into my head. "To be free is very sweet," I said: but she took good care to keep me a slave. I saw her change colour, and I left the room.[35]

Prince nonetheless attempted to build a homelife for herself, and married a free man, who lived in a nearby town. But Prince was not allowed to live with her husband in his home, until eventually, they allowed them to build a cabin outside their own home, where they could live together. Even then, domestic life was fraught, as Prince was entirely occupied with the lives of her enslavers, not even able to wash her own linen, even though she was employed as a washer woman:

> She said that she would not have nigger men about the yards and premises or allow a nigger man's clothes to be washed in the same tub where hers were washed. She was fearful, I think, that I should lose her time, in order to wash and do things for my husband: but I had then no time to wash for myself; I was obliged to put out my own clothes, though I was always at the wash-tub.[36]

In the end, it was coming to London which helped her achieve freedom. But her freedom came at a huge cost: as Prince had nowhere to go in London and she could not go home to her husband and remain free.

Her enslavers, who knew that she had nowhere to go in London, threatened her with expulsion several times. But at first, she was at first reluctant to leave.

> She said, she supposed I thought myself a free woman, but I was not; and if I did not do it directly I should be instantly turned out of doors. I stood a long time before I could answer, for I did not know well what to do. I knew that I was free in England, but I did not know where to go, or how to get my living; and therefore, I did not like to leave the house. But Mr. Wood said he would send for a constable to thrust me out; and at last I took courage and resolved that I would not be longer thus treated, but would go and trust to Providence.[37]

But while Prince wanted her freedom, she also felt she was entitled to the roof over her head that the Woods could provide. She had worked for free there for years, she had not been able to live elsewhere, even though she had wanted to, and she was, moreover, ill, uneducated, felt unable to fend for herself in the streets of a foreign land.

> This was the fourth time they had threatened to turn me out, and, go where I might, I was determined now to take them at their word; though I thought it very hard, after I had lived with them for thirteen years, and worked for them like a horse, to be driven out in this way, like a beggar. My only fault was being sick, and therefore unable to please my mistress, who thought she never could get work enough out of her slaves; and I told them so: but they only abused me and drove me out. This took place from two to three months, I think, after we came to England.[38]

Eventually, exhausted and ill, she sought refuge with members of an abolitionist group.

For Prince, more strikingly than for any of the women discussed in this chapter, perhaps, freedom came at a cost. She never obtained legal liberty from her enslavers, and because of that, was not able to go back to her family in the West Indies. Prince became a servant in a household. She was never reunited with her husband and never had a home of her own. She died shortly after she published her narrative.

In the age of revolutions, men and women fought for freedom, to some extent won, and then began the work of rebuilding their world in ways that was compatible with this freedom. Institutions and practices were abolished, rebuilt, and created. But the home did not, for the most part, figure among the reforms and women began to ask themselves whether the freedom promised by revolutions could in any way be theirs. What was the point of being pronounced free if one still had to cater to the will of a man? How could she participate in the running of the new world if she had to remain confined to the home? And if she broke free, how could she survive? What place in the world was there for a woman without a home? The next chapter looks at how the women of French Revolution tried to resolve this difficulty, by making the home a part of the public space.

6

Revolutionary Matrons

In 1789, the lives of many French women were turned upside down. From subjects to the king, they were suddenly upgraded to citizens of the nation. And almost immediately, they were downgraded again to "passive citizens." This meant that although they would be protected by the nation, they couldn't actually participate in the building or running of the nation. But they did participate. They rose to the occasion on 14 July to take the Bastille. They rioted for bread. They marched from Paris to Versailles to fetch the King and bring him to the Capital. They wrote for newspapers, met in clubs, and donated their jewels to relieve the national debt. French women must have felt like they had a chance to bring about the reforms that their British sisters had merely dreamt about.[1] Very few of them got to occupy the front seat of the Revolution, but even from the back seat, they participated with all their might. And when their hopes fell, eventually, so did their heads.[2]

Women of the French Revolution, despite the violent politics of their time, were not Amazons (with perhaps the exception of a Théroigne de Méricourt, who at least dressed as an Amazon). They were, typically, domestic women who took pride in their marriage, their skills at household management, and, most of all, their maternal virtues. This was not a matter of national character but of philosophical allegiance and historical inspiration. French women read Rousseau, who valued women for their domesticity, and they were inspired by Roman republicanism, which provided them with a ready-made example of a way of combining politics and motherhood, the Roman matron.

From Roman General to Roman Matron (and Back)

Women of the eighteenth century were enthusiastic Rousseau readers. Even those who disagreed with him strongly, like Wollstonecraft, were fans.[3] Rousseau pandered to his audience, making sure he was loved as well as controversial. He was in many ways like a superstar, who was recognized

No Place Like Home. Sandrine Bergès, Oxford University Press. © Oxford University Press USA 2026.
DOI: 10.1093/9780197687413.003.0006

everywhere he went, but cultivated a private persona. Today he would probably be wearing shades and casting insults at Paparazzi.

One reason why Rousseau was so attractive to women readers is that he made them matter, in a way that in old-regime France, they did not. Though Rousseau portrayed women as inferior to men in many ways (in particular regarding their minds), he also wrote that good wives and good mothers made a difference to the well-functioning of the household, and of the political community at large. Even the most basic of mothering act, feeding a child, he said, could influence the state of the nation. If, he wrote in the preface of the *Emile*, a virtuous, healthy mother would breastfeed her child, instead of sending him or her away to a wetnurse, as was the custom then, that child would have a much better chance of becoming a healthy and virtuous individual. This piece of advice, even Wollstonecraft, one of Rousseau's fiercest critiques, took to heart.[4]

It's very puzzling how so many women accepted Rousseau's constant belittling—women are not capable of abstract thought, they are naturally unchaste so must be controlled, etc. But part of the answer has to be the way he exalts mother and breast-feeder.[5] Mothers, in his picture, played the first and most crucial role in building the future of the species. They were responsible for the nation being populated by healthy, capable citizens, rather than weak dissipated ones. In the context of the French Revolution, that made them the foundation stones of the future republic. But that was only half the picture. Rousseau wanted women's domestic role to be foundational for politics, but not for them to take part in politics. Several women who embraced Rousseau's views on motherhood and education did not in fact accept this exclusion. So they worked to adapt Rousseau's views in ways that would allow them to lead a political, as well as a domestic life. This was true of Marie-Jeanne—Manon—Phlipon Roland. Roland embraced Rousseau's views on the virtues of domesticity, aiming to be the perfect wife and mother. But she also somehow managed to become a prominent figure of the French Revolution, through her writings and her participation in decision-making (through her husband's ministry of the interior). By subverting Rousseau's concept of domesticity, Roland was able to become a political actor, as well as a more traditional housewife.

Madame Roland was born in Paris in 1754, and she was executed there in November 1793, as part of the extermination of the members of the Girondin faction by the Montagnards. At the time of her arrest, she was notorious. The Girondins—the political group she belonged too—loved her. The

Montagnards—who came to be known as the architects of the Terror—hated her. Robespierre accused her of being part of a "female triumvirate," who usurped political power from elected men. He called her home, where the Girondins met, a "labyrinth of intrigues."[6] Roland was accused of influencing the male Girondists with sexual favors, and of encourage them to lead France into war despite Robespierre's resistance to it.[7] In the summer 1792, Danton argued against appointing her husband, Jean-Marie Roland, to the Ministry of the Interior, because, he said, everyone knew that it was his wife, not him, who drafted the policies and made the appointments.[8]

Danton, like many men then and now, was not comfortable with a woman on a political platform, so maybe he exaggerated. But we have good reasons to believe Manon Roland was indeed politically active. When she was in prison, waiting for her trial and then her death, Manon Roland wrote *Memoirs* both personal and historical. There she tells us in detail what role she played in the French Revolution, and the rise and fall of the Girondins. And, in case we worry that these Memoirs, written for posterity, don't tell the whole truth, we also have access to letters she wrote to friends, and these show that she was in fact quite involved in the political affairs of the Revolution. She was an activist, then. But what the *Memoirs* also show is that she tried, throughout her life, to excel at domesticity, and that she had very strict views as how a woman should behave and what her daily life should look like. In other words, Manon Roland did everything she could to participate in the political thought that shaped the revolution while attempting to remain faithful to Rousseau's ideals of feminine domesticity.

Roland's first aspirations were not domestic, we know. They were not even womanly. Child Manon wanted to be a man, so she could become a Roman General. She had discovered Plutarch's *Lives* on her parents bookshelves, and at the same time as her republican sentiments were beginning to arise, she dreamt that she too could fight heroically for her country.[9] It was a childhood dream, but it persisted in her twenties still, and she told her best friends, the Cannet sisters, that she wished she could have been born a man, or at least, a Roman.[10] As an adult, she decided that the best she could aim for was the Roman matron, that she could become a powerful woman from within her home, tending republican sentiment in her family and influencing all those who came her way. When she wrote for the revolutionary paper *Le Patriote Français*, she signed herself "Une Romaine."[11]

Why did Manon Roland even contemplate exchanging her dream persona, as a Roman general, and later as a writer, for that of the Roman matron, a wife and mother whose only political role was to support or at most help manage the career of her husband and children? After the death of her mother, when she was grieving and possibly suffering from depression, Manon Roland was given a copy of Rousseau's *New Heloise*. This, the only one of Rousseau's works she had not read, turned out to be a revelation, which in her *Memoirs* she likens to that which she experienced at the age of eight when she first read Plutarch. Plutarch, she said, taught her to be a republican, to value public virtues and liberty. Rousseau, in the *New Heloise*, showed her "the domestic happiness which I could claim for myself, and the ineffable delights I was capable of experiencing."[12]

In *The New Heloise*, as we saw earlier, Rousseau's heroine, Julie, starts off as a bright but morally immature young woman, who is seduced by her tutor. But Julie is forced to give up her lover after her mother dies and made to marry an older man. Rather than end her life in quiet despair, Julie grows in her marriage and becomes a better version of herself. Julie devotes her entire time and energy to domestic pursuits. The couple have children, whom she makes it her business to care for entirely, with the guidance of her wiser husband in designing their education and routines. She also busies herself with the families that live on her husband's property, caring for them and helping them see that the countryside offers them rich and beautiful life, and preventing the inevitable exodus of young peasants to the city. Julie is the "sensible virtue" of the household, that is, in eighteenth-century speak, she is all compassion, while her husband its "living reason."[13] Julie is all "heart," and she finds loving and nurturing those around her a natural extension of her new, truer self. And with this very gendered distribution of roles and natures in place, all in the family are happy (including Julie's ex-lover, welcome as a guest and dear friend by her husband), and the village itself thrives, saved by Julie's care, from the endemic move of peasants to the big city.

Did Roland, when she read *The New Heloise*, finally understand how she could become a Roman without being a man? Was she able to swap an ill-fitting male model of participation for a more achievable female one? As a good Roman wife, she would have done everything she could to support her husband, and, if her husband needed political support, and she was, through her natural gifts and her extensive studies, able to provide it, then so be it.[14] This is the narrative Roland herself pushed. At her trial, when she had to defend herself, she argued that she was a mere housewife, and as such could not possibly present a risk to the political leaders of the Republic.

Fouquier Tinville, who signed Manon Roland's death sentence, must have rolled his eyes when she denied any political activity. Yet it wasn't completely false. Manon Roland had spent much of her marriage supporting her husband, acting as his secretary, editor, and ghost writer. She was the better writer, the better thinker of the two, and she could have put her career first. And at the time she wrote her *Memoirs*, Roland definitely regretted not doing so. Finally, she admitted to herself that the work she had done for her husband was his most valuable contribution to scholarship and politics. After she made that discovery, her enthusiasm for domesticity faded. She realized that she could have had a career as a writer. On her last entry, before she died, she wrote that had she lived, she would have wanted to become a "French Catharine Macaulay"—a republican historian and philosopher, and one of Mary Wollstonecraft's inspirations.[15]

The *Memoirs* offer a complex story of the relationship between Manon Roland and Rousseau's ideals of domesticity. Her narrative juxtaposition of her young self-sublimating of her bereavement pain into admiring Rousseau's New Heloise, and Rousseau's story of a young woman, also losing her mother, sublimating her desire for her young lover into domestic virtue and happiness, is probably not accidental. It suggests that Roland describing a change of direction in her life path. Both she and Heloise suffered trauma, both lost their mothers, and both found a way of surviving, and continuing to improve themselves. Shortly after reading the novel, she wrote to her friend Sophie Cannet to say that any woman above average, she wrote, would find herself improved after reading *Heloise*, or at least desiring to improve herself.[16]

In the narrative of her own life, Manon sees this time of mourning and recovery as transformational: she becomes, not just a child who wishes she were a Roman general, but a young woman who is preparing to take her place in society as a useful homemaker. Domesticity became more important to Roland after she read Rousseau. She welcomed his message that a woman should be useful, become a wife and mother, and put the common good above her own ambitions. She wanted to serve, above all, to matter, and this seemed to be the most realistic way to go about it, if one was neither a man nor a Roman.

But that wasn't the end of the story, and at no point did Roland forget that she had a grander purpose in her. In fact, her discussion of domestic duties is important because it carries a broader political message, namely that domestic happiness ought to guide politics more than general ideas about the common good, and that politicians should study the way in which families are happy or unhappy before deciding on which government is best. But the way in which Roland discusses domestic duties in this passage strongly suggests that she does not, after all, wholeheartedly embrace Rousseau's position in the *New Heloise*.

The biggest difference between Roland and Rousseau is not that Roland wants women to do less domestic work. Roland is very demanding of women: "I expect a woman to keep her family's linen and clothing in good order, to feed her children, order, or herself cook dinner."[17] Even in homes where there are servants, she says, the woman of the house should be involved in the family's upkeep: help with the laundry, pick dinner. Roland came from a middle-class background and married into minor aristocracy. She couldn't rely on servants to run the house, or do all its work, and grew up expected to have some skills in housewifery. She was morally outraged by women who did not, at least, feed their own babies, and was greatly disapproving when a friend and neighbor, Madame d'Eu, sent her newborn out to a wetnurse: "Good God! How strange a newly delivered woman to be found alone without a child seems to me!"[18] In this, if nothing else, she was strongly influenced by Rousseau, who believed that a mothers' milk and care were the best way to start a child's education. Still, there are (at least) two important differences between Roland's and Rousseau's accounts of domesticity.

The first difference is about the amount of time a woman should spend on domestic tasks. Roland requires a lot from a housewife. Just think of the laundry. In the eighteenth century, that would mean washing the entire households bedding and underwear once a month, outside, in water boiled on a fire (which had to be built), scrubbing, treating stains with individual concoctions (no all-in-one detergent!), and finally wringing and hanging. Yet, Roland also insists that domestic work need not take up too much time. The more she'd ever spent on domestic work and organization herself, she says, was two hours per day (presumably she's not counting laundry days). And, she adds confidently, there is no need for anyone who has either help or a small family to spend more time than that on domestic duties. The rest of the time is hers. Rousseau's Julie, on the other hand, always finds some way to use her time for the benefit of others, so that by the time she is to go to bed, she has not done anything for herself.

The second difference between Roland and Rousseau's view of women's domestic duties concerns the place of such duties in a woman's overall life. The time Manon Roland does not spend on her domestic duties, she spends doing what she really cares about: reading and writing. Before she was married, she tells us, she wrote pages and pages of philosophical essays (which were published after her death by a family friend). And afterwards, she worked with her husband on his encyclopedia of textile manufacture, and later on his ministerial speeches and letters. But Rousseau's Julie has no time for that, and Rousseau tells us that this is supposed to be a good thing: "She no longer studies, she no longer reads; she acts."[19]

But Roland was a writer as well as an actor. She enjoyed writing, and her political activism derived from that. During the revolution, she wrote countless letters to male friends, telling them what they ought to do. She also wrote in her capacity as her husband's unofficial secretary at the Ministry of the Interior, drafting several documents that turned out to influence the course of the revolution, including a letter which led to the dismissal by the king of all his ministers. This sort of writing is very much a form of acting. Roland's words were intended to carry a certain weight and to bring about certain consequences. But they were just words, and at the time she died, Roland still considered herself close enough to Rousseau's ideal for women: a quiet housewife who ordered her family's dinner and kept but a few hours to herself each day for private study.

The Republican Home as Political Forum

Manon Roland modeled her version of the political housewife on the Roman matron—a virtuous wife and mother who was devoted to republican ideals. This was something she derived from reading Rousseau, whose writings helped politically inclined female readers define their role as political housewives. Louise Keralio Robert, a friend of Roland and also a republican, was one of these women. Keralio, just like Roland, strove to live a life that was both firmly political and profoundly domestic. Home was a woman's place. But in her picture, home wasn't separate from the public forum: it was central to it. Like Roland she hosted a salon, so politics did happen inside her home, under her supervision. But she also saw deeper ways in which the home, and the women who ran them, were essential to politics. Politics, she thought, began at home.

Roman republican history was a powerful source of inspiration for many actors of the French Revolution. Most had read Plutarch and Livy and cited them generously in their speeches and pamphlets.[20] While most Roman exemplars were men, readers were also aware of the famous women of Roman history. Portraits of women such as Lucretia, who had killed herself rather than let people think her rape was in fact adultery, gave an insight into the role played by the home and the family in Roman politics.[21] One particularly powerful example and role model for the revolutionary hostess was of course Plutarch's Cornelia, the powerful and virtuous Roman matron who gave everything to her country and hosted and even, when all her sons were dead, carried on hosting Rome's luminaries in her villa. Women like Cornelia were central to the making of Roman political and cultural life, and the fact that they were virtuous, and focused only on the public good meant that they were accepted as such.[22] And what is particularly relevant here is that these women were influential from their homes, *qua* mothers or wives, rather than because they took on male roles.

The Roman matron was a model for republican women who wanted to retain their place in the home. Rousseau saw this and his version of republicanism, sometimes called "rural republicanism," also made the home central to the flourishing of the public good.[23] Rousseau's views, developed in his project for a *Constitution of Corsica*, but also in his *Emile* and *New Heloise*, placed the home at the center of politics, on the grounds that it was better for citizens to exercise and develop their virtues close to home than to try and put them to work in the cities, where they would be likely crushed or at least ineffectual.[24]

A good republican citizen could contribute better to the common good by staying at home. Their job was to make sure that all those that lived in and around the home were exposed to virtuous examples and teaching. This was in part the message carried in *The New Heloise*. The Wolmars, Julie and her husband, are not republican—their home, l'Etange, is organized on a feudal model. But they exemplify, to some extent, what Rousseau sees as the ideal form of republic. Julie and her husband not only live exemplary lives themselves, but they also participate in the life of the peasantry in their domain by helping them make the best of their rural existence and dissuading them from abandoning this fruitful and healthy life by running away to the city.

Although it is her husband who rules the domain, Julie's role, as we saw in the previous section, is non-negligible. She is the "heart" of her home, and it is her virtuous love that retains the peasants at least as much as her husband's rational rule.[25] She participates in social transformation, not through direct action, but by using her emotional knowledge to shape the characters of all those around her. The *New Heloise*, in that sense, is central to Rousseau's overall political program, which is to reform the ancient regime by reforming morality and domestic life.[26]

Manon Roland attempted to combine domesticity and republicanism. Keralio Robert argued further that the domestic life that was proper for women was a form of political participation in itself. She did so by appealing to Rousseau's rural republicanism, which held that the home was the heart of the republic, the place where the republic started, and where its flourishing was guaranteed. Women, being the heart of the home, on this model, were therefore very much part of the political life, even if they never set foot in a club. This model suited Keralio Robert, who believed that women must learn to prefer domestic work to politics, and that this distribution of roles was essential to the well-being of the nation. This reasoning enabled Keralio Robert to claim political power for women, without thinking that she was in any way undermining the integrity of the republic or participating in "behind closed doors" intrigues.

Louise Keralio was a historian, political philosopher, and printer. She was elected at the Academy of Arras in 1787, one of the first women to become a member of a French academy. And she was already a published author when the Revolution came: she had written a history of Elizabeth I and an anthology of writings by French women in several volumes, interrupted by lack of funds.[27] At the beginning of the Revolution, Keralio started a newspaper, Le *Journal d'Etat et du Citoyen*. She edited it and contributed articles. Her father, and later her husband, Pierre-François-Joseph Robert also worked for the paper. Keralio was a hard-working journalist and editor, she had written books to publicize women's political and literary accomplishments. Did that mean that she saw the Revolution as a chance to defend the political participation of women? Her views were complicated. In October 1789, Parisian market women walked to Versailles to fetch the King and his family and bring them back to Paris. They delivered the royal family to the Assembly, the first official public forum of the Revolution. Keralio praised them in her paper: they were courageous women and had done their duty as good citizens. But her friend and fellow newspaper editor Jacques-Pierre Brissot challenged her: Was it proper for women to enter the Assembly? Did they not by their presence lower the seriousness of what the new government was trying to do? Surprisingly, Keralio agreed. And she meekly replied that she did not in fact encourage women to be present in the public forum:

[W]omen should not make a great spectacle of themselves. [...] A love of publicity is bad for modesty, from the loss of that comes distaste for domestic work, and from idleness, principles are forgotten and from lack of morals arise all of public disorders. [...] We should be forced [when we need their political input] to pursue women inside their homes, their presence should be hard to obtain, and rare, offered as a favour.[28]

But if Keralio thought women should confine themselves to their homes, she did not believe that women's sociopolitical activity was any less important than men's. When the first French constitution was drafted, women were decreed to be "passive" citizens. This meant that they participate directly in the building and running of the republic but would benefit from its reforms.[29] Keralio's response was immediate and clear: women's work, even in the home, is political. And it should be recognized as such.

Certainly, women and children are not employed. But is this the only way of actively influencing the polity? The discourses, the sentiments, the principles engraved on the souls of children from their earliest youth, which it is women's lot to take care of, the influence which they transmit, in society, among their servants, their retainers, are these indifferent to the homeland?[30]

How did Keralio reconcile her view that women should stay home, with the claim that women had an "active influence on the polity"? Like Roland, she was convinced that there was a place for women in a republic that was central to the flourishing of the nation, even if that place was in the home rather than in the Assembly. State reform, she thought, had to go through the reform of family life, and women had a crucial role to play there nurturing republican values and giving birth to new citizens.[31]

Keralio agreed that women should stay home, rather than participate in debates taking place in public *fora*. But she also believed that the home was just as important a place for the making and cultivating of the republic as the Assembly was. Women participated in the life of the polity by nurturing republican values in their children and husbands, and anyone they came into contact with, that is, servants, tradespeople, neighbors, and friends who came to visit. This meant that it was a good idea for a virtuous woman to host a political salon, as this would help improve the nation. Being at home in the eighteenth century often meant being in the way of a great traffic of ideas and values. The housewife, then, was in a position either to let this traffic run over her or direct it. And by directing it, as Roland and Keralio certainly did, she could participate in the nation's politics.

Roland decided, before she died, that she ought to have been more than just an influential housewife. She had been, but she could have done more if she hadn't been so concerned about keeping to her place. Keralio didn't recant. When she gave birth to her daughter, she retreated further inside her home. But she found out early on that there were serious limitations to her influence as a woman. In 1789, when she first decided to start a newspaper, she tried to set up a press. She petitioned the Bureau of Royal Administration of the Book Trade to set up her own press. She quoted Article 11 of the *Rights of Man*:

> The free communication of ideas and opinions is one of the most precious of the rights of man. Every citizen may, accordingly, speak, write, and print with freedom, but shall be responsible for such abuses of this freedom as shall be defined by law.[32]

But the Bureau responded that Article 11 did not in fact apply to women and that she could only become a printer if she was the widow of a printer.[33] Fortunately for Keralio, her father and, later, her husband were happy to support her career in printing and journalism. But without them, she could not have pursued it.

Mrs. Jellyby as the Modern Mother

The French Revolution, which redefined subjects as citizens, excluded more people than it included in its reforms. The majority of men did not become active citizens, and no woman did. Women were simply not considered capable of taking part in politics. And because they were the support structure for the new republic—needed at home to bring up future citizens—they were not welcome in public fora. This sexist bias, which operated during and after the revolution, is nowhere more visible than in the cases of those who rejected gender norms in their life choices. Manon Roland and Louise Keralio attempted to work with these norms to create an active political life for themselves. They tried to be useful to the nation while remaining paragons of domesticity. Olympe de Gouges took a different path. Widowed at a very young age, she refused to remarry and settle for a domestic life. Instead, she decided to live her life on her own terms, bringing her son with great care, but not sacrificing her talent and career to make a home for him.

Olympe de Gouges was born Marie Gouze in 1748 in Montauban. Her birth father was the local lord and poet Jean-Jacques Le Franc-Pompignan, but she was recognized by her mother's husband and brought up in their home. In 1765, she was married to a man called Louis-Yves Aubry whom she did not like, let alone love. She had one son by him, Pierre, and was widowed a few months later, in 1766. Very soon after she lost her husband, she moved to Paris and changed her name. Taking her mother's first name, giving up her husband's name, and adding "de" to a version of her adoptive father's last name, Marie Aubry became Marie-Olympe de Gouges. For the next ten years, she mixed in Aristocratic and theatrical circles. She acted in the private theater of Madame de Montesson, alongside the famous black composer, Joseph Bologne. Soon she began to write plays, and she toured the provinces with her own company, which included her son. At the eve of the revolution, she started writing texts on political reform. One, a pamphlet about poverty, in which she encouraged rich artists to donate to a public fund to help relieve national debt and feed the poor, was printed on the first page of a national paper and praised by Mirabeau himself. During that time, she and her son moved often, taking rooms and apartments that were partially furnished. There was no sense that Gouges was trying to build a home for herself or her son, and she refused to marry again, rejecting her long-term partner Jacques Biétrix de Rozières's offers of marriage. It was not until the year of her death, in fact, that Gouges decided to settle. Her son was married and had started a family in the south of France. Olympe bought a small house near them, where she hoped to retire and enjoy country life.[34]

During the last five years of her life covering the tumultuous period between the fall of the Bastille and the beginning of the Terror, Gouges devoted herself entirely to politics. She wrote pamphlets that were published in national newspapers; posters, that she paid to be pasted on the walls of Paris; and letters to the King and Queen and to members of revolutionary committees. She printed volumes of her works and kept trying to have her plays performed. These plays became more and more political, dealing with topics such as the abolition of slavery, or divorce. During the Revolution, she became members of clubs, such as the Amis de la Vérite (Friends of Truth) and the Amis des Noirs (Friends of the Black). She kept a salon that moved every time she took up new rooms, and she spent time in other famous salons.

By the time the revolution started, Pierre Aubry, Gouges' son, was twenty-three years old. Her role as a carer and educator was over, but even then, she worked at helping him with his career, writing to influential people, and paying charges for him go into the military (she was even accused of having exchanged sexual favors with the Duke of Orleans for a job offer that was then rescinded). When Pierre was younger, she had paid for tutors for him, to ensure that he received a better education than she had had (she had been taught to read and write at a free religious school in Montauban). She was, by his own accounts, a good mother.[35]

Unlike Manon Roland, who did most of her writing to support others, Gouges wanted to develop her own career rather than living vicariously through a man's. In any case, her son Pierre and her lover Bietrix were not politically inclined: she was. She also knew that political engagement could cost lives. She was not prepared to send her son to his death to fight for the nation—but she was quite willing to go to her own. But that was not good enough mothering by eighteenth-century standards. Not for a woman, anyway. The double standards in operation were extremely clear. The journalist and politician Jacques-Pierre Brissot, for instance, died in poverty, leaving nothing to fund his three son's schooling. But Brissot made a virtue of this, writing to his wife, Félicité, from his prison cell on the day of his death, that she should one day show his writings to his sons, so that they knew that he loved them, but that he loved the republic more.[36] He was not an uncaring father, and in his final letters to his wife and mother-in-law, he also expressed deep regrets for not having had the chance to educate his sons. But he thought that his choice to sacrifice himself for a political cause would be understood by his children, and they did honor his legacy as much as they could.[37]

Gouges' family legacy, despite the fact that she dedicated more of her life to bringing up her son than Brissot did his, is more complicated. Ten days after her death, her son, Pierre, wrote a letter denouncing her as a "monster" and claiming that she was not "républicaine." Aubry said that he wrote and signed this "profession of civic faith" under torture.[38] And three years after the denunciation, once the Terror was over, Aubry recused himself, saying he'd been a victim of the Terror and wanted to protect his own wife and children. He later petitioned the state to have his mother's name and works rehabilitated:

> I am writing to ask you to rehabilitate an illustrious victim. The person I am asking you to recall is Olympe de Gouges, my mother. It is this woman whose only default was to push everything to excess and whose love of her country led to the scaffold. [...] my mother's shadow hangs over your head and is waiting for you to grant her the justice she gave you in her writings.[39]

The ambiguous and sometimes downright hostile attitude to Gouges did not end with her son.[40] One of her grandsons, Jean Hélie Hippolyte Aubry de Gouges (1798–1870), resented his grandmother's political career. He blamed her for the bad luck that seemed to track down her descendants. In a letter to a biographer, Forestié, he called his grandmother a stubborn woman and claimed she was the cause of her son's (his father's) unhappiness. She was "obsessed" with Black people, he said, when she should have been caring for her family. Her "political furies" led her to the scaffold and ruined her son's career. She made the deliberate choice, Hélie goes on, to live a "tempestuous life" when she could have leaved a happy and peaceful one with her grandchildren.[41]

The claim that she chose a "tempestuous life" instead of a peaceful domestic one is particularly damning. It's a choice that her descendants feel they have the right to resent her for. Hélie Aubry also claimed that she had told her son that her head had to roll first for Robespierre to lose his, and that this was why she refused a plea of insanity offered (allegedly) before her trial. "What can a son say, to such a mother, ready to sacrifice her son's safety and future?" he exclaims.[42] The answer that Brissot hoped for (and received) from his wife and son, that he loved his family, but loved the public good more, seems unavailable to Gouges. In her case, there is no suggestion of a heroic attachment to the nation, simply stubbornness, and an "obsessional" love for Black people. It was her abolitionist work, according to Hélie Aubry, which caused his father's ruin. Pierre presented his mother's works on abolitionism to Bonaparte. Shortly afterwards Bonaparte became Napoleon and, in 1802, brought slavery back to the French colonies.

Hélie Aubry claims that Gouges cared more about distant others (in this case the enslaved in the French colonies) than she cared about her own kin. Men and women she had never met, who lived in faraway places she had never traveled to, meant more to her than her flesh and blood. If he's right, Gouge was very much like Dickens's Mrs. Jellyby. A character from *Bleak House* Mrs. Jellyby was a mother who neglected her children and gave all her attention to raising funds for abolitionist schemes in Africa. Mrs.

Jellyby suffered from moral myopia, Dickens suggests: she has "handsome eyes, though they had a curious habit of seeming to look a long way off. As if they could see nothing nearer than Africa!"[43] Moral philosopher Nell Noddings used her example to illustrate a distinction between caring for, which requires having a personal relationship with the person who receives our care, and caring about, which involves a very different set of emotional and practical engagement. Mrs. Jellyby, she says, is failing in her obligation to care for her children, because she is putting all her energy in caring about distant others. "The Mrs. Jellybys of the world are so busy 'caring about' far away and unknown others that they do not even see the misery or joy right in front of them. They fail almost entirely to care for those close to them."[44]

Dickens's account of Mrs. Jellyby suffers from the same double standard that had Brissot's sons praise their father, but Gouges' grandson vilifying her. Had Dickens focused on Mr. Jellyby, he may have criticized for his involvement in fake overseas justice schemes, but would he have blamed him for his children's hair not being brushed properly? Unlikely. Brushing hair was not a father's work.

In *Bleak House*, the scheme Mrs. Jellyby devoted her energy turned out to be a scam. If it hadn't, the portrait of Mrs. Jellyby would not have been so comical. But Gouges's own humanitarian efforts were far from pointless or comical. Her first attempt at political writing for reform, her *Letter to the People, or Project for a Patriotic Tax* 1788, asked women who could afford to do so to donate to the nation in order to help reduce poverty and relieve the national debt. This resulted in a group of women artists following her request and taking their jewels to the Assembly. While this did not solve the problem entirely (the debt was huge), it was momentous, and showed France that women were willing to help and that they could.

Gouges's work on slavery and women's rights was perhaps not as directly effective—she did not single-handedly cause the French public to decide that slavery should be abolished, nor did she obtain the vote for French women. But her writings were discussed and debated, and the reforms she proposed did eventually happen. It's impossible not to think that she had some impact on the slow progress toward emancipation.

Whether or not Gouges' work influenced the world for the better, it was work that had to be done. Slavery had to be abolished, women had to become full citizens, the Terror had to be stopped, and the Republic had to be saved. Gouges couldn't achieve all these, or maybe even a single one of these tasks, by herself, but her work counted. She was not a drop in the ocean.

She was one of a small number of political activists at a time when activism mattered. In that sense, she was very unlike Mrs. Jellyby. But was she like Mrs. Jellyby in other respects? Did she ignore her son for the sake of distant others? This is where changing perceptions of what a home is matter. The home, in revolutionary France, was becoming synonymous with family life, which meant that a wife or a mother had very little time for extracurricular pursuits. A woman had to be willing to take a step back from her political or writing career once her children were born, as Louise Keralio Robert did. Or she had to become super organized so she could do all he housewifely duties in less than two hours a day, as Manon Roland had. But Gouges doesn't seem to have accepted that version of the home. For her, a home was a roof over one's head and regular meals. It is also a place where other necessities, such as clothing and education, are seen to. But most of what was needed for personal development, or flourishing, came from communal life, being involved with others outside the home, exchanging ideas, learning new things, and learning to live and work together. As a child, she had discovered the world by playing with other children in the forest, not be staying home, protected from outside interference. As her son grew up in Paris, his experience had to be different. But Gouges made sure he went out in the world, that he traveled outside Paris, and got to know people who might help him in his career. She didn't just keep him alive; she gave him a rich life.

Pierre Aubry traveled, acted, and was taught by the best tutors. But he was also fed and clothed and always had a roof over his head. Gouges knew that this was the first necessity, and she also knew that many did not have that. For instance, women who lived alone in poverty, unable to heat their homes or obtain sufficient food, did not. This is why Gouges, in yet another piece on social justice, demanded that a hospice may be built for military widows.[45] Many of these women had fallen on hard times, and without education, or independence that comes with it, they could not provide for themselves. A roof over their heads, and a place where they might receive some education, would offer these women the opportunity to grow, form a community, and acquire the skills they needed to survive. This is another place where Gouges differs from more traditional thinkers in her views on home and family. Women were not simply providers of home comfort: they too needed to be homed, and their basic needs seen to and their place in society acknowledged, even if they no longer had husbands or children to care for.

Gouges, despite early royalist pronouncements, was as much of a republican as Roland and Keralio-Robert were. But her view of the world was less imbued with republican ideology. To her, the home was not the hearth of the republic, the woman was not its beating heart. A home was a roof and four walls; a woman was a human creature that needed to be housed and fed. And even if she believed it was a mother's place to raise children, she did not think of it as their most sacred duty, which ought to take up most of their time. A child had to be cared for, but this needn't come at the expense of a mother who had other projects that were important to her. The mother's well-being mattered as much as the child's, and a woman who was childless, or whose children no longer needed her to care for them, still needed to be housed and cared for. Her life mattered, and she ought to have the material comforts she needed in order to do what she could with it.

Exit the Roman Matron—Enter the Angel of the House

Women of the French Revolution could have done one of two things. They could have "forgotten" that they were women, and fought for the rights of men, and gone back home to their subordinate roles once their husbands had achieved independence. Or they could have stood up and asked for their own rights, adding to the growing discontent echoing all over the country. They did both—and some did nothing. Republicans looked for a middle ground. Women, they claimed, were to enact their citizenship in a way that was different from men, but just as important. The Assembly was closed to women, but home, as a political forum, mattered just as much to republic. So women who wanted their influence to reach outside the home hosted salons where they could influence their visitors' political views openly, by talking or writing. Unfortunately, this set up made it far too easy to repress women. They were, after all, already in the home, and they had vowed to be good housewives. So how hard could it be to persuade them to quit all political activity, to order them to go back to their real and proper work, keeping husbands and children fed and clothed? It wasn't hard, and any resistance was overcome with a few drops of the guillotine. The French government told women that a republican woman's job was to help her husband and sons become good citizens. Any woman who did not accept this and who meddled in public affairs was a traitor to the nation. Keralio Robert, sensing a turn for the worse, left France. She survived. Manon Roland and Olympe de Gouges stayed in Paris, and they were executed. Women's political clubs were shut down. The republican home became a place where women taught civic virtues but never exercised them. When the nineteenth century came, the housewife stopped being a Roman matron and became instead a creature we'll read about in the next chapter: a faded husk of republican, whose only worth was her domestic skills (mostly delegated to servants) and purity, the Angel of the House.

7

New Architectures of Domestic Power

North American women did not have to contend with Robespierre and the Terror, but until 1864, many of them were still enslaved. Things could have gone a different way. The path to freedom, started for white men during the American revolution, could have been widened following feminist and abolitionist impulses. And the homes dotted along the way could have been reformed at the same time. But the prevailing domestic ideal for the white American woman was inspired more by Rousseau than by revolutions. The white American home had always been the center of all productive activities. A pioneer would produce most of their own food, build their own furniture and utensils, and school their own children. But as America became industrialized, the white middle-class home stopped being the focus of professional activity. Men spent their days outside the home, in a dissipated world, and women waited for them at home. White, middle-class American women became the guardians of American virtue. It was their job to make sure that their husbands and children read the bible and lived soberly (at least at home). Domesticity became a cult—the Cult of True or Real Womanhood. And women like Catharine Beecher started to proselytize, encouraging other women to become more knowledgeable about domesticity.

This may have been a dominant movement in white America—and in this chapter, I will be talking mostly about white American women—but not all women philosophers gave in to it. Women like Sojourner Truth and the Grimké sisters kept fighting for emancipation—of the enslaved Blacks and of white women—and resisted the passive domestic role that was forcibly assigned to them. They rethought the home as enabling civic life for all, not just men. Some women and men experimented with communal life, Sojourner Truth—discussed in the next chapter—found a home in the learning community of Northampton for several years, making long-lasting friendships that shaped her career. The Angel of the House found less traction with abolitionist women. And while some Black women philosophers

No Place Like Home. Sandrine Bergès, Oxford University Press. © Oxford University Press USA 2026.
DOI: 10.1093/9780197687413.003.0007

argued that the home was central to social progress, they saw their role as rather more substantial than the ethereal angelic creature.

In the next two chapters, we look at the philosophical arguments American nineteenth-century women, Black and white, produced about the home. We'll see how they argued with each other about whether women's role was inside or outside the home (or both). Historically, these exchanges are little more than disputes between the homemakers and the suffragists/abolitionists, a push toward independence for all, and a reaction against it. This is a clash that replicates itself over and over. In the 1980s, "New Traditionalists" were set up against the feminist movement, and in the 2020s, feminists are fighting the #Tradwives movement. But when we look at the actual arguments, we see an important philosophical moment in the conception of the home and its role in social progress. Women thinkers were asking what about the home needed changing so that all (including women) could flourish, and how the home could participate in social progress.

Women's Place

Angelina Grimké (1805–1879) was the last born of a large family living in Charles Town on a South Carolina plantation worked by enslaved men and women.[1] As soon as she could, she moved to Philadelphia to join her older sister Sarah (1792–1873). Because they had seen firsthand what slavery was, they became abolitionists. And then, it didn't take them very long to realize that defending women's rights had to be a part of the fight against slavery. To help others be free, you needed to be free yourself, or, at least, you needed to believe that you deserved to be free. The Grimkés' writings and activism played a role in anchoring thinking about domesticity in gender politics. This is why we start, here, looking at a dispute between feminist and abolitionist thinker Angelina Grimké and one of the most influential thinkers behind the Cult of domesticity, Catharine Beecher.

Angelina Grimké's first published text, *An Appeal to Women in the South* (1836), put forward two radical views and tied them together: the abolition of slavery and the emancipation of women. First, she argues that slavery was entirely against the precepts of Christianity, going through various biblical references and offering an analysis of the relevant Hebrew laws. Then she goes on to argue that women have the power and the duty to bring about change in four ways: (1) reading about slavery, (2) praying for it to end (reading must be done first as prayers need to be informed), (3) talking about it to those around them, and (4) acting, by means of petitions.

Following the publication of her *Appeal*, Angelina Grimké became a well-known speaker. She and Sarah moved away from the Quakers who rejected liberal efforts toward social reform as well as more extreme (read efficient) abolitionist efforts. Instead, they began to interact with more integrated abolitionist groups, such as the Philadelphia Female Anti-Slavery Society (PFASS) where they engaged with and learned from Black women activists such as Grace Douglass, Sarah Douglass, Charlotte Forten, and Margaretta Forten.[2] In May 1838, Grimké gave a speech at the newly consecrated Philadelphia abolitionist venue, Pennsylvania Hall. She was interrupted by anti-abolitionist mobs throwing bricks through the window. The next day, the hall was burned down by those same mobs.

Not everyone who disagreed with Grimké was an enemy or a stone thrower. Catharine Beecher, who had also become quite well known through her writings, and who professed herself a friend of Angelina Grimké, wrote a response to her appeal in which she objected vehemently to her arguments. The people of the North, she said, should not join abolitionist societies. Abolitionist societies were known to provoke negative responses by deliberately choosing to act in showy ways, instead of going for gentle and progressive change. Moreover, Northern abolitionists had no right and no power to meddle in Southern politics, as they belonged to different and competing communities. And, more importantly, it was wrongheaded to expect women to take a leadership role in social or political change as that went against their nature.

Beecher's arguments against the abolitionist effort are appalling and her rhetoric even more so, as she pretends that she is opposing these efforts for the benefit of the movement itself.[3] Her arguments against women's participation in the abolitionist effort seem to be in equal bad faith. But they are constitutive of what Beecher has to say about women and the home. And Beecher's writings on the home, we will see, were extraordinarily influential. Beecher proposes to give a set of objections, together with "some general views" about women's place, to Grimké's claim that women should act in defense of abolition. She begins, just as Grimké does, with an appeal to religion, to "Divine economy"—God's purpose in creating the world, and the ways in which our lives are managed through divine agency with a particular view to salvation. So what is God's plan according to Beecher?

It is the grand feature of the Divine economy, that there should be different stations of superiority and subordination, and it is impossible to annihilate this beneficent and immutable law.[4]

She gives examples: a student must be subordinate to the teacher, a child to a parent, a domestic servant to a master, and a subject to a ruler. This is not dependent on actual intellectual or moral superiority—a student can be cleverer than their teacher, a servant more knowledgeable than their master, and a citizen more virtuous than their leader. But it is, she insists, an "immutable law" set by God himself to regulate human relations. The same arrangement, she continues, applies to gender relations:

Heaven has appointed to one sex the superior, and the other the subordinate station, and this without any reference to the character or conduct of either. It is therefore as much for the dignity as it is for the interest of females, in all respects, to conform to the duties of this relation.[5]

This is not, she says, to deny women influence as long as it is not the sort of influence that is gained through political action.

Woman is to win everything by peace and love; by making herself so much respected, esteemed and loved, that to yield to her opinions and to gratify her wishes, will be the free-will offering of the heart. But this is to be all accomplished in the domestic and social circle. There let every woman become so cultivated and refined in intellect, that her taste and judgment will be respected; so benevolent and feeling in action, that her motives will be reverenced;—so unassuming and unambitious, that collision and competition will be banished;—so "gentle and easy to be entreated," as that every heart will repose in her presence.[6]

If women choose to exert their influence directly onto the public sphere, through petitioning, they will "exasperate" and "be deemed obtrusive, indecorous and unwise, by those to whom they are addressed."[7] They will also, she points out, be acting improperly with respect to the law of the United States, according to which petitioning congress falls "entirely without the sphere of female duty."[8] This does not imply, she then says, that women are not capable of influencing public opinion and help bring the evils of slavery to an end. But they must do so in ways that are "practicable, safe, suitable and Christian."⁹

Angelina Grimké responded to her "friend" in *Letters to Catharine Beecher*. She immediately pointed out that kind of influence Beecher wanted women to have was not really a kind of Christian virtue. Wasn't she simply telling women to use sex as a barter?

> This principle may do as the rule of action of the fashionable belle [. . .] But to the humble Christian, who feels that it is truth which she seeks to recommend to others, truth which she wants them to esteem and love, and not herself, this subtle principle must be rejected with holy indignation.¹⁰

Grimké's objection may well have hit a nerve. But Beecher's view of what a woman should be was not the Southern Belle. A woman, Beecher thought, may not use her sexuality to appeal to men's hearts, only her judgment and feeling, all finely tuned to Christian virtue. In her *Letters on the Difficulty of Religion* (1836), she expanded on this, writing that the

> appropriate character of a woman demands delicacy of appearance and manners, refinement of sentiment, gentleness of speech, modesty in feeling and action, a shrinking from notoriety and public gaze, a love of dependence, and protection, aversion to all that is coarse and rued, and an instinctive abhorrence of all that tends to indelicacy and impurity, either in principles or actions.¹¹

The only way for a woman to be happy, Beecher said, was by exemplifying the virtues of "purity, piety, submissiveness and domesticity" in her relationships to others as mother, daughter, wife, or sister.¹² The purity requirement, when it is understood as sexual purity, creates a paradox of sorts. Women have to be submissive, but without submitting to men's sexual desires. To give in to a man's sensuality would not encourage his virtue. So women have to resist, all along acting in a suitably submissive manner. The idea is that a woman may show herself superior to a man by resisting his sexual advances, even while she is always in fact inferior, by nature and by divine appointment.¹³ Given this part of her intellectual context, it is not surprising that Beecher caused Grimké to respond with sarcasm when she tried to defend women's feminine influence in a non-sexual manner. The "angel in the house" is positioned halfway between an ethereal virtuous being and the Marquise de

Pompadour who conducted her "nocturnal administration" of the French state from underneath Louis XVth's bedlinen.

The Birth of Domestic Science

Catharine Esther Beecher (1800–1878), the eldest of thirteen children, was thrust into a domestic role as her mother's chief helper and trainee early on in life. When she lost her mother at the age of sixteen, she felt qualified to take her place, so she did. This lasted for one full year, until her father, Lyman Beecher, married again, to a woman barely older than Catharine herself. Her father's favorite, Catharine remained close to him all his life. Lyman was a presbyterian minister with progressive ideas on women's education and he encouraged Catharine to read beyond what was normally expected for a young woman. Then in her early twenties, Catharine became engaged to a university mathematician, who also helped her with her education. Sadly, her fiancé died before the wedding could take place, leaving her with nothing but his math books.

At the age of 23, with the encouragement of her father, Catharine Beecher started a school for girls, the Hartford Female Seminary. Lyman advised her to seek his friend Ralph Waldo Emerson's help in designing her curriculum. Catharine defied him and decided to go with her own ideas instead. Since her fiancé's death, she'd spent time reflecting on her own learning, asking herself what was useful, and what other young women would benefit from. Her father had given her access to his philosophy books. She had also followed her younger brother's Latin and Greek lessons. And from her fiancé she'd acquired (some) scientific knowledge. All these traditionally male disciplines, she thought, would benefit young women, so she included them in her curriculum.

There were other aspects of the Hartford Seminary curriculum which made it radical and unusual. Not only did she aim to provide girls with a solid intellectual education, but also insisted on physical education, making sure that their bodies grew as strong and healthy as their minds. Once the school established, and the curriculum tested on a few generations of young women, Beecher started to use her experience to write articles and books on the philosophy of education, with a focus on women's education. She continued to produce those throughout her life, sometimes writing with her sister, the abolitionist Harriet Beecher Stowe.

Beecher's approach to teaching was very close to what earlier feminists, like Mary Wollstonecraft, had pushed for. Women, she said, should receive an education as intellectually and physically challenging as men's. But, unlike Wollstonecraft and others, she did not have a feminist agenda. She argued that women should be educated according to "the distinctive obligations and capacities of woman." These obligations, according to Beecher, put women squarely inside the home, away from politics, and under the authority of men. But the key to performing one's womanly duties well was to gain virtue. And to gain virtue, one needed to develop one's intellect first, so as to gain knowledge of what one's duties consisted of (Beecher had read some Aristotle and Kant, so had good grounds to derive her views on the relationship between intellect and morality from).[14]

Beecher's view was that young women needed a serious well-rounded education in order to become housewives (or work in domestic or caring professions). Before Beecher founded her school in Hartford, young women went to "female seminaries," where they were prepared to become wives and mothers. But this training, Catharine Beecher observed, was not very successful. Young girls came out of seminaries with pious, submissive, and domestic attitudes, but they had no idea how to run a home, and they suffered from it. Beecher decided that if we took domestic duties seriously, then they had to be taught properly, as a science. And that required a solid intellectual background.

Although Beecher did want women to be pious and submissive, this was not the whole story. Beecher thought women should derive power from domesticity, the sort of power that didn't require them to engage in political action. In fact, she thought that the kind of direct political action other women (including Angelina Grimké but also her own suffragist sister Isabella Beecher Hooker) recommended could jeopardize the influence that women had already achieved and any future progress they might make. Domesticity, she thought, had already granted women the power suffragists were fighting for, they just needed to embrace it.

The power exercised by women who stayed home, according to Beecher, was not merely spiritual (and definitely not sexual). Beecher was highly invested in women's domestic power in the sense that she wanted them to be good at what they did and promote the health of the nation through their domesticity. She wrote several books on the science of domestic economy, all containing very practical advice as well as moral and philosophical discussions. She thought that women should be instructed and knowledgeable in all aspects of household management, be it building a house, fixing the plumbing, or preparing a meal. All these topics were introduced and discussed in her and her sister Harriet Beecher Stowe's *An American Woman's Home: Or Principle of Domestic Science* (1869), a book aimed at dispelling the "chief cause of woman's disabilities and sufferings, that women are not trained, as men are, for their peculiar duties."

Beecher's great educational innovation was her argument that domestic science should be taught in schools, that young women should be prepared for their (divinely) assigned social roles, not merely in their own home, but professionally if they did not marry. Beecher thought that women's nature suited them to the caring professions, but that if they ended up caring for people who were not their parent, husband, or children, they ought to get paid for it. So they needed to be trained. In her 1835 "Essay on the Education of Female Teachers," she argued that women's education should be based on "the distinctive obligations and capacities of women" and should aim to "gain virtue" and "qualify a woman for her duties." Thus educated, women can then become "leaders of men" by being their first teachers.[15]

There was a political element to Beecher's program: she wanted women's work to be professionalized and at the same time valued. And what was needed to achieve both these goals was proper training. Women who were trained would take pride in their domestic achievements, and others would recognize the skill that went into these achievements. The skills would be valued, financially in the case of professionals, and through increased respect, in the case of women who cared for their own family's home.

Beecher's program of empowerment is spelt out in an 1865 article Beecher wrote for *Harper's New Monthly Magazine*: "How to Redeem Women's Professions from Dishonor." When men want to develop a profession, she writes, "they endow professorships so as to secure men of the highest culture to study and teach it as a science and art. [. . .] Let woman's profession be thus honored and its disgrace would speedily be ended."[16] There is no reason why a woman who can cut elegant and well-fitting clothes should not be elevated to the status of artist, or why women should not study medicine and become "physicians to their own sex," as well as "skillful and tender nurses of the sick." Women's work is no less important because it is aimed at the comfort, health, and education of others. It should receive the same attention as men's work in terms of educational resources, and the same respect and appraisal in terms of status and pay.

One important aspect of Beecher's educational reforms is her focus on physical education. In order to be a good housekeeper, wife, and mother, women need intellectual and practical knowledge, but they also need strong and able bodies. In the *Treatise on Domestic Economy* (1842), Beecher cites Tocqueville's description of an American woman pioneer: "her delicate limbs appear shrunken, her features are drawn in, her eye is mild and melancholy." Tocqueville goes on to say that there is something admirable in the moral abnegation of these suffering women. Beecher agrees that these women are admirable. But she doesn't think that their bodily suffering is part of what makes them so. On the contrary, she says, their physical weakness is a problem that needs a remedy. Pioneer women would have been better if they'd been healthy: "though American women have those elevated principles and feelings, which enable them to meet such trials in so exemplary a manner, their physical energies are not equal to the exertions demanded."[17] In the *Treatise*, she offers a solution: by teaching American women domestic science, we can make sure that they at least don't waste their energies. Housework and cooking are a lot easier if you know what you're doing, as you don't need to start again, wash up messes, and find ways of fixing things you've ruined through ignorance. This makes sense, but domestic science, Beecher says, must also include physical education. Among the courses to be taught to the American housewife, she lists calisthenics, a set of exercises specifically designed to strengthen the body. Beecher kept on promoting fitness for women, on the grounds that a healthy body would always perform better than an unhealthy one. In 1858, she published *Physiology and Calisthenics: For School and Families*, in which she detailed exercises, how to teach them, and the effects they would have on the body.

Beecher's views on women's education and professional lives were more progressive than the attitude we glimpsed from her exchange with Grimké. Yet it's hard to see Beecher as a feminist: she believed that women's role in the home defined their social power, and that they could only flourish, benefitting themselves and others, if they saw themselves as domestic creatures. And no matter how well educated they were, women would always remain men's subordinates. Still, one may be tempted to see her as a feminist of some sort. She did, after all, try to raise women's social status and help them participate in social progress. But even those who do think we should try and see her as a feminist philosopher, like Catherine Villanueva Gardner, hesitate:

Even within the myriad developments of feminist thought, there does not seem to be much room for a moral philosophy that demands the self-sacrifice and submission of women as the way to a greater good, while offering them in return nothing but a saccharine moral power.[18]

Could Beecher be described as a difference feminist? A difference feminist believes that men and women are equal, equally worthy of respect but different in the ways they can express their humanity. In Beecher's case, men are better suited to a politically or commercially active role, and women to domesticity or the caring professions. Villanueva Gardner warns us against applying our standards of what we are prepared to accept as feminism when looking at philosophers of the past. If we think that feminism is about raising women's status, reducing their systemic oppression, then what counts as feminism will vary with time and place. Christine de Pizan's efforts to persuade men that women are capable of the same intellectual, moral, and physical feats as men—even if she thought that they shouldn't in fact perform them—would seem rather weak if written today. But at the time it was written, it did have the potential to raise women at least in opinion, if not status.

So, the question we should ask is whether Beecher's view of women had the potential to raise women's status at the time she was writing. Perhaps it did—because of its emphasis on education. But her insistence that women must remain subordinate to men does the contrary of raising women. Compared to feminist philosophers that came before her, such as Mary Wollstonecraft or Olympe de Gouges, or her contemporaries—her sister Isabella, the Grimké Sisters, Sojourner Truth, or Frances Harper—she was proposing to bring women down.

The Aunt and the Niece

Proponents of the Cult of True Womanhood thought a home, any home at long as it was run by a woman, was the center of human flourishing and goodness. Beecher also idealized the home as a place of power and influence for women. But she had the grace to see that in many homes, not only women were miserable, but they didn't have a positive influence on anyone else. Homes, she argued, had the potential to become that center of goodness. All that was needed was for women to be educated scientifically in the domestic arts. If they knew what they were doing, their homes would become places where families could safely and happily live and grow. Beecher's great-niece, social philosopher and novelist Charlotte Perkins Gilman, begged to differ. She too saw the domestic misery of housewives who tried over and over to get things right and failed, with no one to help them but plenty to criticize. She saw they were exhausted and weighed down with the feeling that they were failing at something they were supposed to be born knowing how to do. But, unlike her aunt, Perkins Gilman did not think that the home could be redeemed by educating women to become better housewives. The only way to save the home was to free women from domestic work.

Charlotte Perkins Gilman (1860–1935) was Catharine Beecher's great-niece. Her father, Frederic Beecher Perkins, was the son of Catharine's sister Mary. Frederic abandoned his family when Charlotte was still young and her aunts, Catharine, Harriet (Beecher Stowe, the author of *Uncle Tom's Cabin*), and Isabella (Beecher Hooker, a suffragist), helped care for her and her brother in Hartford. Perkins Gilman followed in her aunts' footsteps. She became a writer and a lecturer. She is now known mostly for her short stories (The Yellow Wallpaper) and her novels (especially the feminist science fiction story *Herland*). But she also produced book-length works and articles in social philosophy, including *The Home, Its Work and Influence* published in 1903.

From what must have been a very stimulating, if perhaps intimidating learning environment, Perkins Gilman retained an ambiguous allegiance to her aunts' values. Like her aunt Harriet, she used novels and stories as way of putting forward important social and political messages. Unlike her, she did not take up the cause of Black people, and indeed her writings often carry very racist messages.[19] Like her aunt Isabella, she believed in female suffrage. But she did not, unlike her, place great emphasis on women's property rights. She owed much to Isabella and Harriet. But it's perhaps from her aunt Catharine that she derived the greatest inspiration. Like her she was convinced that women must benefit from a solid education and that this must include physical education. She also agreed with her that domesticity needed reforming. In particular, she agreed that the old-fashioned approach that considered every woman an expert on homemaking, simply because she was a woman, was harmful to everyone, and in particular women. But while Beecher's remedy for this harm was to teach women domestic science, Perkins Gilman believed that we should stop thinking of women as homemakers, and that domestic work should be left to professionals.

It is tempting to think of Beecher and Gilman as ideological enemies. As one scholar remarked, "Gilman [. . .] expended much of her intellectual energy trying to undo the domestic ideology to which her great-aunt so ambitiously contributed. In print and in public lectures, Charlotte Perkins Gilman attacked the nineteenth century's configuration of private space as woman's domain, and its attendant generalizations about femininity."[20] Yet the aunt and the niece had much in common: both believed that the key to social progress, and to the flourishing of women, laid in reforming the home and its work. But while Beecher argued that this meant teaching women to be stronger, and better homemakers, Perkins Gilman went one step further: if domestic work required professional training, it must also require specialization. It makes no sense for each woman to strive to become an expert in cooking, hygiene, architecture, accounting, physical health, plumbing—all topics Beecher thought we should be taught—and more. To expect that much is to set women up for failure. So, instead, why not farm out specific jobs to professionals? That way the home is no longer a place of work, but simply a harbor of peace and a place of rest for all its inhabitants.

Despite their opposition, then, the differences between the niece and the aunt are based on a fundamental agreement. Both wanted to demystify the housewife: a woman who keeps a home and family fed and clean is not an angel. She is a bone and flesh human who is in charge of a very complex and important set of duties, which she needs to be educated and in good health to perform well. Beecher argued all this, and Perkins Gilman built on it: her feminism depended on the (non-feminist) work her aunt had already done.

Perkins Gilman argued that the set of beliefs that were commonly shared about the home, and in particular women's place in it, was harmful. These beliefs consisted of dangerous myths that not only set women up for failure but were likely to harm everybody's physical and mental health. And at the same time, they hampered social and political progress. These myths were so firmly ensconced in our lives that it was futile to expect them simply to go away. Something had to be done.

There is a school of myths connected with the home, more tenacious in their hold on the popular mind than even religious beliefs. Of all current superstitions, none are deeper rooted, none so sensitive to the touch, so acutely painful in removal.[21]

Some of those myths and superstitions were encouraged and propagated by the Cult of True Womanhood. Women were portrayed as angelic creatures, who turned the home into a place of health and virtue by drawing on their natural feminine character: nurturing, patient, and pious. But this is not, we saw, what Catharine Beecher believed. What made the homes of "True Women" comfortable was not their angelic nature or fragility. Instead, domestic women, if properly taught, were well-educated, good critical thinkers, practically minded, and strong-bodied. A "True Woman," according to Beecher, could single-handedly design and build a home, furnish it, keep it clean and in good repair, feed her family, educate her children, and inspire her husband to lead a blameless professional and political life. But despite having a very impressive (and somewhat unrealistic) set of skills, Beecher's women could only be useful to society via their homemaking: by enabling their husbands and sons to go out in the world of money-making and politics. Unmarried women could exert their influence outside their home as long as it was still a domestic influence: they could become teachers who enabled other women to become good homemakers.

Perkins Gilman disagreed with her aunt. What made women useful to society, or powerful, she thought, had nothing to do with the time they spent in their home on domestic work. Domestic work should be contracted out to paid specialists and conducted as much as possible outside the home. This would make the home a safer and more peaceful environment: there'd be no sharp objects or hot ovens, no smoke, no food past its best, and no tubs of soapy water for children to fall into. But also, it would free women to engage in more fulfilling and socially useful activities outside the house. A home where a woman oversaw everything from menu planning to laundry could not, she said, bring about anyone's flourishing, or, more generally, social progress. These were the two main reasons why the home, according to Perkins Gilman, needed to be reformed. The myths to be fought were (1) that the home was the safest and healthiest environment; and(2) that women were at their most useful when they worked in the home.

Let's look at the first myth. Far from protecting citizens health and educating them, the American home, according to Perkins Gilman, prevented them from accessing the safest environments, the healthiest diet, and the best education on offer. Women, no matter how well educated, could not become expert dieticians, cleaners, architects, and educators all at once. There had been enough progress made in all these subjects that experts needed to be specialized. If women tried to do all this, not only would they be performing several distinct and time-consuming jobs that would keep them tied to their home on a permanent basis, but they would flounder. The health and education of their children, their spouse, and themselves would inevitably suffer.

One striking example of the home's failure used by Perkins Gilman is home cooking. Going against (still strong) popular opinion, Perkins Gilman argued that home-cooked meals are not necessarily superior to food that can be bought in restaurants or hotels. In terms of nutrition and disease prevention, they are almost certainly inferior. Professional cooks are more likely to know how to keep a work surface clean, and their ingredients well refrigerated or safely canned. They may also have access to fresher, and more varied ingredients, and to have received a specialized education in food preparation. A housewife could never achieve the standards of food safety and nutrition that well-educated professional caterers could. Perkins Gilman concluded that all we could expect from home-cooked meals was the "slow-poisoning" of our bodies, "Dyspepsia," and "false teeth before they are thirty."[22]

Now for the second myth: an important reason why the home is harmful to social progress, according to Perkins Gilman, follows on from the first. If women are responsible for feeding and educating their families, then women and children spend most of their time at home, in the kitchen and the school room. This means that they miss out on the sort of social interactions that are necessary for social cohesion and, ultimately, social progress. If children are under the control of the home during the period where they should develop—all their lives, if they are women—then they miss out on what attending public institutions and mixing with their peers could teach them. Educating women to become better homemakers and homeschoolers might improve general health and education levels on what they are when insufficiently educated women are in charge of homeschooling and home cooking. But it would still constitute an impediment to human flourishing generally, as, by making the home the central source of early educational practice, and making women universal teachers, the home would block its inhabitants' access to the educational, health, and civic resources that they would need in order to flourish and to contribute to human progress.[23]

The home as the place where we can live safe, happy, and in privacy—where we can retreat from the world and at the same time be educated to live in it—is fundamental to what we understand the home to be. But it's also deeply flawed. There is a feeling, Perkins Gilman says, that "home is more secure and protective than anywhere else," and that feeling, she claims, is at the heart of whatever myths we still believe about the home. These myths, she concludes, must be dispelled, and the home must open up to social progress, and change to accommodate our real needs as human beings and citizens. If we understand this, she says, we might find a way forward.

> In all this long period of progress, the moving world has carried with it the unmoving home; the man free, the woman confined; the man specializing in a thousand industries, the woman still limited to her domestic functions. We have constantly believed that this was the true way to live, the natural way, the only way. Whatever else might change—and all things did—the home must not. So sure were we, and are we yet, of this, that we have utterly refused to admit that the home has changed, has grown, has improved, in spite of our unshaken convictions and unbending opposition.[24]

It is time, Perkins Gilman concludes, for the home to start changing alongside the rest of our lives.

The New, Improved Home

Perkins Gilman was very critical of the American home. But she did not think we should abolish homes. Having a home, she believed, is an essential part of human flourishing, as long it does not force a particular set of living arrangements upon one:

> [E]very human being should have a home. The single person his or her own home; and the family their home. [. . .] The home should offer to the individual rest, peace, quiet, comfort, health and that degree of personal expression requisite; and those condition should be maintained by the best methods of the time.[25]

Unfortunately, these conditions do not in general obtain for most people who do have homes. Homes as they were in nineteenth-century North America did not provide much for children, especially in terms of health, education, or personal development. They provided no peace, rest, or comfort for servants, who lived in a house that was not their home, but that of their employers. And for all women the home meant confinement and labor.

What shape should the new home take, then? Not just one but many. A family, a couple, and a single adult should not live in identical homes. The space should be sufficiently large and well aired to contain and replenish the amount of oxygen each inhabitant requires, and it should be suited to the types of occupation they are more likely to engage in. Children need to run and make noises. They can't do so safely in a home that is full of staircases and high windows. They also need to be under constant supervision: but if their mother is in the kitchen, she will not be able to follow them in their play. And if children play in the kitchen, they may come to harm through the sharp knives, hot ovens, or boiling pots that are there.

A single man coming home from work will not want to get lost in a huge house, waste money on heating it through, and having to hire a multitude of servants to keep it clean and him fed. Young single people may prefer not to live alone, nor to stay in their parents' house: one solution for that (offered in *Moving the Mountain*) is to build communities of flats, where single men and women can share a restaurant, a laundry service, and common rooms and gardens to socialize. If we want all humans to flourish, then we need to rethink the architecture of the places we call homes and stop building everything according to the traditional model of the family home.

One important part of this rethinking, she argues, concerns several of the activities that traditionally take place inside the home such as cooking or laundry. If the home is supposed to be a place of rest, then this kind of work, which is physically demanding and time consuming, should not take place inside the home. And if the home is meant to keep us healthy, then hanging wet clothes to dry and creating humidity, or having food rot in the kitchen, or cooked at the wrong temperature, generating germs, is not a good idea. Such work should instead be performed in specialized buildings by professionals, making the home a safer and cleaner environment and freeing time for its occupants to do other things.

The very realization that home life does not necessarily require what we now tend to regard as regular housework, cooking, or doing laundry may change our expectations as to the shape of the home. Unless cooking is something that is essential to one's flourishing, unless someone enjoys spending time preparing food on a large scale, there is not much need for a kitchen in a home. And if laundry being sent out means that it is picked from our homes, just as our rubbish is, and then delivered clean and folded a few days later, then there is no need for large washing machines and driers, sheets hanging over bedroom doors because it's raining outside, and overflowing laundry baskets blocking the entrance to the bathroom. It means no longer having to chase after odd socks during endless laundry folding sessions. And—this is mentioned in passing in *Home*—bathrooms also stand as candidates for elimination, as they can be replaced by public baths. This is perhaps not as appealing as getting rid of the laundry and cooking duties: the possibility of a hot shower any time we need it is hard to relinquish—and what would we do about lavatories? There is, sadly, no mention of this particular household item in Perkins Gilman's *Home*.

Perkins Gilman's vision of the need to reform the home is both spelt out and put to the test in the third novel of the *Herland* trilogy, *Moving the Mountain*. In that novel, a middle-aged explorer, John, recovers from a long-term memory loss to find that the world he left behind is utterly changed. His sister, also an explorer, guides him in this new world where women are considered men's equals, and every aspect of life, work, and human beings' relationship to nature has been affected by the change. Women perform the same tasks as men but the workday for both sexes is much shorter—only two hours (yes, two hours!)—so that people have time to enjoy life and each other, develop skills and interests, and keep working together at social progress. The home has been reformed alongside the principles spelt out in *Home*, with all the domestic work (cooking, cleaning, laundry, and child-rearing) managed externally by well-paid specialists. Neither women nor children are confined to the home, but the home still retains a particular appeal and all who live there can find comfort and refugee:

> From earliest infancy, they absorbed the idea that home was a place to come out from and go back to; the sweetest, dearest place—for there was mother, and father, and one's own little room to sleep in; but the day hours were to go somewhere to learn and do, to work and play, to grow in.[26]

The only thing missing to make this description identical to what is often presented as the traditional family home (often meaning Western, white, Christian, and middle class) is the smell of home baking and fresh laundry, or the baby brother or sister who has been home all day with mother. These are cut out from Gilman's home. But the fundamental structure—the loving and caring nuclear family—remains the same, carrying with it the domestic function of creating an emotionally supportive environment for the individual. The romantic sentiments that were associated with the apple pie cooling on the windowsill and the freshly washed sheets drying in the garden are replaced by something simpler: the sense of love and belonging that once get from living with a caring family.

Toward the end of *Moving the Mountain*, John, who is still skeptical of the reforms he has seen, particularly those pertaining to gender equality, goes to visit an uncle and aunt whose lives are still anchored in the old world, as they too refuse to accept the new one. At first, John is cheered by recognizing the old ways: "I felt an increasing pleasure in the familiar look of things. [...] My heart quite leaped as I set foot on [the path to Uncle Jake's home]."[27] And once there, he does find comfort for a while, re-discovering the food of his youth and recognizing the more traditional ways of his uncle, aunt, and cousin. There is nothing new to learn and digest, only what he remembers from his childhood. But soon, John realizes that traditional home comforts are not, in fact, as comfortable as the life his sister and her family live. The homespun sheets are scratchy, the crocheted blankets are too thin to keep him warm, and his aunt and cousin, who have lived and worked in the same home their entire lives, have very little conversation.

John, now seeing the progress that his sister's world has brought about, understands that the appeal of old-fashion domesticity was mostly a myth that had been fed him as a child. The reality of the self-contained family home is drab and, rather than producing happiness, stunts the flourishing of its inhabitants and takes away their freedom. John now realizes that he can save not only himself but his spinster cousin by marrying her and embracing the new world together. This realization is Perkins Gilman's way of dispelling the final myths attached to the traditional home. The "angel" who lives there is a bad cook, an indifferent housekeeper, none of its inhabitants are particularly healthy or happy, and the angel herself is miserable. The only thing to do, then, is take her away from home and allow her to flourish in the world.

Professional Cooks and Out-Kitchens

What is the first thing that must go for a gender-just and well-functioning society? According to Perkins Gilman, it is domestic work. All work-related to cooking and cleaning, she says, should be subcontracted to professionals, that is, people (mostly women, a fact we will come back to later) who do not see as drudgery and can do it well, in exchange for a decent salary. In *Moving the Mountain*, she describes professional housework:

The women who liked that kind of work are doing it now, as a profession, for reasonable hours and excellent salaries, and the women who did not like it are now free to do the work they are fitted for and enjoy.[28]

One reason to pay professionals to clean and cook is to reduce the dirt inside houses, accumulated by inefficient housework and generated by its performance (particularly in the kitchen). So, homes which are cared for by housewives or servants are insalubrious because they are dirty. Also, those who do the work are often discontented, which leads to poor mental health. Therefore, eliminating it can only improve the health of the home's inhabitants.

Gilman's particular target, not just in *Home*, but also *Moving the Mountain* and several other stories and essays, is the kitchen. Kitchens, she argues, are dangerous places, where knives and heavy objects are kept, intense heat, and, of course, germs, which require constant and intensive cleaning. In *Moving the Mountain*, Nellie explains to her newly recovered brother, John, why cats are no longer needed to keep down the rodent population:

- And the mouse, the fly, and the croton bug went with the kitchen.
- No homes left?
- I didn't say "home"—I said "kitchen."[29]

She then attempts to explain the benefit of living in kitchenless houses: "We do not live in food warehouses now" (1911, 153), that is, we do not have to take care of our own nutrition from scratch, either growing or shopping for food, storing and preserving it, preparing it, cooking it, and then cleaning afterwards. John, although shocked at the transformation of the home, quickly observes the benefits: "The homes were clean and quiet, too; no kitchen work, no laundry work, no self-made clutter and dirt."[30]

In *Home*, where she is critiquing actual living arrangements, rather than proposing radical reforms, she argues that the home kitchen is irredeemable: not only is home cooking generally unhealthy (because home cooks are not trained dieticians) but kitchens are labor-intensive, resulting in women literally being tied to the home by their apron strings. In many cases, Perkins Gilman suggests, we would be better off eating out than cooking in. She might, one imagines, have become a fan of take-out dinners. Simone de Beauvoir, a few decades later, drew a similar conclusion when she pointed out that single working women often made life more difficult for themselves, compared to their male colleagues, by insisting on cooking their own meals instead of eating out at conveniently located restaurants and hotels.[31] Beauvoir bypasses the question of health (perhaps because French restaurant food at the beginning of the century was no less healthy or balanced than what people prepared at home). But Gilman does not: food from a restaurant will be prepared by professionals who know how to avoid contaminating food and prepare a balanced meal. The point that Perkins Gilman (and Beauvoir) make loud and clear is that not all homes need a kitchen, not all home-cooked food is better, and very little home-cooked food is better than the freedom of not having to cook every day for your entire family.

But freeing one person, we know, often means burdening another. The *Feminine Mystique*, in which Betty Friedan encouraged women to seek work outside the home and step away from domestic work, has been criticized as pushing the burden of domestic work down to poorer, less well-educated, and less white women who would have to clean the deserted homes of suburbia and care for the children whose mothers were at work. As richer women leave housework behind, it becomes even more poorly valued. But is the same problem likely to arise for Perkins Gilman? No, to the extent that homes themselves will have no kitchen, no laundry room, and that children will be taken out to child gardens.

Professionals, she says, who like to cook, wash laundry, and care for babies will oversee these activities, in exchange for a good salary and a short working day. They will not be immigrant women locked inside rich people's house all day, working hard for a pittance. Nor will they have the sort of relationship with their employer that can make such work demeaning: having to clean your boss's toilet, or iron their undies is not dignity enhancing. But cooking or laundering for families one does not know, simply aware that one is contributing to the health and well-being of the population in general, can be rewarding—if it is the sort of work one enjoys and if the pay and conditions are good. Like her aunt, by professionalizing domestic work, making it something that requires rigorous training and education, and insisting that it should be properly rewarded, Perkins Gilman is pushing for a reevaluation of women's work.

This vision of professional domestic work may sound very plausible as far as cooking is concerned—cooking, baking, preserving, or even chopping meat and vegetables for two hours a day is not an unpleasant occupation.[32]

But what about laundry? Nineteenth-century laundry work was hard: there were no machines, no powered soap—just back-breaking work in cold water.[33] We saw the example of Mary Prince, who was in charge of doing the laundry for the family who held her enslaved. The work she did then led to long-term disabilities. But of course, part of the problem was the very long hours: she spent so much time on other people's laundry, that she had to pay someone else to do hers. As an enslaved woman, she did not work two hours a day, she did not have the rest of the time at her disposal to do as she wished, nor did she get paid for it.

The End of Homeschooling

One important criticism of the traditional home Perkins Gilman makes in *Home* is that all houses are built according to a model that is nearly identical, and that those homes that are deemed unsuitable for families by landlords are the very same as those in which families do live. These houses are either unsafe or insalubrious, liable to cause disease or accidents for small children, and unable to provide them with an environment in which they might develop—because, for instance, there are no suitable outdoor spaces in which they might play with other children and exercise.

All these considerations lead her to propose, in *Moving the Mountain*, that children may be better off being brought up outside the home. Babies and young children should be cared for communally in outdoor spaces, which Perkins Gilman calls Child Gardens: "Yes, this is a regular Child Garden, where they are cultivated and grow! And they do so love to grow!"[34] Mothers drop off their babies, still asleep in the morning, and go about their own business, working for two hours—and some might choose to work with at a child-garden—walking with friends, and anything else they care to do. Nellie's brother, John, is shocked at the idea of a home with no children and no mother taking care of them:

> I tried without prejudice to realize the new condition, but a house without a housewife, without children, without servants, seemed altogether empty. Nellie reassured me as to the children, however. 'It's no worse than when they went to school, John, not a bit. If you were here at about 9 AM, you'd see the mothers taking a morning walk, or ride, if it's stormy, to the child-garden, and leaving the babies there, asleep, mostly.'[35]

Aside from the fact that we mostly work more than two hours a day and that if we don't, we can rarely afford to place our children into a nursery, there seems to be little difference between Perkins Gilman's child garden and what we call nursery schools or Kinder Gardens. But at the time she was writing, Perkins Gilman's child garden was a radical innovation. Early childhood was always spent inside the home, with mothers teaching young children to read before they were old enough to be sent to school. Even now, when a child as young as six months can be sent to a nursery, we often hear parents bemoaning the fact that they cannot keep their child at home, that they are too young to be sent out and cared for by outsiders. Others understand that the point of sending children out—aside from allowing parents to work—is to teach them to live and grow outside the home. In doing so, we can minimize the power that home and family have over a child's development, and, instead, we allow them to develop in a healthy outdoor environment, with their peers, and supervised by professionals, rather than by harassed and over-worked parents.

> From earliest infancy, they absorbed the idea that home was a place to come out from and go back to; the sweetest, dearest place – for there was mother, and father, and one's own little room to sleep in; but the day hours were to go somewhere to learn and do, to work and play, to grow in.[36]

The home then still plays a crucial role: it is a place to be loved by one's parents, to belong, to feel safe, and enjoy some privacy—each child has their own room. The home is less cloying when one doesn't have to be in it 24/7.

Perkins Gilman's account here of the role of school and home in a child's education is very close to that put forward by Mary Wollstonecraft in her *Vindication of the Rights of Woman*. Wollstonecraft proposed that day schools become the norm so that boys and girls can learn to develop together, be taught by independent schoolmasters, who can privilege right education over what will impress parents.[37] Children will learn to respect and argue with each other as equals when they are not supervised. And at home in the evenings, they will acquire finer emotions, or "domestic taste" which they would not at a boarding school.[38]

As it did for Wollstonecraft, the family home, for Gilman, still plays a crucial role in human flourishing. It is a more streamlined version of the family home, perhaps, but still one in which parents and children find comfort and safety together at the end of the day.[39]

Freeing All Women?

Despite Perkins Gilman's conception of how the home must be reformed being nearly entirely focused on freeing women from drudgery so that they can participate in social progress, she still suggests that the domestic work they give up will be taken up professionally by women, rather than men. She still believes that women are more likely to enjoy domestic occupations than men—provided they are paid for it and that it does not take up all their time—and that they are also naturally better fitted for it. This applies to cooking and cleaning, but also childrearing. Motherhood, according to Gilman, was both a duty for women and an achievement.[40] Mothers were leaders in evolution, not only because they produced the next generation, but also because they were the first to influence new members of the human race. This role meant, for Gilman, that looking after the well-being of mothers, and ensuring that they were able to flourish in every respect, not just as wives or mothers, was essential for social evolution. "When the mother of the race is free" she said, "we shall have a better world, by the easy right of birth, and by the calm, slow, friendly forces of social evolution."[41]

Perkins Gilman's philosophy of the home was geared toward social progress and the emancipation of women from domestic work. But she did not entirely disagree with her aunt, Catharine Beecher, that it was by exploiting women's motherly aptitudes that we could bring about progress. She disagreed with her that this meant keeping women inside the home. Women could do this job for others, in exchange for a fair salary, and a very short workday. But would this new class or domestic workers, that is, cleaners, caterers, launderers, would truly be women who enjoyed doing such work and wanted to be paid for it? Or they would end up, as always, being the women who are most disadvantaged in society, the poorest, or, as we are talking about nineteenth-century America, the blackest?

Perkins Gilman is suggesting that some women, whether or not they are socially disadvantaged, will choose to become domestic workers. But is this likely to be true in a society where education is free and does not discriminate between social classes, gender, or race, and where there are no examples, at home, of domestic women? Will little girls who share school desks with boys, and whose mothers have professions, sometimes at the highest level, dream of folding laundry or roasting meat? And if not, then will not these jobs, rather than the more glamourous, less physically tiring and more intellectually demanding jobs, go to those who are in some ways disadvantaged? It's clear that Perkins Gilman, no less than her aunt, is thinking about the liberation of women like herself, white and middle class, and not about the poorer Irish immigrants and black women who were in fact doing most of the dirty domestic work. She does not, any more than her aunt Catharine Beecher did, showcase the voices of these women in her writings. This is why, in the next chapter, we turn to American women of the same period who were not white and ask what they had to say about the place of the home in their idea of social progress.

8

The Master's House

The poet Audre Lorde understood that for the oppressed to reconstruct their lives in freedom, using the "Masters' tools" was a perhaps not the safest or most effective tactic:

> Women of today are still being called upon to stretch across the gap of male ignorance and to educated men as to our existence and our needs. *This is an old and primary tool of all oppressors to keep the oppressed occupied with the master's concerns.* Now we hear that it is the task of women of Color to educate white women—in the face of tremendous resistance—as to our existence, our differences, our relative roles in our joint survival. This is a diversion of energies and a tragic repetition of racist patriarchal thought.[1]

Lorde believed that education could bring about social progress, including progress in gender and racial relations, but not without some serious thought about how we educate ourselves. The oppressed, she says, are called upon to educate their oppressors, teach them that what they do is oppressive. But they cannot do so from a position of subordination. They must build a ladder to raise themselves to the platform of their oppressors, learn to speak like them, pass as one of them, so that finally, it is almost impossible for them to speak convincingly about the position of oppression they started from, because they no longer "look" or "sound" like one of the oppressed. And in the meantime, this effort exhausts all their resources and more, so that once they do reach the place where they might speak out, they are too wiped out to do so.

There are many mechanisms in society where this applies, where if we want to argue with those in powers, we are expected to do it in their terms rather than our own, as these are the terms accepted as morally and epistemically correct. To borrow money from a bank, one must pretend to be rich—dress the part. In court, whether as a defendant or a witness, one must look respectable, not show signs of belonging to sections of society that typically attract prejudice. Above all, to succeed, one must "pass," underplay any

No Place Like Home. Sandrine Bergès, Oxford University Press. © Oxford University Press USA 2026.
DOI: 10.1093/9780197687413.003.0008

aspect of not being a rich, white, het-cis man. Only then can a person hope to have some influence on the progress of society.

Progress in human relations, especially when it involves communication across economic, gender, and racial divide, is crucial to social flourishing. But until the social mechanisms that set one kind of people with advantages on arbitrary bases are eliminated, there can be no progress. However, for many oppressed individuals, the struggle is not about changing the way society operates, but simply about surviving. In nineteenth-century United States, people who had previously been enslaved found that they had to make themselves at home in the world of their oppressors, the same world that had considered them property, "chattel," or "contraband."[2] These human beings, while enslaved, had been housed—in order to be kept alive and strong enough to perform free labor. But they had not been allowed homes. Enslaved individuals typically did not live in family units or have resting places to go to for privacy or comfort.

Even those who worked as domestic servants were typically kept away from the home. They isolated from the rest of the family, only sleeping close to them if they were needed at night, to tend to the sick, the young, or to be raped. Domestic work itself typically happened outside the house, in washhouses, milk-houses, and smoke houses. Even plantation kitchens were outbuildings. This was partly to keep heat and fire risk away from the main home, but mostly to ensure that the enslaved did not mix too much with the white plantation owners.[3] The enslaved had no control over their surroundings, or those they shared them with. This included family members, as men and women were forcibly "coupled," and women raped by their white masters, for the purpose of producing more "property." Women could then just as well be told to bring up another's child, as have their own child taken away from them. In no sense was "home" part of their lives and upbringing. And in no way were they prepared to take their place in a society that placed the home at the heart of any society, and the woman as a pale and passive angel at its center. A woman who had grown sugar canes or been forced to do laundry for the family of her enslavers would not fit the picture of "the Angel in the house." As Sojourner Truth reputedly said, in a speech that was transcribed to make her seem less literate than she was, a woman who had been enslaved in this way could be stronger than a man and eat as much as a man.[4] She was not delicate and did not need to be helped into a carriage.

What this meant is that Black women and men, once free, were faced with questions about their new lives. Should they seek to reproduce the living arrangements of their oppressors, in order to best fit into their society? Should they try and recall how their own ancestors, of whom they often had no memory, and—because of broken family ties—perhaps very little oral transmission, had lived together? Or should they try and assert their own preferences, taking the time to figure out what these were? Whatever the answer(s) it seems almost inevitable that the debate over women and domesticity would have seemed very different from the perspective of a Black woman than it would from that of a white American, whether southern or northern. But we needn't speculate: Black women of that period did write about domesticity, either as part of philosophical arguments for social progress or reflecting on their own experiences. Among them the four women I discuss here: Frances Harper Watkins, Anna Julia Cooper, Sojourner Truth, and Harriet Jacobs.

"Today I Am Puzzled Where to Make My Home"

Frances Harper Watkins was born of free parents in Baltimore, a slave state, in 1825. Orphaned at the age of 3, she was brought up by her aunt and uncle (who was a church minister) and went to school till the age of 13. Then she took a job in a family who ran a bookshop and was able to complete her education informally during her spare time. Harper became a well-known poet and novelist, and an activist for abolitionism and women's rights. Her position on both reflected her gender and race. As a Black woman, she did not experience oppression in the same way the white suffragists did. And, speaking on behalf of Black men and women who were or had been enslaved, she saw the path to progress quite differently than her white counterparts did.

She explained her position in a speech to the 1866 National Woman's Rights convention in New York. In the audience were abolitionist and woman's rights activist sisters, Lucretia Mott and Martha C. Wright, Elizabeth Cady Stanton presided. Harper opened with a clear statement of what it feels like to participate in a convention for women, as a woman, but also as an outsider because she is Black:

> I feel I am something of a novice upon this platform. Born of a race whose inheritance has been outrage and wrong, most of my life had been spent in battling against those wrongs. But I did not feel as keenly as others,

that I had these rights, in common with other women, which are now demanded.[5]

Then Harper offers an example drawn from her life. Her husband had died in debt, two years before. Immediately after he died, the debt collectors came and emptied her home of everything of use or value, including what she would need to make butter (as was her trade). They left her a mirror and some basic furniture. She went out with her four children and stepchildren to find work, and during her absence a neighbor reported her as a non-resident. The neighbor seized whatever furniture she had left, and she was evicted. She found herself homeless, and the sole carer for four children. Had she been a man, she says, this would not have happened to her. People would not have broken into her home. They would been sympathetic to her plight, and maybe even helped her find a new partner to care for the children. Had she been white, she does not need to add—she would have been protected or at least left alone. But the fact that she was a Black woman meant that she was prevented from performing the most basic duties that nineteenth-century mothers were expected to do—put her children to bed at night or sit them around a table to feed them.

This experience of racist oppression, Harper says, never let off. A little later in the same speech she describes her journey to New York to attend the convention: she was, she tells the women present, forced out of her seat for being Black. Harper drew on her experience of being set apart, because of her gender and her color, of being wronged when she was at her most vulnerable, or when she was attempting to address these wrongs (coming to speak at the convention). Society, she argued, cannot ignore the plight of some in order to benefit others. All human beings are interdependent, she says, regardless of race, gender, or class, and this means that oppressing one group will have negative effects on the others:

> We are all bound up together in one great bundle of humanity, and society cannot trample on the weakest and feeblest of its members without receiving the curse in its own soul. You tried that in the case of the negro. You pressed him down for two centuries; and in so doing you crippled the moral strength and paralyzed the spiritual energies of the white men of the country. When the hands of the black were fettered, white men were deprived of the liberty of speech and the freedom of the press. Society cannot afford to neglect the enlightenment of any class of its members.[6]

Harper believed that "justice is not fulfilled so long as woman is unequal before the law." But she was not convinced that universal suffrage was the solution. Her priorities were elsewhere: human ties needed to be restored before we could focus on individual actions. Otherwise, there is no guarantee that individuals will act for the benefit of all, as opposed to their own. And this is true of women, she says, as much as it is true of men:

> I do not believe that giving the woman the ballot is immediately going to cure all the ills of life. I do not believer that white women are dew-drops just exhaled from the skies. I think that like men they may be divided into three classes, the good, the bad, and the indifferent. The good would vote according to their convictions and principles; the bad, as dictated by prejudice or malice; and the indifferent will vote on the strongest side of the question, with the winning party.[7]

Many suffragists did believe that women—white women—were exceptional, and that giving them the vote would help bring about justice. This was not merely because it was unjust that women should not vote, but because women's actual votes would weigh on the side of the good. It was a good idea to bring women to politics because women were more virtuous than men. Just as Catharine Beecher thought that women in the home could influence men's political judgment (and vote) for the better, some suffragists thought that if women were given the vote, they would choose the right candidates and the right policies. This was the basis of Elizabeth Cady Stanton's argument for allowing white women the vote before Black men and women. White women were "educated" she said, but Black men "degraded" and "ignorant."[8] Stanton went on to make more obnoxious racist statements in her campaign to give white women the vote before Black men (and presumably, Black women would come last).

Basing the vote on education was controversial. Some women argued that it was dangerous to give the vote to the sort of woman who might want it. Women's role, they thought, following Beecher, was a domestic one, and the vote belonged outside their realm. Women who had received the sort of education that made them political were not virtuous and therefore they would use their vote unwisely. One proponent of this view was Laura Ingalls Wilder, the famous children author. She worried about the effect of giving women the vote and encouraged the anti-suffrage women to use their own vote to prevent the ill effect of these "rough" women's vote:

It is easy to forecast the effect of woman suffrage on politics if the home-loving, home-keeping women should refuse to use their voting privilege, for the *rougher class of women* will have no hesitancy in going to the polling places and casting their ballots.[9]

The respectable domestic woman, Wilder thought, had a duty to balance out the vicious politics of the wild woman suffragist. But in the best possible world, no woman would vote.

It is tempting to divide up nineteenth-century American women into two camps, the suffragist and the "angel of the house." Either women were political beings and should have the vote, or they were domestic beings and they should stay home while their husbands voted. But the question of Black suffrage, and the presence of Black women on the political platforms which argued for and against it, means that things were far more complex. Frances Harper, like Wilder, was skeptical about the vote for white women. But this was not because she questioned whether their virtue was best suited to the home. Her reasons were far less elitist: she simply did not have as high an opinion of white women's virtue as white women themselves did. For one thing, their agenda failed to take in the perspective of the women they had oppressed and enslaved:

> You white women speak here of rights. I speak of wrongs. I, as a colored woman, have had in this country an education which has made me feel as if I were in the situation of Ishmael, my hand against every man, and every man's hand against me.[10]

Harper also thought that giving every woman the vote would not help fix the evil that had been conducted against Africans. Nor would it help them live in America as free men and women. Having the right to cast a vote, we know, does not guarantee being able to do so, and voting does not guarantee results. A person could vote and still fail to obtain work, schooling, healthcare. A person could vote and still be lynched. Voting, however much of a priority it may have been for white American women, did not seem, to Harper, the most crucial step toward Black emancipation. And granting white women the vote did not strike her as more of a priority than helping redress the wrongs committed against Black people.

What then did Harper think was the way forward, the reform that would help repair some of the wrongs that were inflicted on Black Americans, and ensure that all classes of society could pursue enlightenment together? The way forward, she believes, is domesticity: ensuring that everyone who is freed from slavery can live in a home, with a family.

> While I am in favor of Universal suffrage, yet I know that the colored man needs something more than a vote in his hand: he needs to know the value of a home life; to rightly appreciate and value the marriage relation; to know how and to be incited to leave behind him the old shards and shells of slavery and to rise in the scale of character, wealth and influence. Like the Nautilus outgrowing his home to build for himself more 'stately temples' of social condition. A man landless, ignorant and poor may use the vote against his interests; but with intelligence and land he holds in his hand the basis of power and elements of strength.[11]

Part of Harper's concern is with men and drinking: as a temperance activist, she fears that the whole human race is at risk of hereditary depravity and that black people, more vulnerable to social ills because of their recent insertion in free American society, are particularly to be protected. A good home, she thought, where you can come to after a day's work, where you can be happy surrounded by a loving family, and where churchgoing and bible reading are common pastimes, is the best remedy against alcoholism.

But temperance aside, why would Harper want the newly freed Black men and women to replicate the living arrangements of their abusers? Why should the home be a priority for someone who had had no freedom of movement, someone who was forced to live and work on the land of a men and women who had the right to beat them, rape them, or sell them? Why should such people, upon becoming free, seek to live in the way of their oppressors, adopting the same notions of respectability, the same structures, and the same values?

Harper's arguments came from a different position than Beecher's and the American cult of domesticity. Her position took into account the lives of Black men and women, their attempts at making a place for themselves in American society. It also takes into account the backlash they were confronted with. White Americans, even those who fought to abolish slavery, didn't seem particularly keen for Black people to live among them as equals. And looked for every opportunity to show that they were not. Harper illustrated this backlash to the participants in the 1866 New York convention for women's rights by telling them of her experience of Black widowhood. But she also made sure they knew how pervasive and current the abuse was by recounting her travels to New York for the Convention:

> Let me go to-morrow morning and take my seat in one of your street cars—I do not know that they will do it in New York, but they will in Philadelphia—and the conductor will put up his hand and stop the car rather than let me ride.

> A Lady—They will not do that here.

> Mrs. Harper—They do in Philadelphia. Going from Washington to Baltimore this Spring, they put me in the smoking car. (Loud Voices—"Shame.") Aye, in the capital of the nation, where the black man consecrated himself to the nation's defence, faithful when the white man was faithless, they put me in the smoking car! They did it once; but the next time they tried it, they failed; for I would not go in. I felt the fight in me; but I don't want to have to fight all the time. [...] Have women nothing to do with this? Not long since, a colored woman took her seat in an Eleventh Street car in Philadelphia, and the conductor stopped the car, and told the rest of the passengers to get out, and left the car with her in it alone, when they took it back to the station. One day I took my seat in a car, and the conductor came to me and told me to take another seat. I just screamed "murder." The man said if I was black I ought to behave myself. I knew that if he was white he was not behaving himself. Are there no wrongs to be righted?[12]

To be Black means that one should "behave oneself," that one should live under everyday abuse while remaining calm, quiet, and perfectly polite at all times. The consequences of not observing this are dire: lynching—the practice of murdering Black men, women, and children without trial, often on trumped-up accusations. Lynching began in earnest with the reconstruction the year before Harper's New York speech. She understood protesting, as white women did, and asserting oneself as political presence, was more likely to result in torture and death than social progress. But domestication would perhaps enable Black men and women to fly under the radar of the oppressors in a way that voting wouldn't. One can stay at home, come home, and generally avoid being seen or heard in a way that could lead to a pretend offence. A home is also a way of entering society from a stable position, that is not only a home, a church, but a school, a job, shops, and perhaps even access to medical care. But this only works if one finds a place to call home: and Harper makes it very clear that this is a difficult choice:

> To-day I am puzzled where to make my home. I would like to make it in Philadelphia, near my own friends and relations. But if I want to ride in the streets of Philadelphia, they send me to ride on the platform with the driver. (Cries of "Shame.")[13]

And even if a black woman does have a home, there is no guarantee, we saw, that this home will remain hers. Harper knew this from experience. Harper's vision of free Black domesticity is not so much moralizing (as one might think reading it from the temperance angle) as aspirational. Aspirational and disillusioned: it simply was not clear to her that there would be anywhere in America anytime soon, where Black Americans could make their home and flourish. Unfortunately, Harper turned out to be right, for the distant as well as the near future. In the twentieth century, Black women were blamed for Black people's lack of success in American society. The fact that some Black women did not bring up their children in stable homes with a gainfully employed father was cited as a reason why Black Americans were not availing themselves of the privileges of American life.[14] Harper predicted that this would be so, and that the obstacles placed in the way of Black women who sought to create a good domestic environment for themselves and their family would make it harder for Black people to settle in free America. But perhaps she did not predict that, instead of being removed, these obstacles would increase over the years so that Black families, when they still needed to recover from the trauma and the harms of slavery, would be crippled by disadvantageous laws and policies that, still today, dictate their choice of housing, education, career, health, and finances.

The Cult of Black Womanhood

Anna Julia Cooper (1858–1964) was born into slavery. But was freed as a young child and immediately started going to school. A promising student, she continued on to a teacher training college in North Carolina. There she met fellow student George Cooper who was studying to become a church minister. They married, but George died two years later, leaving Cooper child free and eager to continue her studies. For a few years she taught at the school she had graduated from. And then she joined Oberlin College, where she studied for a Bachelor of Arts degree, and then a master. She became a writer, a teacher, and a Black activist. She started the Colored Women's League in Washington, DC, together with Ida B. Wells (1862–1931), Charlotte Forten Grimké (1837–1914), and Mary Church Terrell (1863–1954). She worked as a teacher for most of her life, and for some time principal at Chicago's M Street School. In 1930, she joined Frelinghuysen University as Director. As well as her best-known work, *A Voice from the South* (1892), Cooper wrote essays and delivered public speeches. When she was in her sixties, she wrote a doctoral thesis at the Sorbonne on slavery in the French Revolution, at the same time caring for the five orphaned nieces and nephews she had just adopted.[15] Active until her death at the age of 105, Cooper remained involved in promoting the education of the African American community.

Domesticity, in particular women's domesticity, is central to Cooper's work. In *A Voice from the South*, she extolls the virtues and benefits that contribute to and derive from taking domestic duties seriously. Cooper shared Harper's belief that domesticity is essential for social progress. But while Harper's argument is centered on how the home consolidates women and men's places in society, Cooper focuses on how domesticity empowers women to bring about progress. In *A Voice from the South*, Cooper makes the argument that women's voices, and in particular Black women's voices, are needed to bring about social progress in the United States in the years following the abolition of slavery. This argument goes hand in hand with the view that it is because of their womanly essence, which is tied to domesticity in much the same way as Beecher's concept of True Womanhood is: women have the power to bring about change. But the resemblance with Beecher stops here. Beecher's intended audience was the white middle-class women of America, because she thought they could exert their influence indirectly, working on the moral and political attitudes of the men in their lives. But this sort of influence supposes that those men must be in a social position to wield enough power to influence the course of progress. Cooper, on the other hand, was addressing Black American women who, at the end of the nineteenth century, were not, on the whole, married to men who could influence the market or the government. So why did she think that Black women were in a key place to bring about social progress? Part of the answer is that Cooper does not see women's influence as needing to be quite as indirect as Beecher did. But also, it lies in the fact that Black women were situated in such a way that they had a much richer and wider perspective on the rights and wrongs of nineteenth-century America. Cooper saw, long before the term "intersectional" was coined, that Black women stood at the intersection of two marginal positions:[16]

> The colored woman of today occupies, one may say, a unique position in this country. In a period of itself transitional and unsettled, her status seems one of the least ascertainable and definitive of all the forces which make for our civilization. She is confronted by both a woman question and a race problem.[17]

But more than simply bringing about the realization that Black women face problems that are distinct from those of the two classes they intersect with, Cooper believes this places them in a position of "cognitive authority."[18] Because Black women are ignored both by white women suffragists and Black men activists,[19] they are the best possible observers, and, being acquainted with both sets of problems, as well as their own, they are also the best-informed judges:

> The colored woman, then, should not be ignored because her bark is resting in the silent waters of the sheltered cove. She is watching the movements of the contestants none the less and is all the better qualified, perhaps, to weigh and judge and advise because not herself in the excitement of the race.[20]

Black women are intimately acquainted with the problems of Black people and those of women. They deal with both, sometimes separately but mostly together, throughout their lives. At the same time, they are left out of the battles that white women and Black men fight. In the May 1869 meeting of the American Equal Rights Association in which Elizabeth Stanton and Frederick Douglass clashed over the 15th amendment, Black women were left out of the debate altogether. Douglass argued that Black men needed the vote more urgently than white women, and Stanton that white women would use it better than Black men. But since Sojourner Truths' last appearance at a meeting of the American Equal Rights Association in 1867, no one had bothered to ask whether Black women might need or deserve the vote. This is what Cooper meant when she said that Black women are not part of the race: all that is left for them to do is quietly observe and judge. And their judgment is likely to be less biased than either Black men's or white women's because they have little to gain. Black women are the judge of progress, the only section of society capable of observing and deciding what must be done without their judgment being clouded by their own self-interest. Yet, far from arguing that Black women should be given proper political situations from which they can exercise this judgment, Cooper advocates for their influence to be dispensed from within the home.[21]

> Woman, Mother—your responsibility is one that might make angels tremble and fear to take hold! To trifle with it, to ignore or misuse it, is to treat lightly the most sacred and solemn trust ever confided by God to humankind. The training of children is a task on which an infinity of weal or woe depends.[22]

But motherhood is not the end of women's domestic duties, according to Cooper. Like Beecher, Cooper seems to see women as guardians of morality and religion:

> Her kingdom is not over physical forces. Not by might, nor by power can she prevail. Her position must ever be inferior where strength of muscle creates leadership. If she follows the instincts of her nature, however, she must always stand for the conservation of those deeper moral forces which make for the happiness of homes and the righteousness of the country. In a reign of moral ideals she is easily queen.[23]

The phrase "instincts of her nature" suggests that Cooper is appealing to a form of essentialism: women are by nature domestic, by nature destined to stay home and look after children. A woman who does not do this would not be a real woman. This, however, doesn't chime well with what we know of Cooper, her commitment to working together with other highly educated women, to make America a better place for Black people, and her insistence that women should be educated, not just to primary level, but that they should aim for higher university degrees.

One author, Chike Jeffers, suggests that rather than refuse to accept Cooper's essentialism, we should treat it as central to Cooper's message.[24] This message, according to Jeffers, is a version of what he calls elsewhere the Black Gift thesis, that is, the idea defended by several Black philosophers including Cooper and W. E. B Du Bois that Black people have a special contribution to make to social progress.[25] Under his interpretation, what Cooper is arguing then, is that in order for America to progress, it ought to embrace all the gifts its people have to offer, accepting conflict as a means toward resolution, peace, and a better state for the nation. The Black Gift is "tropical warmth and spontaneous emotionalism," which provides "ballast" for "the cold and calculation Anglo-Saxon."[26] For Jeffers, then, Cooper's gender essentialism means that she is also proposing a Female Gift thesis, whereby women's participation in human progress would also bring balance of some sort to an entirely male panel of participants. Again, Cooper opposes an emotional character to a calculating one: "side by side with the cold, mathematical, selfishly calculating, so-called practical and unsentimental instinct of the businessman, there comes the sympathetic warmth and sunshine of good women."[27]

If we follow Jeffer's interpretation of Cooper's essentialism as part of a Black Gift or a Woman Gift thesis, is it less problematic? It is, in the sense that it plays a much-needed role in diversifying perspectives. Women's essential difference and their intimate understanding of everything domestic are not reasons for their exclusion. On the contrary, their essence means that they need to participate in human progress. Far from putting shutting their access to the public space, women's position at the center of home life is a position of power:

> A stream cannot rise higher than its source. The atmosphere of homes is no rarer and purer than sweeter than are the mothers in those homes. A race is but a total of families. The nation is the aggregate of its homes. As the whole is the sum of all its parts, so the character of the parts will determine the characteristics of the whole. These are all axioms and so evident that it seems gratuitous to remark it; and yet, unless I am greatly mistaken, most of the unsatisfaction from our past results arises from just such a radical and palpable error, as much almost on our own part as on that of our benevolent white friends.[28]

Cooper sees the home as the building block of civilization. And she observes that, as things stand, it is women who have the most influence within the home. This is mostly because they are in charge of educating the young, but also because the home, with its works, is their domain. But while Beecher believes that domesticity is essentially female, and that women should take pride in the role they play as "angel of the home," Cooper acknowledges that there is no necessary connection between domestic virtues and womanhood. Ideally, masculine and feminine characteristics should be shared among men and women. And certainly, they should figure equally in the education of children:

> Now please understand me. I do not ask you to admit that these benefactions and virtues are the exclusive possession of women or even that women are their chief and only advocates. [. . .] All I claim is that there is a feminine as well as a masculine side to truth; that these are related not as inferior and superior, not as better and worse, not as weaker and stronger, but as complements—complements in one necessary and symmetric whole. That as the man is more noble in reason, so the woman is more quick in sympathy. [. . .] That both are needed to be worked into the training of children, in order that our boys may supplement their virility by tenderness and sensibility, and our girls may round out their gentleness by strength and self-reliance. That, as both are alike necessary in giving symmetry to the individual, so a nation or a race will degenerate into mere emotionalism on the one hand, or bullyism on the other, if dominated by either exclusively.[29]

The main difference between the Cult of True Womanhood and what Cooper is proposing can be found in Cooper's arguments for the education of women. To promote progress from within the home, women need to be educated at the highest level, Cooper argues. She does not claim that they need simply to know enough to teach their children to read and count, and to know the Bible, but that they need to attend university and pursue higher degrees. This is crucial to unleashing women's power.

> There is, then, a real and special influence of woman. An influence subtle and often involuntary, an influence so intimately interwoven in, so intricately interpenetrated by the masculine influence of the time that it is often difficult to extricate the delicate meshes and analyze and identify the closely clinging fibers. And yet, without this influence—so long as woman sat with bandaged eyes and manacled hands, fast bound in the clamps of ignorance and inaction, the world of thought moved in its orbit like the revolutions of the moon; with one face (the man's face) always out, so that the spectator could not distinguish whether it was disc or sphere.[30]

Women's influence, Cooper makes very clear, is not simply to bring emotion or warmth to men's cold reason, but to show a different side of truth, to help the "world of thought" orbit differently. As well as the place where we can find rest and the loving influence of a family, the home should become a center for philosophy and progressive thinking. Cooper distances herself clearly from Beecher, who claims that women exercise their influence through their gentler nature, and Perkins Gilman, who wanted the home to become merely a retreat from society, but not a place where social reform happened. For Cooper, women can exert direct, non-domestic influence from within the home.

Resisting Black Domesticity

Harper and Cooper advocated for a Black resistance and growth into power that was domestically rooted. This was perhaps surprising: Black people, when enslaved, had not had homes, and what they had lacked, first and foremost, was freedom. So why confine themselves to a town, a neighborhood, a room or two, when one was at last free to go where one chose? And why risk investing into a home, a neighborhood, and make oneself vulnerable to expulsion—as had happened to Harper—or worse? Douglass had made this when he'd argued against Elizabeth Cady Stanton at the May 1869 Association for Equal Rights in America, when she was insisted that (white) women be granted the vote before Black men:

> I do not see how any one can pretend that there is the same urgency in giving the ballot to woman as to the negro. With us, the question is a matter of life and death, at least, in fifteen States of the Union [in reference to the former slave states]. When women, because they are women, are hunted down through the cities of New York and New Orleans . . . when they are in danger of having their homes burnt down over their heads; when their children are not allowed to enter schools; then they will have an urgency to obtain the ballot equal to our own.[31]

Why, when this is the reality of a Black person trying to make a home in the United States, make that choice instead of traveling the world, spreading the word about slavery and its aftermath? This was the attitude of two women—both contemporaries of Douglass—whose testimonies we have: Sojourner Truth and Harriet Jacobs.

Born Isabella, (Belle) to James and Elizabeth Baumfree in 1797, enslaved to a Dutch family in New York State, Truth was sold at the age of nine. She was sold three more times, and bore five children, as the result of both rape and forced marriage. In 1826, after being falsely promised emancipation, she escaped with her baby daughter. Two years later, she was able to recover one of her sons through a difficult legal process.

During her freedom, Truth became a devout Christian and, in 1843, de-cided to give over her life to God and religion. She changed her name to Sojourner Truth and became an itinerant lecturer. For two years, she was a follower of William Miller, a Christian Adventist, who fell out of favor when the second coming he predicted failed to materialize. Then she joined an abolitionist commune, the Northampton Association of Education and Industry, and lived there for four and half years. There her thinking ex-panded from religion to slavery and women's rights. She met William Lloyd Garrisson and Frederick Douglass, and later Olive Gilbert. Gilbert and Truth became friends and, in 1850, collaborated on the writing of Truth's *Narrative of a Northern Slave*, published by Garrisson. Truth used her earnings from the book to finance her life as an itinerant lecturer, speaking all over America on slavery and women's rights.

The *Narrative* is told by Truth and recorded by Gilbert. Occasionally, Gilbert comments as herself. Her inserts usually suggest that Gilbert disagreed with Truth about the relative significance of some incident, or the conclusions that ought to be drawn from it.[32] One place where Gilbert's voice is clear and distinct from Truth's is when she bemoans the fact that Truth did not try and build a home for herself and her children. Instead, after she freed herself and her daughter and regained custody of her son, she found a place for her son working with a lockkeeper and went off to stay with her sister and other acquaintances. Gilbert, instead of accepting that this was what Truth wanted, tries to make excuses:

> Of course, it was not in her power to make to herself a home, around whose sacred hearth-stone she could collect her family, as they gradually emerged from their prison-house of bondage; a home, where she could cultivate their affection, administer to their wants, and instill into the opening minds of her children those principles of virtue, and that love of purity, truth and

benevolence, which must forever form the foundation of a life of usefulness and happiness.[33]

Gilbert implies that had she been able to, making a home would have been Truth's first care. She is anxious to prove that her friend was a good mother, and we sense her discomfort when Truth's attitude to her children's well-being departs too much from the nineteenth-century ideal of mother-hood. But Truth's first concern was not to oversee her children's upbringing. Perhaps she felt that others, who had received a better education than she had, would stand as better teachers and examples. Or perhaps she thought that any adult that did not outright mistreat her children would be an ad-equate tutor. Traveling and preaching was her priority because she'd had a dream that she ought to do that. So rather than place roots for herself and her family, she set out on her travels, not even bothering at first to plan her journey, but simply heading "east" as her dream had said she should.

Although domesticity was not her calling, Truth did rely on it being others'. During her itinerant lecturing years: "she sought for lodgings-free, if she might—if not she paid; at a tavern, if she chanced to be at one—if not, at a private dwelling; with the rich, if they would receive her—if not, with the poor."[34] This doesn't mean that she was piggy backing off a system she disapproved of: there's nothing to suggest that Truth disapproved of domes-ticity in general. She simply did not have the urge to build a home, and did not think that this made her any less human than those who did.

Truth also experimented in alternative living arrangements, spending time at a commune in Northampton—the Northampton Association for Education and Industry, which welcomed abolitionist and women's rights activists, where William Lloyd Garrison and Frederick Douglass often vis-ited. At the Northampton Association, she met like-minded people who helped her further her career as a lecturer for women's rights and aboli-tionism. The commune itself turned out to be a better fit for Truth than any dreams of a home of her own she might have had. A friend reports: "She wrote to me from thence that she had found the quiet resting place that she had so long desired."[35] But Truth did not merely appreciate the Northampton com-mune as a domestic arrangement. For her, it was first and foremost a place where rich conversation could be had at any time of day, without having to walk miles to find it. She had found what she needed: a way of living that fulfilled her intellectual and spiritual needs and allowed her to be useful by helping educated others.

Harriet Jacobs (1813?–1897) was born into slavery in North Carolina. Sexually threatened by her male employer, and punished for it by his wife, she decided to try and go north and have her children join her there. In order to minimize the chances of her children being harmed, she hid for seven years in a crawl space in her grandmother's house. Eventually, when she thought her children were safe, she escaped to the North and reunited with her children. But like Truth, instead of settling down in a home with her children, she chose to become an itinerant lecturer.

Her story, which she powerfully relates in *Incidents in the Life of a Slave Girl*, is similar to Truth's in some ways. Having finally escaped her tyrants in the South, found her way to Boston, and succeeded in getting both her children to join her, all at great cost and risk, Jacobs did not make a home for them. She says that she "longed for a hearthstone of [her] own" at least for her children's sake. But she felt bound to the Bruce family, who had helped her when she first ran away to the North, and wanted to work with her, as much as possible. She left her daughter in boarding school, hoping she would receive enough of an education to work as a teacher, and her son joined her brother in California. None of this was ideal. But she needed to work, and she needed to work toward the emancipation of others. But note that she expresses regrets for not settling down in a home on behalf of her children, not herself. It is freedom that she values before all else, for herself and her children. The last words of her narrative offer a reversal of the typical nineteenth-century romance (with perhaps a nod to *Jane Eyre*): "Reader, my story ends with freedom; not in the usual way, with marriage. I and my children are now free!"[36]

So might we have another proposition to consider, namely that some previously enslaved individuals did not share all the moral priorities of respectable America. In particular, could it be that they were underwhelmed by the ideal of domesticity, the imperative to have a home, make it the center of one's moral and spiritual life? Both Jacobs and Truth needed to travel to fulfill their moral, political, and spiritual priorities. Both needed to see the world, meet people, and share their experiences and observations of slavery. Perhaps they were in that sense exceptional: not all who escaped slavery became touring lecturers—and not all touring lecturers were unmarried. Frederick Douglass was married and had a family. But Frederick Douglass was a man and could leave his wife to take care of children while he toured. When we read Truth's and Jacobs' narrative, we get the sense that having a home was never a goal in the first place but that freeing their children is very clearly one.

One further question is whether, had they not been born into slavery, they would not have wished for a home of their own? That is indeed likely, but the question can be reversed: had Olive Gilbert and Frances Harper not been born into nineteenth-century American society, would they have found the need for a home so compelling? Is the resistance to domesticity "the shards and shells of slavery," as Harper said? Or is it simply the absence of a certain kind of moral and social conditioning? What the contrast between Harper and Cooper, on the one hand, and Jacobs and Truth, on the other, may show is simply that the priorities may have been different for those people who had been recently enslaved and those who had either been born free or become free very early on in their lives. But this would discount the fact that both Harper and Cooper were also lecturers and writers as well as homemakers. So maybe the answer is simply that they felt the world needed homes and homemakers, but that it also needed spokespeople and advocates to make it possible for these homes and their inhabitants to flourish. After all, Catharine Beecher was a writer before she was a homemaker—a real homemaker has no time to write about the experience.[37]

Whether or not that is the case, we should note that there is a clear distancing in both Jacobs and Truth's narratives from the domestic ideal. Did they think that domesticity, having a home in the traditional sense, was perhaps not essential to human flourishing, but that there may be other ways of living one's life as a productive member of a community. In particular, those who have not been brought up in a home, or whose only domestic membership has been as servants to those who were cared for in the home, are unlikely to develop an association between flourishing and domesticity. As Frederick Douglass wrote in his autobiography:

> The ties that ordinarily bind children to their homes were all suspended in my case. I found no severe trial in my departure. My home was charmless; it was not home to me; on parting from it, I could not feel that I was leaving anything which I could have enjoyed by staying. My mother was dead, my grandmother lived far off so that I seldom saw her. I had two sisters and one brother, that lived in the same house with me; but the early separation of us from our mother had well nigh blotted the fact of our relationship from our memories.[38]

But while Perkins Gilman makes a case for women's flourishing outside of traditional domestic settings, and Cooper argues that such settings make women invisible, both are more concerned with the effect of the home on social progress than on individual flourishing. And while it's clear that Truth and Jacobs's activism relied on travel, and that domesticity may have prevented them from doing the good they did, it does not follow that social progress can do without homes altogether. What we learn from Perkins Gilman and Cooper is that progress necessitates the reform of the home and of women's place in it. But both still believe that homes are necessary, and that traditionally feminine traits (but exercised in non-domestic contexts according to Perkins Gilman, and shared by men, according to Cooper) are still useful for the sake of educating children and engendering a culture of sympathy and care. The home remains, but it must be reformed. It is essential, but escapable. It is a woman's place, but also a man's. It's complicated.

9

The Feminist at Home

When short story author Katherine Mansfield went on a writing retreat with her partner, John Murry, she wasn't able to get any work done because her head was full of "saucepans and stoves." But it was not them she blamed or resented, so much as the person who made them take up residence inside her head, her partner. Murry spent their time in the country writing and entertaining friends. Mansfield—the superior writer of the couple by far—was expected to clean and cater for all.

What Mansfield's story suggest to us is that it's not having a home that leads to the overburdening and oppression of women: it is being a woman in a household shared with men—and women—who expect to be served. Mansfield alone would have almost certainly managed to keep herself fed and happy without it interfering with her work: a few cups of tea, a sandwich, the odd trip to the local pub for a hot meal—none of this requires much work. But it is the presence of Murry and his guests, their expectation that she should prepare regular meals for them that oppresses her.

"I Wish Her Well": Friedan *Contra* Beauvoir

Katherine Mansfield's predicament wouldn't have come as much of a surprise to many of the women we talked about in this book. Women philosophers, when they were in a position to make decisions about their homes, didn't pay so much attention to where they lived, as to whom they lived with. Sei Shōnagon would only contemplate sharing a home with family if they were the non-nagging kind, and if they didn't control who came in and out of the house at night. Mary Wollstonecraft lived in rooms, never putting down roots by purchasing a home. She kept her own lodgings even when she married. She and William Godwin did not live far from each other, but they lived in separate homes. Of course this was partly for his benefit. If they'd lived together, he would have had to spend all his time in cramped quarters with Wollstonecraft's three-year-old daughter and her maid. But it was

No Place Like Home. Sandrine Bergès, Oxford University Press. © Oxford University Press USA 2026.
DOI: 10.1093/9780197687413.003.0009

also a way of preventing the accumulation of domestic duties which every family incurs, and to protect their working time from each other. Simone de Beauvoir and Sartre had a similar arrangement: both lived most of their lives as a couple apart, in hotels, and then separate apartments. For Beauvoir, this was the only way of avoiding taking on domestic responsibilities. Being a married woman, in the first half of the twentieth century, still meant being forced into a domestic and subservient role. Shared responsibility for a home meant that a wife—who will after all have been "trained" into domesticity as a child, while her husband will have been expected to remain oblivious— would have to take over. Beauvoir resisted domesticity all her life. In her forties, she eventually acquired an apartment. She invited friends over for dinner, and she was exceedingly proud to be able to produce boiled pasta and sliced sausage, along with a tin of pudding.[1] Had she lived in a shared household with Sartre, she would have been expected to feed friends and strangers more regularly, and perhaps would have come to resent Sartre in the way that Xanthippe came to resent Socrates, and Katherine Mansfield, Murry.

Beauvoir's opposition to traditional marriage comes across most strongly in an exchange with Betty Friedan, which took place twenty-six years after the publication of *The Second Sex* and twelve years after *The Feminine Mystique* came out. Friedan traveled to Paris to interview Beauvoir in her home. She felt that the feminist movement in the United States was floundering, and that an alliance between herself and the most famous French feminist in France might help revive it or at least give her some potential solutions to think about.[2] The feminist movement in the States needed to be unified, Friedan thought: it was losing strength due to the dissociation of some "extreme" feminists, possibly "agents provocateurs" who wanted to make "a political ideology out of lesbianism" and were "down with men, childbearing and motherhood." How can we ensure that the majority of women are empowered while "extremists" are taking the movement away from them, Friedan wondered? One solution she thought was to argue for a minimum wage for housework. And this was what wanted Beauvoir to endorse.

Beauvoir was clearly not in a good mood that day.[3] Sartre was sick and in hospital, so that she'd had to rearrange the interview already, and she would not give Friedan more than an hour of her time. She also strongly disagreed. The problem with feminism, she thought, was not that it was fragmenting, but that the necessary widespread societal changes was not happening. She was hostile to Friedan's suggestion that middle-class women ought to go to work to compete with their husbands. This would only affect a very small proportion of women—the educated middle-class. She also thought that in many ways, women are better off taking humble jobs as teachers than they are becoming presidents of universities as this is more likely—through sheer number—to bring overall change. In an interview conducted four years later with Alice Jardine, Beauvoir comes back to that point:

> Yes, that "we want to be just like men," that is, men as they are today, when in truth we need to change the society itself, men as well as women, to change everything. It is very striking in Betty Friedan: What she wants is for women to have as much power as men do. Obviously, if you are truly on the left, if you reject ideas of power and hierarchy, what you want is equality. Otherwise, it won't work at all.[4]

Beauvoir didn't want women to become what men are: she wanted both men and women to change. So, when Friedan proposed the minimum wage for housework idea, Beauvoir rejected it immediately: it would reinforce the division of the spheres. It would make it much harder to bring the sort of societal change that means women are no longer seen as domestic creatures. Friedan objected that the women who currently did this work and had been doing it for years should nonetheless be rewarded for it. But Beauvoir didn't budge. Women should not be offered the choice of staying home to raise children, "precisely because if there is such a choice, too many women will make that one. It is a way of forcing women in a certain direction." Instead, she argued, household chores should be held in common, shared among all those who are capable of learning to do them, regardless of class or gender.

Friedan tried to refute what she saw as Beauvoir's oppressive ideology by appealing to a "pluralistic situation of real options." It makes no sense to try and erase the special role that women have in the home because:

> the sense of individual family and the values of motherhood are so strong in people that I don't see any viable or even valuable political attempt to wipe them out. If people should choose a communal lifestyle such as you spoke of, that possibility should soon be open to them.[5]

Beauvoir takes no prisoners. She replied that what we needed to do, instead, was to destroy the "myth of the family and the myth of maternity and of the maternal instinct."

Friedan, clearly disappointed by the interview, published in the same issue a short article where she distances herself from Beauvoir. The piece, entitled "No Gods, No Goddesses" traces her history with Beauvoir: it was her *Second Sex* which introduced her to Existentialism (not feminism), but it also caused her to be depressed for years—until she wrote her own book. As Sandra Dijkstra (1980) notes, this is a clever way of not acknowledging Beauvoir's very clear influence on Friedan's on book. Friedan continues to deal with her disappointment by launching accusations on Beauvoir. Her disagreements with Friedan are merely a product of her repeating Sartre's Maoism—just as she had once repeated his existentialism.[6] Beauvoir's repudiation of elitism, she says, elevates "the anonymous working-class woman in the abstract" and her praise of anonymous feminist writings doesn't stop her from collecting her royalties.[7] Also, although she says women should make do with normal teaching jobs so as not to fall into the "equality with the top men" interpretation of feminism, she herself has had "exceptionally good jobs"—this is not entirely true as Beauvoir spent part of her life teaching in high schools. Finally, Beauvoir wanting to keep the interview with Friedan down to one hour because she wants to visit Sartre in hospital demonstrates her lifelong dependency on a man, which is hypocritical in the light of her rejections of the traditional values of marriage and motherhood. Friedan ends by saying "I wish her well."

Beauvoir's leftist attitude, in hindsight, should have served as a warning to what Friedan was doing. Friedan rejected some parts of domesticity as a form of dependence that kept women from participating in public life. For some of her privileged readers, this stance must have felt very liberating (at least until they figured that "having it all" meant "doing it all"). But really, was a rejection not of domesticity as such, but of middle-class white women's domestic work. And while some (socioeconomically privileged, typically white) women were liberated, this was at the cost of passing down the burden of housework and childcare to poorly paid working women. In other words, what Sheryl Sandberg called "leaning in," pushing through until one gets to the position one wants to be in at work, means also "leaning on" those women who are not in a position to compete with men for high flying jobs.[8] Simply arguing that household chores held women back but without offering to revise the system that makes it necessary—that is, small families living in their own self-sufficient space, having to keep it clean and at the same time keep the whole family fed and healthy—is unlikely to work without enlisting other women to do the despised work of cleaning. But must one do away with marriage and family to resolve the problem? Can't some women simply embrace domesticity as their life's work? And whether they do so willingly or out of necessity, should not reward their labor financially?

Choosing the Home

The #tradwife movement, which emerged on social media over the last decade, is composed of a group of (mostly white, mostly Christian) middle-class women who advocate old-fashion submissiveness and domesticity. They wear flowery aprons to prepare elaborate meals and then change into sexy outfits before their husbands come home. They do not work outside the home, except as online influencers. They refer to their husbands in all things, because he is their God-appointed master. They argue that theirs is a "valid" choice, which feminists ought to respect if they want women to make independent decisions about their lives. Feminists tend to disagree. #Tradwives, they think, encourage sexist and racist attitudes, taking over social media with their performance of white woman submissiveness.[9] Some #tradwives deny that they are in fact sexist or racist, but they don't provide any argument that would incline one to believe them. Perhaps their chosen media for expressing their views, Instagram, TikTok, or YouTube, aren't conducive to argumentation. But their message is clear: to be a good woman, and a good citizen, means obeying one's husband, one's elders, and one's religious and (in some cases) political leaders. It means not challenging the *status quo*, siding with the patriarchy, and the white supremacy that enables it. It means avoiding independence at all costs, and the education that would facilitate it. It means thinking less of a woman who has to fend for herself, who must fight to be recognized, or even to stay alive. More than a personal choice, it's a public statement, signed by as many women as there are Instagram #tradwives accounts, and the message it carries is that real women stay home.

What we may find appealing in the #tradwives message is their claim that by relinquishing the "second shift"—working for pay during the day and housekeeping and parenting at night and weekends—they have a better chance at happiness and fulfillment. They are less stressed, less tired. They can spend their entire time doing what they were expected to do in their off hours. And they can expect, in exchange, to be provided for by their husband. This became more attractive during the Covid epidemic. During these months, women, men, and children, who'd been accustomed to being out of the house during the day, at work or school, suddenly found themselves not only confined, but having to manage the home and each other full time. That was hard. But for #tradwives, it seemed that their aptitude for the domestic life was a real booster. Alena Kate Pettit, who writes on her website: "It's ok to be a housewife. Chasing a career isn't for every woman. Feminism is about choice, and this one is just as valid, and valued!" posted on her defunct Instagram account, @darlingacademy:

> Suddenly "looking to the past" and doing things the #TradWife way doesn't seem quite so crazy. I can happily care for & teach my child without complaint, cook a meal from scratch, minimise, economise and budget—AND I actually like spending time with my family. Born for this! (April 2020)[10]

But sometimes you look to the past and it stares right back at you, long and hard. And in the last eight chapters, we've been holding that stare, and trying to understand what's behind it. One key feature of the #Tradwife lifestyle is submission to the husband. Some call it "biblical submission." Submission, however, one presents it, is the relinquishing of freedom and independence. It is about obeying one's husband, whatever he decides. In the words of another Instagrammer, it's about "trusting his leadership over your marriage and family and to make the ultimate decision that will be best."[11] Even though that need not mean that wives are not allowed to argue, in the sense of trying to persuade their husband to make a different decision, it does mean that they will have to go with whatever her husband ultimately decides, trust that his arguments are best, even when theirs seem perfectly fine to them. In that sense arguing is not going to help make a #tradwife feel better about her submission: it will make her second guess her own reasoning, because the husband has to be right.

The fact that a #tradwife must submit to her husband also brings into question the claim that being a #tradwife is consistent with feminism because it's about choice. Can one choose to relinquish one's independence irreversibly (given that divorce is not part of the #tradwife ethos)? Even women who in the past accepted that their proper mode of life was submission to a husband, and defended it in writing, such as Lucrezia Marinella and Mary Astell, did not choose this status. If Mary Astell did not marry, we might be tempted to assume that it was because she focused entirely on her writing career. But that would be to ignore the realities that led her to the decision to become a writer. Because her father died when she was twelve, there had been no time to build up a dowry for her to marry. And in any case, without her father, it would have been difficult to organize the sort of social interactions that would have helped identify a suitor. There is a world of difference, we saw, between choosing submission and trying to make the best out of submission we cannot avoid. Astell, although she defended the institution of marriage and a wife's submission to her husband, also realized that this was a form of slavery imposed on women. What she proposed, we saw, was women should educate themselves. If they did, they could hope to build a tolerable life for themselves, their husbands, and their children, despite this condition of dependence. She did not think that married women were happy because they were dependent on their husband, but that they had a chance of happiness in spite of it. Marriage and dependence were more or less unavoidable for women. Their only hope was to temper this through self-development. Had Astell been born into a world where women could choose not to marry, or to marry on their own terms, would she have still defended the view that women must submit to husbands? There is no way of finding out, and no indication in her actual arguments that she thought this choice would one day exist.

Even if choosing to relinquish one's freedom were a viable choice, it is not one that wives of the past had to make. They married because their fathers told them to. They did not relinquish a life of independence in order to do so: that was never an option in the first place. The point at which Beauvoir and Friedan started to question whether being a housewife was a worthwhile life for women was the beginning of an era in which women could conceivably choose—although it is only recently that choice has become a practical option in some parts of the world, and it is still not an option at all in others. In that sense, #tradwives are not traditional at all: they are choosing to live their lives as if they did not have a choice. Very few women before the mid-twentieth century were ever in that position.

Getting Paid for Housework

Whether or not #tradwives, or any woman who chooses a domestic rather than a professional life, have anything in common with women of the past, should we respect their choice and help make their lives more livable? Many women who are housewives do not choose this life because of any ideology, but for more prosaic reasons. They cannot afford childcare if they work, or their husbands, who may have had more linear careers—unbroken by pregnancy—make more money than they do. Or they make that choice because their couple is not sufficiently egalitarian for the housework and childcare to be divided, and they end up doing a "second shift" at home when they finish work. In any of those cases, it seems to make sense for a woman to become a housewife. But then, isn't Friedan's suggestion that these women be paid for the work they do at home straightforwardly fair?

When Friedan asks why women shouldn't be paid for their housework, Beauvoir returns the question: Why women? Why not get both men and women and indeed everyone in the community to share the work, and then, why pay everyone separately for their contribution to the necessary upkeep of the community? Why—using Beauvoir's own example—should darning your socks be something you get paid for? What's wrong, for Beauvoir, is not that women do not get paid for cleaning the family home, and cooking for the family. It's that they have full responsibility for the work of upkeep of men as well as their own.

While Beauvoir's point is persuasive, it also leaves women who live before the necessary societal changes have taken place in a very unfair position: they are the victims of inegalitarian social structures and being downtrodden and exhausted is not going to help them fight for a better world. Let's clarify Friedan's proposal, then, and see whether it can in fact become something acceptable from a revisionary feminist perspective. If women keep house for their own families, and we recognize that this is symptomatic of a deeply inegalitarian society, does this mean that we should not count what these women do as work, and pay them for it? This question, and this proposal, did not in fact originate with Friedan. Nor was it a proposal designed to recenter the feminist movement toward the white middle-class married woman. The feminist movement "Wages for Housework" started in Italy, the United States, and the United Kingdom in the early seventies, led by Silvia Federici, Mariarosa Dalla Costa, and Selma James. They argued that women, in particular working-class women, should be financially compensated for the work they do in their homes. Compensation is due to them, not because their work is undervalued and prevents them from developing their full professional or creative potential, but because they are exploited by a capitalist system.

> It is important to recognize that when we speak of housework we are not speaking of a job like other jobs, but we are speaking of the most pervasive

manipulation, and the subtlest violence that capitalism has ever perpetrated against any section of the working class.[12]

The solution is not to treat women as if they were in fact professionals choosing to work from home because that is the work they are naturally best suited for, of that they enjoy, but to recognize this exploitation. Claiming wages for housework is a political statement:

> But the wage at least recognizes that you are a worker, and you can bargain and struggle around and against the terms and the quantity of that wage, the terms and the quantity of the work. To have a wage means to be part of a social contract, and there is no doubt concerning its meaning: you work, not because you like it, or because it comes naturally to you, but because it is the only condition under which you are allowed to live. Exploited as you might be, you are not that work.[13]

Federici's solution is temporary—it is meant to raise awareness of working-class women's exploitation. It also doesn't address a different systemic reason why some women choose to stay at home: the fact that social infrastructures are such that it will be easier for a professional couple to fall back on an inegalitarian model of living. The husband will make more money and progress faster up the career ladder, because men are usually privileged by employers, and because he will not have taken as much time off work as his female partner for procreation. The wife will therefore have a smaller income if she works, and that income will not be sufficient to cover necessary childcare expenses while she is at work. Financially it therefore makes more sense for her to stay home. So should she not be compensated if she does?

One worry is that increasing the ease with which women could choose to become paid housewives would simply re-enforce existing gender prejudices, and make it less likely that those prejudices could ever be made to disappear or diminish.[14] Paying women to pick up after men, to feed them, and make sure they have a comfortable home life is tantamount to giving them a good reason not to pursue their own career goals. If they live in a society that normalizes women as housewives, then rewarding them financially for doing it will reinforce the idea that this is what they are supposed to do. It will also make it harder to try something else: after all, what guarantee of success is there outside the home? Very little. And if staying at home means getting a regular income, thereby adding to one's current comfort and future security, then the risk of losing this may not seem worth taking.

Here it is helpful to come back to Federici's argument that the "Wage for Housework" is, more than a financial boost for poor and exploited women, a political statement designed to enable change. Women, in gender-asymmetrical societies, or patriarchal societies, who perform domestic work without being paid for it accept—actively or passively—that this is their natural role, that which they are born to do, and that which will make them, and everyone else, happiest. Federici argues, wanting to be paid for it amounts an expression of a refusal that this work is "the expression of our nature." And accepting payment for this work, conversely, is at least a willingness to consider that cleaning and mothering is not a natural calling, and to grapple with the reality of exploitation. On that same line of argument, if we refuse to be paid for the work we do in the home, we are accepting a *status quo* in which women are submissive dependents: "It is also clear that if we think we do not need that money, it is because we have accepted the particular forms of prostitution of body and mind by which we get the money to hide that need."[15] This can be read as a terrible indictment of the #tradwive: submission might be their calling but it is also the only way they can survive if they do not have financial independence.

The Smart Home and the Care-Bot

Housework is not just the plague of the housewife: the second shift means that even working women have to clean their homes and care for children. And even if that work is equitably shared with a partner, it remains time consuming. I've often heard people tell me that housework wouldn't be a problem if only men did their share. But it still needs to be done! And organizing a sharing schedule is also work! When we come home from work in the evening, the last thing we want to do is argue about whose turn it is to do the washing up, and who'd rather spend their weekend doing laundry and cleaning floors than enjoying a good rest? Why not aim to get rid of housework altogether, and why not rely on machines to do it for us? We already do that. But it's unclear whether domestic robots do in fact save time or labor. Dishwashers must be loaded and unloaded; laundry needs to be dried and folded (and sometimes ironed!). Robot vacuums are fun to watch, especially in cat households, but they do need to be watched and the room they are set to work in need to be prearranged so they don't get stuck and start chewing bits of carpet or electric wiring. But it's more than that. The very concept of a housewife is someone who must be kept busy—or else she'll turn to drinking and daytime TV. This means that for every time-saving device introduced in the home, there is a new expectation that time should be spent on something domestic: Don't have to wash the dishes? Why not make cupcakes for the school fair?

This observation is documented and has a name: the Cowan paradox. The paradox, explored by Hester and Srnicek (2023) in their book *After Work: A History of the Home and the Fight for Free Time*, states that increase in domestic technology does not decrease the amount of housework that needs doing. Studies by Ruth Schwartz Cowan showed that time spent on housework between the 1870s and the 1970s had not diminished, while domestic technology had increased a great deal. Another study comparing countries at different stages of development (with more or less home technology) showed that technology did not seem to affect time spent on housework.[16]

One explanation for the failure of domestic technology to relieve the housewife of some duties is simply that it is not meant to be labor saving. Consider the bread machine. A woman in possession of a bread machine, if she is conscientious, will try to use it, because it would be a waste of money not too, because she can make bread that is more nutritious, and free of harmful additives, and because her family will enjoy the smell of fresh bread when they get up in the morning. This means more time spent at home, in the kitchen. In some countries (such as France), this means losing out on the daily routine of going to the bakers to buy the day's bread, meeting with friends and neighbors. In other cultures (such as rural Turkey), it would mean no longer going out to do weekly communal baking. In brief, the bread machine not only creates more work, it is also isolating: where we would have gone to the shops and met with neighbors, we stay home to bake.

The example of the bread machine reveals another hidden cost of domestic technology. As Hester and Srnicek note, there is, in parallel to technological advancement, a movement toward increasing the demands of housework designed to sell more products. This corresponds to what they call the raising of "Standards," in particular around cleanliness and food safety. The more we rely on highly effective cleaning products or machines, the more we are made aware of the germs that threaten our children's health, the more work we have to put in cleaning our home.[17]

Is there no alternative to this vicious circle of knowledge and technology? Are we doomed to learn more about the presence of our enemies the germs, as the technology to destroy them develops? There is at least one alternative: we saw in that Charlotte Perkins Gilman's response to germs was to argue that we should close down private kitchens. You can't, she said, educate every woman to be a germ-fighter. It requires specialized medical and technical knowledge. But you can take the work of preparing food from them and outsource it to specialists. Families will eat healthily, and women will have time on their hands to do something more productive than scrubbing the work surface. This is the sensible approach. What we in fact do is not the sensible approach. It is an approach designed to keep women bound to unpaid domestic work and to sell products and machines.

As well as domestic robots, we can imagine—and we are beginning to test—care-bots, AI structures designed to do some of the legwork work in hospitals, and in some cases to care for the elderly at home. These robots can potentially replace labor that is mostly conducted by women, either at home, or women who work on poorly paid nursing jobs. We can picture a future where very few nurses will be needed, and people won't have to choose between living their own life and caring for their elderly relatives. Silvia Federici, the advocate of wages for housework, responded to this picture by simply asking "is this the world we want?"[18] Do we want to take human beings away from the work of care, living those who are suffering more isolated than ever? Why not simply revalue the work that women do in caring, and teach men to take equal part in it? Are men so unprepared to do their share of care work that they had rather their elderly relatives be cared for by robots? This—not whether care-bots should replace human nurses—is what is at stake. It only requires fairness, and no technology, to relieve women of the burden of care by sharing it equally with men. There is no need to take humans out of the equation: there are plenty of humans around to care for the elderly once we look past the requirement that carers should be female.

But this is not the only way of looking at the situation. Care-bots don't have to be humanoids or pretend to be nurses. A human live-in or home-visiting nurse or carer needs to be able to do everything for their patients: drive, monitor vitals and intake of medicines, cook and design appropriate menus, shop, and make sure that the patient is getting suitable exercise and human contact. But this is a lot for one person to do well, and it does require at least one full-time human nurse. But a humanoid robot that can do all these things without getting tired is not the only alternative. There are also AI devices that each help with one area of care. Coin and Dubljević (2020) argue that a self-driving car, a smart home linked to a virtual assistant, devices that can connect to friends and professionals *via* video calls, and a smart watch that helps monitor medicine intake and exercise, can all help an elderly person continue to live in their own home independently. And this is valuable in itself. Rather than a replacement for a live-in nurse (and possibly a night nurse), it enables people to continue doing things for themselves. Having a live-in nurse is not only prohibitively expensive, but it also diminishes the independence of the person who is cared for. They lose the sole use of their home, they have to share with someone they don't know well, and they are constantly monitored and told what to do. Robots can help to some extent retain independence, but they can be (for the most part) ignored, and at the very least, one doesn't have to be polite or grateful to them.

Obviously very few elderly people will be in a position to set up the latest AI technology by themselves. Even those of us who were brought up in the computer age will probably find it hard to understand how new machines work by the time we need them, that is, by the time we are struggling to perform everyday tasks. So, a human will still need to be on call to help solve tech problems. But one good thing is this: tech knowledge—unlike care—is typically coded masculine rather than feminine, so that a son, rather than a daughter, may end up doing the residual care work: regular visits to help their elderly parent cope with their independence giving technology. And if the need for women as carers persist, then at least women will come to be thought of as tech savvy individuals, not just as nurturing ones. This is probably a world we would want to live in.

The Joyful Housewife—Or Husband

Simone de Beauvoir may well be right about the futility of the fifties' housewives' lives. They have little control over their surroundings, and no purpose in life other than keeping them habitable for members of the family who actually go out in the world. The same tasks have to be done again and again, in the full knowledge that the same dust, the same stain, the same mud tracks will inevitably be back. To be a housewife, in that sense, is to be prisoner of the home and its work. It is not something that anyone should find enviable, and, we saw earlier, women who claim to enjoy submission have trouble understanding what submission actually means. And yet, women and men often confess that they would sometimes enjoy being home from work a bit earlier to spend time in domestic activities. Is this a flashback to earlier oppression, and leftover "bad faith," a sign that we are unable to let go of the roles that were imposed on our foremothers?

One alternative is to grant that some people (mostly women still) are finding that quiet focus on their immediate surroundings is actually a good way of being in the world, and that at times it can be as meaningful as being engaged in a professional pursuit, or in social interactions.

Marie Kondo, the Japanese organizing consultant known for her books and her Netflix series, definitely thinks so. Her highly influential method for tidying the home, known as the KonMari method, has meant that millions of people who were happily folding their clothes in their drawers or shelves are now rolling them up, lining them by color, and hoping they don't collapse into a messy pile of shirts or a nest of unpaired socks. Marie Kondo doesn't just want us to be neat. She asks us to engage with our surrounding, not scurry along, but stop in one place, get everything out into a pile, sort it, then arrange it according to category, function, color, etc. It's an emotional engagement: we need to ask ourselves whether a particular item "gives us joy." This aspect of the KonMari method has received a lot of criticism: not everything we must keep gives us joy. The stick I use to walk because of arthritis does not give me joy. But do I want to get rid of it? No, because then the quantity of joy in my life will be even smaller, there will be more pain and less movement. But maybe, if I focus on the stick long enough, if I reflect on my reaction to it, I will realize that it is not the stick's purpose to bring me joy, but to enable me to continue living my life as fully as possible until I can receive surgery. I am grateful to my stick for this. And if there is something that bothers me, it's that I have been a bit slow about doing the things I need to do for surgery to happen. This is a useful thought, and one that's brought about by considering Marie Kondo's question mindfully: Does that stick bring me joy?

Ruth Ozeki, Buddhist nun, journalist, and novelist, brought her own take to the KonMari method in her novel, *The Book of Emptiness and Forgetting*. Tidying and cleaning can be a way of engaging with the world fully. In her novel, which tells the story of a teenage boy and his mother who lose a father and husband, everyday objects take center stage. The boy hears them speak, and the mother becomes a hoarder. A third character is a Marie Kondo-inspired character, an environmentalist Japanese Buddhist monk who becomes a media celebrity through her work on clean and tidying. The story is resolved when the two central characters manage to negotiate their own place in the world by taking care of the objects around them.

Cleaning and tidying are not the same thing. As Marie Kondo herself puts it:

> While tidying requires careful deliberation, cleaning can be a meditative act—your mind empties while your hands move. In Buddhist temples and shrines, monks and nuns clean throughout the day as part of their spiritual practice—dusting, polishing and sweeping their way toward inner peace.[19]

Tidying is about a relationship to the objects we gather around ourselves, our choices, and our habits, but cleaning about our relationship to our environment. At the same time, because tidying requires planning ahead—when will I next use this? And reflection—why did I buy this in the first place?—cleaning, after the initial product selection, does not. It is, as Beauvoir claimed, as much a repetitive habit as Sisyphus pushing up his rock to top again and again. But one may wonder why Beauvoir chose this analogy, rather than other repetitive things we enjoy doing time after time, such as gardening. The weeds we pick out will grow again, the ground we water will dry out. Flowers and vegetables will need sowing every year, trees and bushes will have to be trimmed. Yet, those of us who enjoy gardening do not see this as an unpleasant type of repetition. It is not mindless repetition, such as one might experience on a production line. It is mindful, in the sense that the mind empties, but remains focused on the activity at hand, or rather, on the environment that the activity centers on.

But one might say, while it's very noble to focus on the natural environment, even a garden, is the same true of the kitchen floor? Or even, while we might feel some respect for a vintage linoleum, or some beautiful, reclaimed tiles, what about a cheap vinyl covering that curls in corners? Can we give this our mindful attention? It would be hard to do so and not wish to tear it up and replace it. And it's likely, if one has that sort of cheap dilapidated floor covering, that one is not in a position to replace it. The same is true if one has damp patches on the walls that won't go away, or black mold that has to be scrubbed with bleach and will reappear in a few days anyway. Misery is not a friend to mindfulness.

Mindfulness is also an expression of freedom: a dominated mind cannot choose to focus unilaterally on something: it might be called to attention anytime. So in a sense, Beauvoir is right that the housewife, who is dependent on her husband, cannot enjoy the repetitiveness of housework. To her it is a Sisyphean activity. For it not to be, she would have to assume that her work was respected, valued, and, to some extent, chosen.

Perhaps Ruth Ozeki's take on Kondo may help us address Simone de Beauvoir's worry: a housewife, who cleans the living room carpet day in, day out, but rarely dirties it herself because she does not leave the home, or when she does, she is never so fully taken up by her activities that she would forget to take off her shoes on coming home, is not in a position to engage with the world. She is not in the world. Or if she is, it is not as herself, but an accessory, a domestic robot, whose sole function it is to facilitate others' being in the world. Calmly waxing the floor, even with a Mr. Miyagi "wax-on wax-off" movement, will not teach her how to be a better person, or how to respect herself and her environment, because she is prevented from having the sort of free interaction with the world where questions of respect arise.

What Next for the Home?

None of the issues we've identified with housework will go away until parity between men and women is achieved, and until economic inequalities are small enough that no one need feel obliged to scrub somebody else's toilet for a pittance. Equally, housework must not be glorified until those who claim to enjoy it are free, and until all who must do it have, or are in position to acquire, surroundings worth caring for.

Some people will never find the thought that cleaning and tidying are mindful and liberating activities. To them, the home will forever remain simply a place to put one's things down, and to avoid being trapped by expectations of coupledom or family life.

Whatever our take on domesticity, one thing is unavoidable: the home is, and always has been a place of political struggle, that is a place where men attempted to keep their equals in a state of subservience, and where women struggled to live a full human life despite the bonds men imposed on them. The home was never a retreat from the busy life of the city, but, as Marinella argued, a city in itself, either ruled by women or where men enslaved women.

The home is not, either, that extra layer of skin, designed to keep the individual or the family safe from the cold air. This is only one aspect of the home, and it can be reproduced by other modes of living. Sor Juana de la Cruz kept warm and cooked her meals in a convent; Sei Shōnagon, behind the paper-thin walls of the imperial palaces, where doors were always open; and Sojourner Truth, under the roof of strangers she met when she traveled the country to lecture on religion, slavery, and women's rights.

Finally, the home need not be a place of domestic labor. As Charlotte Perkins Gilman argued, there is no reason for individual women to become expert builders, cleaners, nutritionists and cooks, nurses, and educators just because they move into their husband's home. The work of keeping people alive and thriving can and should be outsourced to those who are trained for specific parts of it, and whose work is respected and valued.

Given that Perkins Gilman's vision has not yet been realized (and perhaps never will be), and the social structures that make the home a place of oppression have yet to be eradicated, what can we do to make the home less problematic and less oppressive?

We can learn to be thoughtful about our living arrangements, to seek fairness in them and communicate with our living companions.

We can remember that the condition of the white, middle-class occidental woman does not define the condition of the woman in the home, that other women have different experiences of being at home, and different struggles that must be understood from their own perspectives.

We can accept that women have always struggled to make space for themselves in the public sphere, to live fully human lives, and that the confinement and expectations of the domestic sphere had always prevented them from doing that as well as they could.

Finally, for those who can and choose to, let them enjoy the privilege of a beautiful, safe, and comfortable home—as long as they do not participate in the oppression of others through their choices.

For those who do not chose to live in this way, let them be allowed to enjoy the itinerant life, and not have expectations placed on them that they should settle down with their family.

For those who must work in others' homes to earn enough to care for themselves and their family, let the work they do be respected, and through decent working conditions and retributions, let them be granted some of the freedom they create for others through their work.

Postface

Under the Rubble

Fifteen years ago, we received a phone call in the middle of the night. Our building was on fire and we needed to evacuate. The smoke was thick in the corridor, but, after a brief panic, we made our way to the escape stairs. We walked down from the ninth floor, our nine-year-old leading the way, with me behind her, and my husband carrying our six-year-old at the back. When we got to the ground, we realized that both my husband and son only had one shoe each. Also, we were all wearing our pajamas and it was cold. Graduate students lent the children blankets. As we watched the fire brigade go in, I suddenly remembered that we'd left one living being behind: Elvis, our turtle. I was horrified. But it was only much later, once we'd realized that the fire was located in one single apartment, and that the worst that happened was one melted fridge and a stench of smoke for several weeks afterwards, that I started to grieve for our nearly lost stuff: our books, our children's toys, our important papers, and the beautiful carpets we'd began to collect: in other words, our home. At the time, that wasn't what struck us as urgent. What mattered was that we weren't adequately clothed, and that we'd left our pet behind to die a potentially horrible death.[1]

Our ordeal lasted a couple of hours at most, after which we reintegrated our smelly but safe beds, with plenty of food for thought. While our home and all the things that make it up matter enormously to us, none of it matters as much as the lives within it, even that of a pet turtle. In a matter of minutes, the home can go from being the heart of your life to just stuff—only some of which is necessary to your survival. Living in Turkey, where earthquakes happen, we have an emergency bag ready: it contains clothes, dry food, blankets, phone chargers and lamps, and copies of important papers. That night it stayed by the door: we forgot we had it. Preserving our lives was all we could think of.

People lose their homes in tragic circumstances all the time. Over a hundred and fifty thousand homes were destroyed in Ukraine between February

2022 and June 2023. Since October 2023, seventy percent of Gaza's homes have been damaged or destroyed by bombing. In South-Eastern Turkey and Northern Syria, the February 2023 earthquake destroyed over two hundred and fifty buildings, leaving fifteen million people without a home. For Syrians, the losses compounded those of the war. Losing a home to war or natural disaster means losing everything. One woman from Antakya described running outside with her six-month-old twins when the earthquake started: the twins didn't even have blankets to protect them from the rain that was falling. Over a year later, they live in a tent, together with their grandparents, depending on charity for all their material needs.[2]

Some of the women I write about did lose their homes, and sometimes their properties. When Margaret Cavendish was a young woman, her family home was invaded by a regiment of Cromwell's soldiers, the "Roundheads," and they ransacked it, even destroying family graves. Later, her husband's property was confiscated. But she was never entirely destitute, never had to live in a makeshift shelter or rely on the kindness of strangers to protect her body from the cold. She and her husband were aristocrats, which meant they were offered what they needed when they needed it. A century later, Mary Prince was sent out into the streets of London when she decided to claim her freedom from the man and woman who had enslaved her. But she had already made friends who were in a position to find a place for her that she could, after a while, call home. But she never did make it home to her husband and family, so she remained, until her death, a displaced person. Frances Harper, when she talked at the Women's Rights Convention in New York in 1866, told the story of how, as a new widow, she was kicked out from her home, all her property confiscated or stolen, left with nowhere to go, and no means to feed her children. Her case was not an isolated one. As Frederick Douglass confirmed, a few years later at the American Equal Rights Convention, Black men and women were used to being thrown out of their homes, or having their homes burned down while they were asleep in them. In peace-time America, Black people lived in a state of war and emergency. Many still do.

What to make of all this loss and misery when thinking about the home? In a novel I read, a Ukrainian woman expressed her impatience about English people's obsession with their homes: who cares what color your bathroom tiles are when they could so easily become rubble through a twist of fate?[3] Still, we do care. The people who currently live in tents in South-Eastern

Turkey will, as soon as they can, try and rebuild a home, making it comfortable and pleasant for their children and themselves. Or perhaps they won't. Perhaps, like Sojourner Truth and Harriet Jacobs, they will decide to use their experience to help those who live through some of the same horrors they experienced.

Notes

Chapter 1

1. "Wouldn't It Be Loverly?" music by Frederick Loewe; lyrics by Alan Jay Lerner. The song was in fact performed by a "ghost-singer" Marni Nixon.
2. Possibly he was hoping that the marriage wouldn't last, and that he would get to keep Eliza for himself.
3. https://www.weforum.org/publications/global-gender-gap-report-2024/digest/
4. Or, post-Covid-19, inside the home, but earning money.
5. See Rogers (1978) for a review of women's place in anthropological literature in the nineteenth and twentieth centuries.
6. Rousseau (1997b, 164).
7. Graeber and Wengrow (2021) argue, based on recent knowledge, that accounts linking the origin of inequality to the beginning of human settlement:

   1. "Simply aren't true;
   2. have dire political implications;
   3. make the past needlessly dull" (p. 3).

   Instead, what research shows is that:

   > human societies before the advent of farming were not confined to small, egalitarian bands. On the contrary, the world of hunter-gatherers as it existed before the coming of agriculture was one of bold social experiments, resembling a carnival parade of political forms [. . .] Agriculture, in turn, did not mean the inception of private property, nor did it mark an irreversible step towards inequality. In fact, many of the first farming communities were relatively free of ranks and hierarchies. (p. 4)

8. *The Second Shift* is a 1989 book by Arlie Hochild, arguing that working women who are also wives or mothers tend to perform two full work days: one at their place of work and one at home, taking care of children and housework.

Chapter 2

1. The Peloponnesian War, between Athens and her allies and Sparta and her allies, took place between 431 and 404 BCE and was documented by the contemporary historian Thucydides.
2. Thucydides, II.45
3. *Menexenus* (236a). Miletus was a city-state on the Turkish Aegean coast, near Ephesus.
4. See Arlene Saxonhouse (2018, 610–635, 617) for an insightful discussion of Xanthippe's role in shaping the idea of philosophical wives.
5. Xanthippe is discussed in Diogenes Laertius Book 5, chapter 2, paragraphs 26 and 38.
6. And indeed, her reputation as a shrew survived and flourished, at least as far as the sixteenth century, as Shakespeare's Petruchio compares Katherina to Xanthippe (*The Taming of the Shrew*, Act 1, scene 2, lines 68–69).
7. See Saxonhouse (2018, 617) for an insightful discussion of Xanthippe's role in shaping the idea of philosophical wives.
8. On the signification of Xanthippe's anger, see De Gandt (2017, 38).
9. Xenophon's *Symposium*, 2.10, discussed in Saxonhouse (2018, 613–614).

10. Her life may have been not unlike that of Abby May Alcott, mother of novelist Louisa May and wife of the transcendentalist Bronson. Bronson took his family to live in a commune, Fruitlands, where the women worked day and night to make sure the philosophers did not starve.
11. See Graeber and Wengrow (2021), Widerquist and McCall (2017), and Solometo and Moss (2013).
12. Daybell (2010) and Marik (2004, 54).
13. Fermon (1994) and Trouille (1991).
14. Bergès (2022).
15. Welter (1966, 9).
16. Vickery (1993, X).
17. On Aristotle's sexism, see Connell (2015) and Deslauriers (2022).
18. There are texts and authors that it might be surprising I don't spend any time on. Of course part of the reason is length—I have to be selective. But there are also more principled reasons. So I don't look at Plato because his most extent writings on family life is to take it out of the home, in *Republic* V. I don't look at Xenophon's *Economics*, because I look at Aristotle's which is important for my later discussion, in the following section and later in Chapter 4, of Lucretia Marinella.
19. Note that while the *Economics* is commonly regarded as a work wrongly attributed to Aristotle, there is no compelling evidence that he did not write it, or indeed that someone else did (Valente 2011).
20. All citations from *Politics* and *Economics* are taken from Barnes and Lane (2016).
21. It is a translation of "plethos."
22. Barnes and Lane (2016, 252). Book III is perhaps the most unlikely part of the *Economics* to have been written by Aristotle. We only have a Latin version of the text, so no way of dating it or comparing to other texts. Valente (2011, 31).
23. Barnes and Lane (2016, viii). See also Valente (2011).
24. Nussbaum (2002), Hill (2001), and Engel (2003).
25. The edition I use is Lutz (1935).
26. Fragment XIIIa, "What Is the Chief End of Marriage," Lutz (1935, 89).
27. Lutz (1947, 35), fragment 4, "On the Education of Daughters."
28. This claim is what gave rise to the revival of interest in Musonius. Philosopher Martha Nussbaum suggested that Musonius, and indeed the old stoics (Zeno and Chrysippus), defended a form of proto-feminism, because, unlike Aristotle, they did not believe that men and women were essentially different, at least in terms of mental capacities. For the comments on the old Stoa, see Nussbaum (1994, 322–324).
29. Engel (2003, 288).
30. Lutz (1947, 49)
31. Ramelli (2009).
32. Ramelli (2009, 73–75).
33. Ramelli (2009, 95). Note that the full passage contains a rather transphobic statement about non-masculine men who like to perform womanly tasks. I've omitted it because it's not strictly relevant to what he has to say (and it's offensive).
34. Pomeroy (2013, 45–46), Le Dœuff (1991), and Waithe (1987, vol. 1, 68–71).
35. In the last hundred years, Diotima has been described as a "fiction" (Bury 1932, xxxix) "fictional beyond any reasonable doubt" (Rowe 1998, 173), "a Deus ex machina," and "an expository device" (Prior 2006, 149).
36. See Huffmann (2005, 93–96) for an argument that the letters are example of pseudo-epigraphia.
37. Dorota Dutsch, in her 2020 *Pythagorean Women Philosophers, Between Belief and Suspicion,* suggests that the treatises and letters were part of the "familiar genre of Greek paraenetic epistle, as practiced under the Roman empire," that is texts offering moral advice (135). And it is striking, she notes, the extent to which these texts correspond to treatises on household management and marriage, written by male philosophers from that period, whose texts are more easily (and perhaps with more willingness) established: Ocellus, Callicratidas, Bryson, and the Stoics Musonius and Hierocles. Dutsch (2020, 139, 151–152).
38. Huffmann (2005, 93–96).
39. Dutsch (2020, 130).
40. Dutsch (2020, 232).
41. Dutsch (2020, 234–235).
42. Dutsch (2020, 239).
43. Dutsch (2020, 231).

44. Dutsch (2020, 247–248).
45. Dutsch (2020, 250).

Chapter 3

1. "Imperial porphyry" is a purple colored stone, which was mined in Egypt and used in Imperial Rome for Imperial monuments and statues, and for the Porphyra in Constantinople.
2. Here again we need to be cautious in our reading: while Komnene, unlike Plutarch, wrote about recent events, she was also creating a legend for her father, while protecting her own reputation, and that of her mother and grandmother, as virtuous women. See Neville (2016) on the rhetoric of the *Alexiad*. I will discuss some issues related to this below.
3. Neville (2016, 92).
4. Neville (2016, 111).
5. Interesting parallel with Manon Roland, who Mary Shelley described as a doer, not a writer (despite her many writings) and who was branded as a conniving overly ambitious woman. See also Manne (2017) on the treatment of Hilary Clinton.
6. Komnene (2009, 3).
7. Laiou (2000, 5).
8. Komnene (2009, 150).
9. Komnene (2009, 45).
10. Trizio (2021).
11. George Tornikes' funeral oration of Anna Komnene, quoted in Trizio (2021, 12).
12. Trizio (2021, 12).
13. Neville (2016, 17).
14. Ward (2008, 39).
15. See Howard-Johnston (1996, 285–289). However his claims were discredited by Macrides (2000).
16. Neville (2016, 16–17).
17. Neville (2016, 18).
18. Neville (2016, 137).
19. Byzantine women were expected to live in women's quarters, and only come out veiled, much like women in ancient Greece. Conditions worsened in the sixth century, but were somewhat better during the reign of Alexos.
20. Komnene (2009, 93–94, my emphasis).
21. Neville (2016, 81).
22. Willard (1984, 336).
23. All this we know through a thorough guidebook to housewifery written anonymously by an older husband for his young, inexperienced, and presumably soon-to-be widowed and remarried wife. (Anon 1846).
24. I call the author by her last name "Pizan," which is controversial historically but justified in a book where one tries to makes a case for women's history to be taken as seriously as men's. Even the historical justification is a little dubious. No one calls Abelard "Peter," but when I refer to her quasi-autobiographical character, I use the name she uses—Christine.
25. Gutt (2020, 454).
26. Following Gutt (2020, 456).
27. Note that in the Middle French text, the metamorphosis is marked with gendered grammar. The first participles are feminine and the later one masculine. [*Livre de la Mutacion de la Fortune*, gallica.bnf.fr / Bibliothèque nationale de France. Bibliothèque de l'Arsenal. Ms-3172, 29].
28. Hobbins (2005, 33). Charlie Josephine's play, *I, Joan*, which premiered in the summer 2022 at the Globe theater in London, portrays Joan as non-binary, taking its cue from Joan's own claim that "it was necessary" to change into men's clothes. The play has raised controversy for portraying a catholic figure as trans, and for "canceling" a historical female heroine. https://www.shakespearesglobe.com/discover/blogs-and-features/2022/08/08/it-was-necessary-taking-joan-of-arc-on-their-own-terms/

29. *The Book of Deeds of Arms and Chivalry*, 1410, a military manual about strategy and the correct use of war technology.
30. We also know she was rival to Murasaki Shikibu, the author of the *Tale of Genji*, who was lady-in-waiting to another of Emperor Ichijo's consorts (McKinney 2006, 39).
31. Weiss (2008, 28).
32. Weiss (2008, 38).
33. Shōnagon (1991, 411).
34. McKinney (2006, 19).
35. Shōnagon (1991, 384).
36. Shōnagon (1991, 284).
37. Shōnagon (1991, 286–287).
38. McKinney (2006, 23).
39. Shōnagon (1991, 184).

Chapter 4

1. Mansfield (1977, 43–44). The passage, as excerpted, is from Russ (2005, 8).
2. Pizan (1982, 254–258).
3. For more biographical detail, see Marinella (1645/2012), Introduction.
4. Sinclair (2019, 441–442).
5. Sinclair (2019, 433, 434).
6. Marinella (1645/2012, 6).
7. Cavendish (1664, Letter 150).
8. Hopkins (2013, 556).
9. Hunter and Hutton (1997, 3).
10. A recipe for the Boke of Gode Cookery suggests that for a quart of new Cream, one should use seven eggs. http://www.godecookery.com/engrec/engrec53.html
11. Wilkins (2014).
12. Scott-Bauman (2008, 89).
13. Sor Juana wrote recipes herself. Chuck Goldhaber informs me that her chicken and plantain mole is delicious.
14. See, for instance, Sambursky (1956, xii) and Kuhn (1976, 55). But see also Byrne (2020) for an argument that Aristotle did in fact conduct experiments, in particular with salt water.
15. "Males have more teeth than females in the case of men, sheep, goats, and swine; in the case of other animals observations have not yet been made," Parts of Animals, Book III.
16. Paz (1998, 105).
17. Paz (1988, 98).
18. Trueblood (1988, 206–243, 212).

Chapter 5

1. *Rule 1*: "Acquaint our selves thoroughly with the State of the Question, have a Distinct Notion of our Subject whatever it be, and of the Terms we make use of, knowing precisely what it is we drive at." *Rule 2*: "Cut off all needless Ideas and whatever has not a necessary Connexion to the matter under consideration." *Rule 3*: "To conduct our Thoughts by Order, beginning with the most Simple and easie Objects, and ascending by Degrees to the Knowledge of more Compos'd." *Rule 4*: "Not to leave out part of our Subject unexamin'd." *Rule 5*: "Always keep our Subject Directly in our Eye, and Closely pursue it thro all, our Progress." *Rule 6*: "To judge no further

than we Perceive, and not to take anything for Truth, which we do not evidently Know to be so'" (Astell 2002, 176–179).

2. Astell (2015, 94).
3. Mancini (2008).
4. https://collections.louvre.fr/en/ark:/53355/cl010091806
5. Astell (2015, 6).
6. Astell (2015, 4).
7. Astell (2015, 11).
8. Broad (2015, 145).
9. Astell (2015, 32).
10. Astell (2015, 32–33).
11. Preface to the 3rd edition of *Some Reflections Upon Marriage* (1706) in Astell (1996).
12. Astell (2015, 82).
13. Astell (2015, 29).
14. Astell (2015, 97).
15. To what extent is a woman broken by a bad marriage in control of her faculties? Astell touches on this in the *Reflections*, but the thought is not developed. We'll come back to this when we look at Charlotte Perkins Gilman in Chapter 7.
16. John Knowles (1881, pp. 164–165). "Fuseli found in her (what he most disliked in woman) a philosophical sloven: her usual dress being a habit of coarse cloth, such as is now worn by milk-women, black worsted stockings, and a beaver hat, with her hair hanging lank about her shoulders. These notions had their influence also in regard to the conveniences of life; for when the Prince Talleyrand was in this country, in a low condition with regard to his pecuniary affairs, and visited her, they drank their tea, and the little wine they took, indiscriminately from tea-cups."
17. Hunt Botting (2021, 35).
18. Godwin (1798, 92–93).
19. Wollstonecraft (2014, 21).
20. Amartya Sen (2005, 1–9, 6; 1992, 55).
21. Khader (2011, 7).
22. Wollstonecraft (2014, 31).
23. Wollstonecraft (1975, 56–57).
24. On Rousseau, femininity, and Wollstonecraft, see Pateman (1980, 20–34).
25. Wollstonecraft (2014, 175, 181, 221).
26. Wollstonecraft (2014, 171).
27. Wollstonecraft (2014, 175).
28. Though she does not say anything of the kind in either *Vindications*, she comes very close to it in *An Historical View of the French Revolution* when she says that: "Nature, having made men unequal, by giving stronger bodily and mental powers to one than to another, the end of government ought to be to destroy this inequality by protecting the weak" (1993, 289).
29. Wollstonecraft (2014, 223).
30. Wollstonecraft (2014, 223).
31. There have been several discussions of this aspect of Wollstonecraft's feminist take on domesticity, see Sandrine Berges (2013, 269–284, 277–279) and Eileen Hunt Botting in Wollstonecraft (2014, p. 268).
32. Wollstonecraft (2014, 24).
33. Wollstonecraft (2014, 209).
34. Prince was partially literate and her narrative was transcribed by Susanna Strickland and edited by the abolitionist writer Thomas Pringle. There are some questions about the nature of her authorship, just as there are in the case of Sojourner Truth's Narrative, taken down by Olive Gilbert. But in Prince's case, it seems that most one can question is how much was censored (either by herself or by her editors) of her treatment by her enslavers.
35. Prince (2004, 118).
36. Prince (2004, 117).
37. Prince (2004, 122).
38. Prince (2004, 123).

Chapter 6

1. Again, this does not apply across the board. Mary Wollstonecraft seems to have been involved, or about to be involved, in a project of educational reform led by Condorcet and Paine. Letter to Ruth Barlow, 1793, in Wollstonecraft (2003, p. 221f).
2. Parts of this chapter, especially parts of Sections 1 and 2 are reproduced—with some modifications—from my Political Research Quarterly article "At Home with the Jacobin Women" (Bergès 2022).
3. Wollstonecraft says that she was "half in love" with Rousseau Wollstonecraft 1989, vol. 6, 387. See also Trouille (1997).
4. Bergès (2016a).
5. On Rousseau's negative take on women, see Pateman (1989), Rosenblatt (2002) and Weiss (1987).
6. The identity of Robespierre's female triumvirate is unclear. Linton (2013) suggests that the three women are Manon Roland, Louise Keralio-Robert, and Sophie de Grouchy. Her source is a footnote in a 1939 edition of Le Defenseur de la Constitution by Gustave Laurent. May (1964) also names those three women (using the same source).
7. Linton (2013, 157).
8. Danton to the Convention, September 29, 1792. Cited in Reynold (2012, 221).
9. Roland (1905, vol. 2, 22).
10. Roland (1913, 374).
11. Roland (1791). Letter to Brissot April 28, 1791, edited by Brissot and published in the Patriote Français on April 30, 1791.
12. Roland (1864, vol. II, 169).
13. Rousseau (1997a, 432).
14. Marisa Linton (2013, 156) notes that Manon Roland was the most politically acute of the Girondins.
15. Roland (1905, vol. 2, 264).
16. Roland (1864, 168, note).
17. Roland (1864, 344).
18. Roland (1913, 53).
19. Rousseau (1997a, 455).
20. Sellers (2003).
21. Plutarch, in particular, discusses virtuous women in On the Bravery of Women, but also in several chapters of his Parallel Lives. See my Chapters 2 and 3.
22. See Barnard (1990, 383–392).
23. See Eileen (2006, 29).
24. On this and the influence Rousseau's republicanism had on Roland, see Bergès (2016b).
25. Rousseau (1997a, 432).
26. Fermon (1994).
27. For a description of Keralio's anthology, see Mistacco (2021).
28. Keralio (1789), MS Archives Nationales, 446AP/7, 31—my translation.
29. Sieyes made sure to emphasize that this was a temporary measure only, and did not have principled objections to women's political participation.
30. Keralio (1789), Le Mercure National, August 20, 1789, my translation.
31. This has led some readers to qualify her branch of republicanism as "sexist" though it is not clear whether she could not also be called a difference feminist. See Geffroy (2006) and Green (2014, 211).
32. https://avalon.law.yale.edu/18th_century/rightsof.asp
33. See Hesse (1989, 479). Note that Keralio did found a press, with the help of her father and later her husband.
34. Unless indicated otherwise, biographical details come from Blanc (2003).
35. Blanc (2003, 38).
36. Brissot (1912, 394).
37. By all accounts those of Brissot's children who survived understood that he had to make that sacrifice. One of his sons published a version of his memoirs of the revolution in his 1830s.

38. Accounts of his later life in French Guiana show him in a most unfavorable light. See Olivier Blanc (2003, 233): Victor Hughes claimed that Aubry asked him to cause trouble so that they could take over plantations and pillage.
39. Archives Nationales Pierrefite, AB/XIX/3470, my translation.
40. I am grateful to Andrew Groome, a descendent of Olympe de Gouges, who wrote to me and shared information about his ancestors with me.
41. From a letter printed in Edouard Forestié, *Olympe de Gouges*, printed by the author in Montauban, 1901, 96–97, my translation.
42. Forestié (1901, 97).
43. I took the characterization of Mrs. Jellyby as suffering from moral myopia from Matthew A. Lapine's (2023) blog post, https://matthewalapine.com/2015/05/07/telescopic-philanthropy-covers-a-multitude-of-sins/ consulted January 25, 2023.
44. Noddings (1999, 36). Noddings did somewhat revise her account of Mrs. Jellyby in a later text, adding that her attitude was pathological, rather than typical of parents who want to try and re-live the sufferings of distant others. Noddings (2013, xv).
45. Gouges (1789/2014, pp. 18–29).

Chapter 7

1. For biographical details, see Greenidge, 2022.
2. For an exposition of the Grimké's interactions with the Douglasses and the Fortens, see Greenidge (2022, chapter 4).
3. Abolitionism in nineteenth-century America came in many different strengths, levels of commitment, and willingness to act. Lydia Maria Child was one of the few abolitionists who understood this and sought good will from all kinds of abolitionists. See Moland (2022).
4. Beecher (1837, 98).
5. Beecher (1837, 99).
6. Beecher (1837, 100–101).
7. Beecher (1837, 103).
8. Beecher (1837, 104).
9. Beecher (1837, 110).
10. Grimké (1838, 104).
11. Beecher (1836, 22).
12. Welter (1996, 152).
13. Welter (1966, 156, 159).
14. See Therese B. Dykeman and Dorothy G. Rogers's General Introduction to their 2002, Vol. 1, v–xxxi.
15. For a sketch of Beecher's philosophy of education, see Therese B. Dykeman with Dorothy G. Rogers (2002, v–xxxi).
16. Beecher (1865, 712).
17. Beecher (1845, 25).
18. Gardner (2004, 3).
19. Newman (1999, 29).
20. Gill (2004, 17).
21. Gilman (2002, 36).
22. Gilman (2002, 125). Perkins Gilman also attacks the myth that "mothers know best" when it comes to curing childhood ailments, arguing that all mothers do is perpetuate the mistakes committed on them in their own childhood, and that this was bound to result in ill-health, and more generally stunted development (231–232).
23. Beecher's proposal that girls and women receive a school and university education in the domestic sciences would somewhat mitigate the harms of confinement. But once educated, women would be so busy with the myriads of responsibility they face in the home that they would no longer be in a position to engage with the outside world.
24. Gilman (2002, 6).
25. Gilman (2002, 3).

26. Gilman (1911, 206).
27. Gilman (1911, 279).
28. Gilman (1911, 159).
29. Gilman (1911, 70). The same theme, with the same example, is also present in an essay Perkins Gilman published in her own magazine, *The Forerunner*, in 1910: "The Kitchen Fly": "And every home that keeps a kitchen, with its attendant staples, helps to maintain and disseminate this scourge of humanity, this purveyor of infectious disease—The Kitchen Fly."
30. Gilman (1911, 213).
31. Beauvoir (2009, 817).
32. This is not to say that there is nothing problematic about Perkins Gilman's proposal. Her image of the kitchen as being built outside the home is borrowed from the out kitchen of the plantation, where slaves were expected to spend their time cooking for the family, all the while maintaining their distance from the home where the whites lived.
33. The early twentieth century saw the invention of the washing machine, with the first laundromat opening in the United States in the thirties. In Europe, at least, there were still washer women working their trades by hand.
34. Gilman (1911, 156).
35. Gilman (1911, 160).
36. Gilman (1911, 206).
37. Wollstonecraft (2014, 194).
38. Wollstonecraft (2014, 198).
39. The lack of kitchen or nursery is not the only radical proposal Perkins Gilman makes. Another is that she suggests there may other living arrangements aside from the family home, including single living for the unmarried, and communal living (see Hayden 1981 for a fuller discussion of the innovative living arrangements she proposed).
40. Hayden (1981, 188).
41. Gilman (1966, 340).

Chapter 8

1. Lorde (1984, 114).
2. This was the term adopted by Northern soldiers to denote Black men and women who sought refuge in their military camps, and offered to help fight the war against the South. (Moland 2022, 369). Those people were compared to goods, like tobacco, or cotton, illegally smuggled from the South.
3. Charlotte Perkins Gilman sometimes talks of out-kitchens as liberating for women. That she probably had the plantation kitchen in mind as a model does lead one to question whether she meant the out-kitchen to be liberating for all women. For an account of plantation kitchen, see Fanto Deetz (2017).
4. See https://www.thesojournertruthproject.com/compare-the-speeches/, accessed March 20, 2024. The transcription by Frances Gage also had Truth speaking with a Southern accent. But Truth had been brought up speaking Dutch in New York.
5. Harper (1866).
6. Harper (1866).
7. Harper (1866).
8. Dudden (2011, 71).
9. Wilder (2007, 182).
10. Harper (1866).
11. Still (1886, 775).
12. Harper (1866).
13. Harper (1866).
14. Hannah-Jones (2021, 55).
15. For an English translation of her dissertation, see Cooper (1998).
16. bell hooks described Cooper as "one of the first black activists to urge black women to articulate their own experiences and to make the public aware of the way in which racism and sexism

together affected their social status" (hooks 1981, 166). Kimberley Crenshaw mentions Cooper briefly in her work (1989, 160). She cites the same sentence Du Bois used (without attribution) in Darkwater (Du Bois 2004, 134): "Only the black woman can say 'when and where I enter, in the quiet undisputed dignity of my womanhood, without violence and without suing of special patronage, then and there the whole Negro race enters with me.'" Cooper (1998, 31).

17. Cooper (1998, 112).
18. May (2007, 79).
19. Cooper's quote, cited in fn4 "when and where I enter," is a direct criticism of Martin Delany's own sentence, in which he refers to black men only.
20. Cooper (1998, 138).
21. In fact, Vivian May (2004, 82; 2007, 69) argues that this appeal is merely strategic, playing into her readers' belief in separate spheres to only to show them that these characterizations of the sexes as essentially different are not inevitable.
22. Cooper (1998, 59).
23. Cooper (1998, 112).
24. Jeffers (2016, 92).
25. Jeffers (2009, 58). Jeffers also argues that Cooper influenced Du Bois's own formulation of the Black Gift thesis in "The Conservation of Races" and the *Soul of Black Folk* (Jeffers 2016, 83).
26. Cooper (1998, 173).
27. Cooper (1998, 131). Jeffers also argues, convincingly, that Cooper does not propose a Black Female Gift, but believes that what is distinctive and important about Black female voices is the fact of their unique and non-universal experience, which models what it is like to exist at the intersection of two dominated groups, that is, "doubly enslaved." This is key to understanding Cooper and shows her as a precursor of intersectionalism.
28. Cooper (1989, 63).
29. Cooper (1998, 78).
30. Cooper (1998, 76).
31. Douglass (2018, 271).
32. See Humez (1996, 29–52) and Painter (1994).
33. Truth and Gilbert (1875, 71).
34. Truth and Gilbert (1875, 101).
35. Truth and Gilbert (1875, 114).
36. "The first history of the U.S. woman suffrage movement celebrated Brontë as 'part of the great uprising of women [and] the complete revolution a thousand pens and voices herald at this hour' (Stanton, Anthony, and Gage 1889, p. 42). Anti-lynching activist Ida B. Wells 'formed her ideals' in part from reading Jane Eyre, and M. Carey Thomas, later president of Bryn Mawr College, selected passages from Jane Eyre for her girlhood copybook" (Homans 2015, 27).
37. Except perhaps on social media, as witness the trend of #tradwives accounts on Instagram.
38. Douglass (1851, 31).

Chapter 9

1. Beauvoir (1999, 251).
2. Beauvoir and Friedan (1975, 14). Thanks to Manon Garcia for alerting me to the interview of Beauvoir by Friedan.
3. And perhaps she was not terribly well predisposed toward the woman who had published a popular "digest" of her own work, without acknowledging its influence. See Dijkstra (1980).
4. Jardine (1979, 226).
5. Beauvoir and Friedan (1975, 20).
6. Friedan (1975, 16).
7. Friedan (1975, 17).
8. Sandberg (2013).
9. Proctor (2023, 21).
10. Because this account is no longer active, and posts have been deleted, there is no reference.

11. The Tradwives Club, @thetradwivesclub, February 11, 2022.
12. Federici (2012, 44).
13. Federici (2012, 76).
14. This is an argument made by Anca Gheaus in a 2008 paper.
15. Federici (2012, 44).
16. Hester and Srnicek (2023, 30).
17. Hester and Srnicek (2023, 61).
18. Hester and Srnicek (2023, 23).
19. https://konmari.com/cleaning-is-not-tidying/ consulted June 17, 2024.

Postface: Under the Rubble

1. Elvis grew to be a healthy and very fat turtle. When we eventually adopted a cat, Elvis no longer felt safe in our home—we would find him on the floor every morning—so he was taken in by friends who gave him a bigger aquarium where he grew to giant proportions.
2. These figures were obtained at the time of writing, in spring 2024.
3. Griffiths (2024).

References

Anon. 1846. *Le Ménagier de Paris, traité de morale et d'économie domestique composé vers 1393 par un bourgeois Parisien*. Paris: Crapelet.

Astell, Mary. 1996. "Some Reflections Upon Marriage" (1706). In *Astell: Political Writings*, edited by Patricia Springborg, 1–80. Cambridge Texts in the History of Political Thought. Cambridge: Cambridge University Press.

Astell, Mary. 2002. *A Serious Proposal to the Ladies. Parts I and II*. Edited by P. Springborg. Peterborough, ON: Broadview Literary Texts.

Astell, Mary. 2015. *Some Reflections Upon Marriage*. Introduction by John A. Dussinger. Champaign, IL: University of Illinois Press.

Barnard, Sylvia. 1990. "Cornelia and the Women of Her Family," *Latomus* 49(2): 383–392.

Barnes, J. and Lane, M., eds. 2016. *Aristotle's Politics: Writings from the Complete Works: Politics, Economics, Constitution of Athens*. Princeton, NJ: Princeton University Press.

Beauvoir, Simone de. 1999. *Lettres à Nelson Algren*. Paris: Folio.

Beauvoir, Simone de. 2009. *The Second Sex*. Translated by Constance Borde and Sheila Malovany-Chevallier. Vintage E-Book.

Beauvoir, Simone de and Friedan, Betty. 1975. "Sex Society and the Female Dilemma. A Dialogue Between Simone de Beauvoir and Betty Friedan," *Saturday Review*, June 14, 1975, 12–21. (Reprinted in Friedan, Betty. 1976. "*A Dialogue with Simone de Beauvoir,*" *It Changed My Life: Writings on the Women's Movement*. New York, NY: Random House, 304–316.)

Beecher, Catharine E. 1835. *Essay on the Education of Female Teachers*. New York, NY: Van Nostrand & Dwight.

Beecher, Catharine E. 1836. *Letters on the Difficulty of Religion*. Hartford, CT: Belknap & Hamersley.

Beecher, Catharine E. 1837. *An Essay on Slavery and Abolitionism, with Reference to the Duty of American Females*. Philadelphia, PA: Henry Perkins.

Beecher, Catharine E. 1842. *Treatise on Domestic Economy*. Boston, MA: T. H. Webb, & Co.

Beecher, Catharine E. 1845. *Treatise on Domestic Economy*. New York, NY: Harper and Brothers.

Beecher, Catharine E. 1858. *Physiology and Calisthenics: For School and Families*. New York, NY: Harper.

Beecher, Catharine E. 1865. "How to Redeem Women's Professions from Dishonor," *Harper's New Monthly Magazine*, xxxi, 710–716.

Beecher, Catharine E. and Stowe, Harriet Beecher. 1869. *American Woman's Home: Or Principle of Domestic Science*. New York, NY: J. B. Ford and Company.

Berges, Sandrine. 2013. "Mothers and Independent Citizens," *Philosophical Papers* 42(3): 269–284.

Bergès, Sandrine. 2016a. "Wetnursing and Political Participation, the Republican Approaches to Motherhood of Mary Wollstonecraft and Sophie de Grouchy." In *The Social and Political Philosophy of Mary Wollstonecraft*, edited by S. Bergès and A. Coffee, 201–218. Oxford, UK: Oxford University Press.

Bergès, Sandrine. 2016b. "A Republican Housewife: Marie-Jeanne Phlipon Roland on Women's Political Role," *Hypatia* 31(1): 107–122.

Bergès, Sandrine. 2022. "Domesticity and Political Participation: At Home with the Jacobin Women," *Political Research Quarterly* 76(1): 213–223.

Blanc, Olivier. 2003. *Marie-Olympe de Gouge: Une humaniste a la find du XVIIIe siecle.* Paris: Editions Rene Vienet.

Brissot, Jacques-Pierre. 1912. *Memoires* tome 3 (1754–1784). Edited by Claude Perroud. Paris: Alphonse Picard et Fils, 394.

Broad, Jacqueline. 2015. *The Philosophy of Mary Astell.* Oxford: Oxford University Press.

Bury, R. G. 1932. *The Symposium of Plato.* Cambridge: Cambridge University Press.

Byrne, C. 2020. "Aristotle and Scientific Experiments," *Dialogue* 59(4): 527–537.

Cavendish, Margaret. 1653. *Poems and Fancies.* Retrieved from https://quod.lib.umich.edu/e/eebo/A53061.0001.001/1:8?rgn = div1;view = toc

Cavendish, Margaret. 1664. *The Sociable Letters.* Retrieved from http://digitalcavendish.org

Coccia, Emanuele. 2020. *Philosophy of the Home: Domestic Space and Happiness.* London: Penguin Random House UK.

Coin, Allen and Dubljević, Veljko. 2020. "Carebots for Eldercare: Technology, Ethics, and Implications." In *Trust in Human-Robot Interaction,* edited by Chang S. Nam and Joseph B. Lyons, 553–569. London: Academic Press, Elsevier.

Connell, Sophia M. 2015. *Aristotle on Female Animals: A Study of the Generation of Animals.* Cambridge: Cambridge University Press.

Cooper Anna J. 1998. *The Voice of Anna Julia Cooper Including A Voice from the South and Other Important Essays, Papers and Letters.* Edited by Charles Lemert and Esme Bahn. Lanham, MD: Rowan & Littlefield Publishers.

Crenshaw, Kimberley. 1989. "Demarginalizing the Intersection of Race and Sex: A Black Feminist Critique of Antidiscrimination Doctrine, Feminist Theory and Antiracist Politics," *University of Chicago Legal Forum* 1: 139–167.

Daybell, J. 2010. "Gender, Obedience, and Authority in Sixteenth-Century Women's Letters," *The Sixteenth Century Journal* 41(1): 49–67.

De Gandt, M. 2017. "Xanthippe, l'anti-logos," *Les Lettres de la SPF* 38: 45–56.

Deslauriers, Marguerite. 2022. *Aristotle on Sexual Differences.* New York, NY: Oxford University Press.

Dijkstra, Sandra. 1980. "Simone de Beauvoir and Betty Friedan: The Politics of Omission," *Feminist Studies* 6(2): 290–303.

Diogenes Laertius. 1925. *Lives of the Philosophers, Volume I: Books 1–5.* Translated by R. D. Hicks. Loeb Classical Library 184. Cambridge, MA: Harvard University Press.

Douglass, Frederick. 1851. *Narrative of the Life of Frederick Douglass, and American Slave, Written by Himself.* London: H.G. Collins.

Douglass, Frederick. 2018. *The Speeches of Frederick Douglass: A Critical Edition.* Edited by John R. Mckivigan, Julie Husband, and Heather L. Kaufman. New Haven, CT: Yale University Press.

Du Bois, W. E. B. 2004. *Darkwater.* New York, NY: Washington Square Press.

Dudden, Faye E. 2011. *Fighting Chance: The Struggle over Woman Suffrage and Black Suffrage in Reconstruction America.* New York, NY: Oxford University Press.

Dutsch, Dorota. 2020. *Pythagorean Women Philosophers, Between Belief and Suspicion.* New York, NY: Oxford University Press.

Dykeman, Therese B. with Dorothy G. Rogers. 2002. *The Social, Political and Philosophical Works of Catharine Beecher,* 6 volumes. Bristol: Thoemmes Press.

Engel, David M. 2003. "Women's Role in the Home and the State: Stoic Theory Reconsidered," *Harvard Studies in Classical Philology* 101: 267–288.

Fanto Deetz, Kelley. 2017. *Bound to the Fire: How Virginia's Enslaved Cooks Helped Invent American Cuisine.* Lexington, KY: The University Press of Kentucky.

Federici, Silvia. 2012. *Revolution at Point Zero.* Binghampton, NY: PM Press.

Fermon, Nicole. 1994. "Domesticating Women, Civilizing Men: Rousseau's Political Program," *The Sociological Quarterly* 35(3): 431–442.

Forestié Edouard, 1901. *Olympe de Gouges,* Printed by the Author in Montauban.

Friedan, Betty. 1975. "No Gods No Goddesses," *Saturday Review,* June 14, 1975, 16–17.

Gardner, Catherine Villanueva. 2004. "Heaven-Appointed Educators of Mind: Catharine Beecher and the Moral Power of Women," *Hypatia* 19(2): 1–16, 3.

Geffroy, Annie. 2006. "Louise de Keralio-Robert, Pionnière Durépublicanisme Sexiste," *Annales Historiques de la Révolution Française* 344: 107–124.

Gheaus, Anca. 2008. "Basic Income, Gender Justice and the Costs of Gender-Symmetrical Lifestyles," *Basic Income Studies* 3(3): 1–8.

Gill, Valerie. 2004. "Catharine Beecher and Charlotte Perkins Gilman: Architects of Female Power," *Journal of American Culture* 21(2): 17–24.

Gilman, Charlotte Perkins. 1911. *Moving the Mountain*. New York, NY: Charlton Press.

Gilman, Charlotte Perkins. 1966. *Women and Economics*. New York, NY: Harper and Row.

Gilman, Charlotte Perkins. 2002. *The Home, Its Work and Influence*. Lanham, MD: Rowan & Littlefield.

Godwin, William. 1798. *Memoirs of the Author of a Vindication of the Rights of Woman*. London: J. Johnson.

Gouges, Olympe de. 1788. *Lettre au people ou projet d'une caisse patriotique. Letter to the People, or Patriotic Purse Project*. Translated by Clarissa Palmer. https://olympedegouges. eu/docs/a.Lettre-au-peuple.pdf

Gouges, Olympe de. 1789/2014. "Projet Utile et Salutaire." In *Femme reveille-toi! Déclaration des droits de la femme et de la citoyenne et autres écrits*, edited by Martine Reid, 18–29. Paris: Gallimard.

Graeber, David and David Wengrow. 2021. *The Dawn of Everything: A New History of Humanity*. London: Signal.

Green, Karen. 2014. *A History of Women's Political Thought in Europe, 1700–1800*. Cambridge: Cambridge University Press.

Green, Karen. 2021. *Joan of Arc and Christine de Pizan's Ditié*. London: Lexington Press.

Greenidge, Kerry. 2022. *The Grimkes*. New York, NY: Liveright.

Griffiths, Elly. 2024. *The Last Word*. London: Quercus.

Grimké, A. 1836. *Appeal to the Christian Women of the South*. New York, NY: American Anti-Slavery Society.

Grimké, A. 1838. *Letters to Catherine E. Beecher, in Reply to an Essay on Slavery and Abolitionism, Addressed to A. E. Grimke*. Revised by the Author. Boston, MA: Isaac Knapp.

Gutt, Blake. 2020. "Transgender Mutation and the Canon: Christine de Pizan's Livre de la Mutacion de Fortune," *Postmedieval: A Journal of Medieval Cultural Studies* 11: 451–458.

Hannah-Jones, Nikole, Roper, Caitlin, Silverman, Ilena, and Silverstein, J. (eds). 2021. *The 1619 Project*. New York, NY: One World.

Harper Watkins, Frances. 1866. "We Are All Bound Up Together," May 1866. https://awpc.cat tcenter.iastate.edu/2017/03/21/we-are-all-bound-up-together-may-1866/ last consulted June 24, 2020.

Hayden, Dolores, 1981. *The Grand Domestic Revolution: A History of Feminist Designs for American Homes, Neighborhoods, and Cities*. Cambridge, MA: MIT Press.

Hesse, Carla. 1989. "Female Authorship and Revolutionary Law in France, 1750–1850 Special Issue: The French Revolution in Culture," *Eighteenth-Century Studies* 22(3): 469–487.

Hester, Helen and Srnicek Nick. 2023. *After Work: A History of the Home and the Fight for Free Time*. London: Verso.

Hill, L. 2001. "The First Wave of Feminism: Were the Stoics Feminists?" *History of Political Thought* 22(1): 13–40.

Hobbins, Daniel, trans. 2005. *The Trial of Joan of Arc*. Cambridge, MA: Harvard University Press.

Hochschild, Arlie Russell and Machung, Anne. 2012. *The Second Shift*. New York, NY: Penguin.

Homans. M. 2015. "Jane Eyre, Incidents in the Life of a Slave Girl, and the Varieties of Nineteenth-Century Feminism." In *Literature and the Development of Feminist Theory*, edited by R. Goodman, 27–41. Cambridge: Cambridge University Press.

hooks, bell. 1981. *Ain't I a Woman, Black Women and Feminism*. Abingdon: Routledge.

Hopkins, Lisa. 2013. "Point, Counterpoint, Needlepoint: The Tapestry in Margaret Cavendish's *The Unnatural Tragedy*," *Women's Writing* 20(4): 555–566.

Howard-Johnston, J. 1996. "Anna Komnene and the Alexiad." In *Alexios I Komnenos*, edited by Margaret Mullett and Dion Smythe, 260–302. Belfast: Byzantine Enterprises.

Huffman, Carl A. 2005. *Archytas of Tarentum*. Cambridge: Cambridge University Press.

Humez, Jean M. 1996. "Reading 'The Narrative of Sojourner Truth' as a Collaborative Text," *Frontiers: A Journal of Women Studies* 16(1): 29–52.

Hunt Botting, Eileen. 2006. *Family Feuds*. Albany, NY: State University of New York Press.

Hunt Botting, Eileen. 2021. *Portraits of Mary Wollstonecraft, Vol. I*. London: Bloomsbury.

Hunter, Lynette and Hutton, Sarah. 1997. *Women, Science and Medicine*. Thrupp, Stroud, Gloucestershire: Sutton Pub.

Jacobs, Harriet. 1861. *Incidents in the Life of a Slave Girl*. Edited by Lydia Maria Child. Boston, MA: Printed for the Author.

Jardine, A. 1979. "Interview with Simone de Beauvoir," *Signs* 5(2): 224–236.

Jeffers, Chike. 2009. "Black Civilization and the Dialogue of Cultures: Senghor's Combination of Cultural Nationalism and Cosmopolitanism." In *Negritude, Legacy and Present Relevance*, edited by Isabelle Constant and Kahiudi C. Mabana, 54–64. Newcastle upon Tyne: Cambridge Scholars Publishing.

Jeffers, Chike. 2016. "Julia Cooper and the Black Gift Thesis," *History of Philosophy Quarterly* 33(1): 79–97.

Khader, Serene. 2011. *Adaptive Preferences and Women's Empowerment*. New York, NY: Oxford University, p. 7.

Knowles, John. 1881. *Life and Writings of Henry Fuseli, Vol. 1*. London: Samuel Bentley.

Komnene, Anna. 2009. *The Alexiad*. Translated by E. R. A. Sewter. London: Penguin.

Kuhn, Thomas. 1976. "Mathematical Versus Experimental Traditions in the Development of Physical Science," *Journal of Interdisciplinary History* 7: 1–31.

Lapine, Matthew A. 2023. Blog post, https://matthewalapine.com/2015/05/07/telescopic-philanthropy-covers-a-multitude-of-sins/ consulted January 25, 2023.

Le Dœuff, Michèle. 1991. *Hipparchia's Choice: An Essay Concerning Women, Philosophy, etc.* Cambridge, MA: Blackwell.

Linton, Marisa. 2013. *Choosing Terror*. Oxford: Oxford University Press.

Lorde, Audre. 2007. "The Master's Tools Will Never Dismantle the Master's House" (1984). In *Sister Outsider: Essays and Speeches*, edited by Audre Lorde, 110–114. Berkeley, CA: Crossing Press.

Lutz, Cora. 1947. *Musonius Rufus, "The Roman Socrates"*. London: Yale University Press.

Macrides, Ruth. 2000. "The Pen and the Sword: Who Wrote the Alexiad?" In *Anna Komnene and Her Times*, edited by Thalia Gouma-Peterson and Laiou Angeliki, 63–81. New York, NY: Garland Publishing.

Mancini, Hortense. *Memoirs by Hortense Mancini and Marie Mancini*. Edited and translated by Sarah Nelson. Chicago, IL: University of Chicago Press, 2008.

Manne, Kate. 2017. *Down Girl*. New York, NY: Oxford University Press.

Mansfield, Katherine. 1977. *The Letters and Journals of Katherine Mansfield*. Edited by C. K. Stain. London: Allen Lane.

Marik, S. 2004. "Christopher Hill: Women Turning the World Upside Down," *Social Scientist* 32(3/4): 50–70.

Marinella, Lucrezia. 1601/2000. *The Nobility and Excellence of Women and the Defects and Vices of Men*. Translated by A. Dunhill. Chicago, IL: Chicago University Press.

Marinella, Lucrezia. 1645/2012. *Exhortations to Women and Others If They Please*. Translated by L. Benedetti. Chicago, IL: Chicago University Press.

May, Gita. 1964. *De Jean-Jacques Rousseau à Manon Roland: Essai sur la Sensibilite Preromantique et Revolutionaire*. Geneva, Switzerland: Droz.

May, Vivian, M. 2004. "Thinking from the Margins, Acting at the Intersections: Anna Julia Cooper's *A Voice from the South*," *Hypatia* 9(2): 74–91.

May, Vivian, M. 2007. *Anna Julia Cooper, Visionary Black Feminist: A Critical Introduction*. New York, NY: Routledge.

McKinney, Meredith. (ed). 2006. *Sei Shōnagon, The Pillow Book*. London: Penguin.

Mistacco, Vicki. 2021. "Encountering Women Writers and Their Texts: Louise de Keralio's Pioneering Anthology." In *Encounters in the Arts, Literature and Philosophy: Chance and Choice*, edited by J. Brillaud and V. Green, 93–106. London: Bloomsbury.

Moland, Lydia. 2022. *Lydia Maria Child: A Radical American Life*. Chicago, IL: Chicago University Press.

Neville, Leonora. 2016. *Anna Komnene: The Life and Work of a Medieval Historian*. New York, NY: Oxford University Press.

Newman, Louise Michele. 1999. *White Women's Rights*. New York, NY: Oxford University Press.

Noddings, Nel. 1999. "Two Concepts of Caring," *Philosophy of Education* 55: 36–39.

Noddings, Nel. 2013. *Caring*. Berkeley, CA: University of California Press.

Nussbaum, Martha. 1994. *The Therapy of Desire: Theory and Practice in Hellenistic Ethics*. Princeton, NJ: Princeton University Press.

Nussbaum, Martha. 2002. "The Incomplete Feminism of Musonius Rufus, Platonist, Stoic, and Roman." In *The Sleep of Reason: Erotic Experience and Sexual Ethics in Ancient Greece and Rome*, edited by Martha C. Nussbaum and Juha Sihvola, 283–326. Chicago, IL: University of Chicago Press.

Painter, Nell Irvin. 1994. "Representing Truth: Sojourner Truth's Knowing and Becoming Known," *The Journal of American History* 81(2): 461–492.

Pateman, Carole. 1980. "The Disorder of Women: Women, Love and the Sense of Justice," *Ethics* 91: 20–34.

Pateman, Carole. 1989. *The Disorder of Women: Democracy, Feminism, and Political Theory*. Stanford, CA: Stanford University Press.

Paz, Octavio. 1988. *Sor Juana, or the Traps of Faith*. Translated by Margaret Sayers Peden. Cambridge, MA: Harvard University Press.

Pennell, Elizabeth. 1885. *Mary Wollstonecraft Godwin*. London: W.H. Allen & Co.

Pizan, Christine de. 1982. *The Book of the City of Ladies*. Translated by Earl Jeffrey Richards. New York, NY: Persea Books.

Pizan, Christine de. 1997. *The Selected Writings*. Translated by Renate Blumenfield-Kosinski and Kevin Brownlee. New York, NY: Norton.

Pomeroy, Sarah B. 2013. *Pythagorean Women: Their History and Writings*. Baltimore, MD: Johns Hopkins University Press.

Prince, Mary, 2004. *The History of Mary Prince*. London: Penguin Classics.

Prior, W. J. 2006. "The Portrait of Socrates in Plato's Symposium," *Oxford Studies in Philosophy* XXXI: 137–166.

Proctor, Devin. 2023. "The #Tradwife Persona and the Rise of Radicalized Domesticity," *Persona Studies* 8(2): 7–26.

Ramelli, Ilaria. 2009. *Hierocles the Stoic: Elements of Ethics, Fragments, and Excerpts*. Leiden: Brill.

Reynold, Sian. 2012. *Marriage and Revolution*. Oxford, UK: Oxford University Press, 221.

Rogers, Susan Carol. 1978. "Woman's Place: A Critical Review of Anthropological Theory," *Comparative Studies in Society and History* 20(1): 123–162.

Roland, M. J. 1791. "Letter to Brissot April 28, 1791." Edited by Brissot and published in *Le Patriote Français* on April 30, 1791.

Roland, M. J. 1864. *Mémoires de Madame Roland*. Edited by François Alphonse Faugères, New Edition, Vol. II. Paris: Hachette.

Roland, M. J. 1905. *Mémoires de Madame Roland.* Edited by Claude Perroud. Paris: Plon.

Roland, M. J. 1913. *Lettres de Madame Roland* (1767–1780). Edited by Claude Perroud. Paris: Imprimerie Nationale.

Rosenblatt, Helena. 2002. "On the 'Misogyny' of Rousseau: The Letter to d'Alembert in Historical Perspective," *French Historical Studies* 25: 91–114.

Rousseau, Jean-Jacques. 1997a. *Julie, or, The New Heloise: Letters of Two Lovers Who Live In in a Small Town at the Foot of the Alps.* Edited by Roger D. Masters and Christopher Kelly. Hanover, Germany: Dartmouth College Press.

Rousseau, Jean-Jacques. 1997b. *The Discourses and Other Political Writings.* Edited by Victor Gourevitch. New York, NY: Cambridge University Press.

Rowe, Christopher. 1998. *Plato's Symposium.* Liverpool: Liverpool University Press.

Russ, Joana. 2005. *How to Suppress Women's Writing.* Austin, TX: Texas University Press.

Russell, Bertrand. 1953. *The Impact of Science on Society.* New York, NY: AMS.

Sambursky, Samuel. 1956. *The Physical World of the Greeks.* Princeton, NJ: Princeton University Press.

Sandberg, Sheryl. 2013. *Lean In: Women, Work and the Will to Lead.* New York, NY: Alfred A. Knopf.

Saxonhouse, Arlene. 2018. "Xanthippe: Shrew or Muse," *Hypatia* 33(4): 610–635.

Scott-Baumann, Elizabeth. 2008. " 'Bake'd in the Oven of Applause': The Blazon and the Body in Margaret Cavendish's *Fancies,*" *Women's Writing* 15(1): 86–106.

Sellers M. N. S. 2003. "Republican Influences on the French and American Revolutions." In *Republican Legal Theory,* 6–15. London: Palgrave Macmillan.

Sen, Amartya, 1992. *Inequality Re-Examined.* Oxford: Clarendon Press.

Sen, Amartya. 2005. "Mary, Mary, Quite Contrary!" *Feminist Economics* 11(1): 1–9.

Shaw, George Bernard. 2004. *Pygmalion and Three Other Plays.* New York, NY: Barnes and Nobles.

Shōnagon, Sei. 1991. *The Pillow Book.* Translated and edited by Ivan Morris. New York, NY: Columbia University Press.

Sinclair, A. 2019. "Insinuatio in Lucrezia Marinella's *Essortationi alle donne* (1645): Exhorting Marital Harmony and Insinuating Feminist Critique," *Renaissance Studies* 34(3): 430–446.

Snively, Samantha. 2015. " 'The Quintessence of Wit': Domestic Labor, Science, and Margaret Cavendish's Kitchen Fancies." In *Newberry Essays in Medieval and Early Modern Studies, Vol. 9, Selected Proceedings of the Newberry Center for Renaissance Studies. Multidisciplinary Graduate Student Conference,* 21–28. Chicago, IL: The Newberry Library.

Solometo, J. and Moss, J. 2013. "Picturing the Past: Gender in National Geographic Reconstructions of Prehistoric Life," *American Antiquity* 78(1): 123–146.

Stanton, Elizabeth Cady, Gage, Matilda Joslyn, and Anthony, Susan B. 1889. *History of Woman Suffrage.* Rochester, NY: Charles Mann.

Still, William. 1886. *The Underground Railroad,* Revised Edition. Philadelphia, PA: William Still Publisher.

Trizio, M. 2021. "Eustratius of Nicaea and the Nicomachean Ethics in Twelfth-Century Constantinople: Literary Criticism, Patronage and the Construction of the Byzantine Commentary Tradition." In *The Reception of Greek Ethics in Late Antiquity and Byzantium,* edited by S. Xenophontos and A. Marmodoro, 193–211. Cambridge: Cambridge University Press.

Trouille, Mary Seidman. 1991. "The Failings of Rousseau's Ideals of Domesticity and Sensibility," *Eighteenth-Century Studies* 24(4): 451–483.

Trouille, Mary Seidman. 1997. *Sexual Politics in the Enlightenment: Women Writers Read Rousseau.* Albany, NY: SUNY Press.

Trueblood, Alan S. 1988. *A Sor Juana Anthology.* Cambridge, MA: Harvard University Press.

Truth, Sojourner and Olive Gilbert. 1875. *Narrative of Sojourner Truth: A Bondswoman of Olden Time.* Boston, MA: Published for the Author.

Valente, Marcello. 2011. *Aristotele, Economici. Introduzione, testo rivisto, traduzione e commento.* Alessandria: Edizioni dell'Orso.

Vickery, A. 1993. "Golden Age to Separate Spheres? A Review of the Categories and Chronology of English Women's History," *The Historical Journal* 36(2): 383–414.

Waithe, Mary Ellen. 1987. *A History of Women Philosophers, Vol. 1.* New York, NY: Springer.

Wallengren-Lynch, M., Dominelli, L., and Cuadra, C. 2023. "Working and Learning from Home During COVID-19: International Experiences Among Social Work Educators and Students," *International Social Work* 66(4): 1045–1048. doi: 10.1177/00208728211051412.

Ward, Ann. 2008. "Mothering and the Sacrifice of Self: Women and Friendship in Aristotle's Nicomachean Ethics," *Third Space: A Journal of Feminist Theory and Culture* 7(2): 32–57.

Weiss, Penny. 1987. "Rousseau, Antifeminism and Woman's Nature," *Political Theory* 15(1): 81–98.

Weiss, Penny. 2008. "Sei Shônagon and the Politics of Form," *Journal of Political Philosophy* 16(1): 26–47.

Welter, Barbara. 1966. "The Cult of True Womanhood: 1820–1860," *American Quarterly* 18(2): 151–74.

Widerquist, Karl and McCall, Grant S. 2017. *Prehistoric Myths in Modern Political Philosophy.* Edingburgh: Edinburgh University Press.

Wilder, Laura Ingalls. 2007. "The Farm Home." In *Laura Ingalls Wilder, Farm Journalist: Writings from the Ozarks*, edited by S. W. Hines, 181–183. Jackson, MS: University of Missouri Press.

Wilkins, Emma. 2014. "Margaret Cavendish and the Royal Society," *Notes and Records* 68: 245–260.

Willard, Charity. 1984. "The Franco-Italian Professional Writer: Christine de Pizan." In *Medieval Woman Writers*, edited by K. M. Wilson, 333–361. Athens, GA: University of Georgia Press.

Wollstonecraft, Mary. 1975. *Maria or the Wrongs of Woman.* New York, NY: Norton.

Wollstonecraft, Mary. 1993. "An Historical View of the French Revolution." In *A Vindication of the Rights of Men and A Vindication of the Rights of Woman*, edited by Janet Todd. Oxford: Oxford University Press.

Wollstonecraft, Mary. 2003. *The Collected Letters.* Edited by Janet Todd. New York, NY: Columbia University Press.

Wollstonecraft, Mary. 2014. *A Vindication of the Rights of Woman*, edited and with an introduction by Eileen Hunt Botting. New Haven, CT: Yale University Press, p. 21.

Index

For the benefit of digital users, indexed terms that span two pages (e.g., 52–53) may, on occasion, appear on only one of those pages.

angel of the house, 14–15, 110–11, 112–13, 116–17, 124, 129, 137, 141, 148–49
anthropology, 10–11
architecture, 123, 127
Aristotle, 13–14, 19, 21–25, 26, 27–28, 35–37, 49, 57–58, 68–69
Aspasia of Miletus, 17
Astell, Mary, 74, 75–82, 83, 161–62

bathroom, 5, 62–63, 127–28, 174–75
Baumfree, Isabella. See Truth, Sojourner
Beauvoir, Simone de, 10–12, 37–38, 54–55, 130–31, 156–60, 170–71
Beecher, Catharine, 14–15, 114, 116–26, 140, 145–46, 148–49
Black Gift thesis, 147–48
Brissot, Jacques-Pierre, 102, 106, 108
budget, 18–19, 161

care-bots, 165–68. See also robots
Cavendish, Margaret, 13–14, 61, 62–68, 174
child garden, 132, 133
childcare, 12, 159–60, 162–63, 164
children, 17–19, 25–26, 30, 54–55, 60, 63, 71, 74, 75, 79–81, 87–88, 89, 103, 125, 127, 132–33, 144, 147, 148–49, 151–52, 153–54, 158
Christianity, 36–37, 52–53, 56, 76, 79, 115–16, 151
citizenship, 29–30, 87, 89–90, 94, 101, 103, 110–11, 115, 160
city, 21–25, 44–45, 46–47, 58–59, 60, 97, 171
Coccia, Emanuele, 5, 7–8
comfort, vii, 11, 16, 18–19, 37–38, 39–40, 50, 56, 109, 126, 128, 133, 137, 164–65
communal life, 21, 71, 108–9, 112–13, 158, 166
convent, 33–35, 36–38, 41–42, 55–56, 69–73, 78, 171–72
cooking, 56, 62–69, 120, 123, 125, 127–28, 129–32
Cooper, Anna Julia, 144–50
Cornelia, 100–1

Covid, CP, 6, 7–8, 160–61
Cowan paradox, 166
Cruz, Sor Juana de la, 68–73, 171–72
cult of domesticity, 113, 142–43
cult of real or true womanhood, 112, 121–22, 124, 149

Dalassene, Anna, 33, 38–39, 40
Descartes, René, 7, 62, 75
diet, 124–25, 130–31
difference feminism, 121
divine economy, 114, 115
division of labor, 9–10, 46
domestic arts or crafts, 57–58, 63, 73, 121–22
domestic duties, 79–80, 84, 88, 98–100, 101–2, 145–46, 147, 156–58
domestic economy, 118–19
domestic science, 14–15, 117–21, 122
domestic sphere, 20, 172
domestic virtue, 28–29, 86, 98, 148–49
Douglass, Frederick, 146–47, 150–51, 153, 174
Du Bois, WEB, 147–48
Duchess of Mazarin. See Hortence Mancini

education, 14–15, 37, 60, 62–63, 72–73, 75, 76, 79–80, 87–88, 95, 99, 106, 109, 117, 121, 124–25, 133, 136, 140, 144–45, 148–49, 150
emancipation, 2, 108, 112–13, 134, 141, 151, 153
enslaved, 15, 75, 80–82, 85, 91, 107–8, 112–13, 131–32, 137–38, 141, 150, 151, 153–54, 171–72, 174
Existentialism, 6, 10, 159
exploitation, 84, 164, 165

family resemblance, 4–5, 7–8
Federici, Silvia, 163, 164, 165, 167
fifteenth amendment, 146–47
Forten, Charlotte, 114, 144–45
freedom, 9–10, 12–15, 19, 50, 70, 75, 78, 81, 83, 91–93, 104, 129, 130–31, 136, 142, 150, 153, 161, 162, 170–71, 172

French Revolution, 14, 20, 39–40, 93, 94–
  111, 144–45
Friedan, Betty, 16, 131, 156–60

garden, 41–42, 50, 90–91, 127, 170
Gilbert, Olive, 151–52, 154
Gilman, Charlotte Perkins, 6, 14–15, 121–35,
  154–55, 167, 172
Girondins, 39–40, 95–96
Global south, 84
Gouges, Olympe de, 104–11, 121
Grimke, Angelina, 14–15, 112–17, 118, 120

happiness, 21–22, 24, 58, 79, 82, 91, 96–97, 98,
  129, 147, 151–52, 160–61, 162
Harper, Frances, 15, 121, 138–44, 150, 154, 174
Hierocles, 25, 26–28
Hobbes, 10–11, 62
household, 8–10, 21, 22–25, 30–31, 37–38, 46–
  47, 52, 60, 66–67, 89, 97, 156, 158, 159–60
household management, 19–20, 22, 26–27, 37–
  38, 41–43, 68–69, 94, 118–19, 123, 125, 132,
  160–61, 162–63, 165–66
housewife, 19, 30, 31, 46, 52–53, 62–63, 95, 97,
  99, 103–4, 110–11, 120, 168–71
housewifery, 61, 65–66, 99. See also huswifery
human development, 19–20, 80
human flourishing, 15, 21, 22, 23, 121–22, 125,
  126, 133, 154
huswifery, 61, 64. See also housewifery

income, 76–77, 78, 88–89, 164
independence – financial, 88, 165

Jacobs, Harriet, 15, 150–51, 153–55
Joan of Arc, 40–41, 43, 46–48

Keralio Robert, Louise, 100–4, 108–9, 110–11
kitchen, 11–12, 54–55, 64, 66–69, 127–28, 129–
  32, 137, 166, 167, 170
Kiyora no Nagiko. See Shonagon Sei
Komnene, Anna, 33–40, 48, 55–56, 69–70
KonMari method, 46

laundry, 54–55, 99, 124, 127–29, 130, 131–32,
  137, 165–66
letters, 28–29, 30, 31, 50, 58, 96, 99–100, 105
Lorde, Audre, 136
Lucretia, 100–1, 138

Macaulay, Catharine, 98
Mancini, Hortence, 74, 75–82
manners, 87–88, 116

Mansfield, Katherine, 55, 156, 157
Marinella, Lucrezia, 56–61, 63, 73, 161–62, 171

motherhood, 10, 89, 90, 94, 95, 134, 147, 152,
  157, 158, 159
Musonius Rufus, 25–27
My Fair Lady, 1
myths, 20, 28, 123–24, 125–26, 129

neo-Pythagorean women, 19, 28–30
neo-Pythagoreanism, 21, 25, 28, 31
nurse, 67–68, 167–68

Oikos, 22
Ozeki, Ruth, 169–70, 171

palace, 32, 34, 37–38, 48–53, 70
patriarchy, 32, 52–53, 136, 160, 165
Pericles, 17–18
Perictione, 28–30
Pizan, Christine, 40–48, 54–56, 72, 79–80, 121
plantation, 15, 91, 113, 137
platform, 2, 48, 96, 136, 138–39
Plato, 17–18, 19–20, 28–30, 49, 57–58, 75
Plutarch, 96–97, 100–1
polis, 22, 42–43
political association, 22–23
Prince, Mary, 91–93, 131–32, 174
profession, 78, 88, 90, 119, 130
progress, 2, 14–15, 108, 112–13, 118, 120, 123–
  26, 128, 134, 136–37, 138, 143–44, 145–46,
  147–48, 154–55
public life, 22–23, 26, 32, 48, 58, 83, 159–60
Pygmalion, 1, 2. See also My Fair Lady

Quakers, 114

race, 134–35, 138–39, 142, 146–47, 148, 149
racism, 122, 136, 139, 140, 160
reform, 14–15, 27–28, 78, 83, 93, 94, 101–2,
  103, 108, 114, 120, 122–23, 128, 130–31,
  141–42, 154–55
republicanism, 81, 94, 96, 100–4, 109–11
reputation, 17–18, 49–50, 56–57, 76–77
robots domestic. See care-bots
Roland, Marie-Jeanne, 39–40, 94–100, 102,
  104, 108–9
Rousseau, Jean-Jacques, 10–11, 86–87, 88, 94

salon, 34–35, 39–40, 76–77, 100, 103–4, 105–6,
  110–11
Sanderg Sheryl, 159–60
Sartre, 157–58, 159

second shift, 12, 160–61, 162–63, 164–65
servants, 7–8, 51, 56, 64, 77, 99, 103–4, 126, 130,
    132, 137, 154
sexism, 25, 28, 35–36, 44–45, 58, 104–5, 160
Shonagon Sei, 48–53, 156–57, 171–72
slavery, 15, 81–82, 91–93, 108–9, 113–14,
    115–16, 141–42, 144–46, 151, 153–54,
    161–62
slaves, 21, 22–23, 80–81, 93. See also enslaved
Socrates, 4, 17–19, 156–57
Stanton Elizabeth Cady, 138, 140, 146–47, 150
State-of-nature, 10–11
stoicism, 19, 25–28, 29–30
Stowe, Harriet Beecher, 117, 122
submissiveness, 79, 116–17, 118, 165

Talleyrand, 82–83, 88
technology domestic, 166–68. See also robots

temperance, 142, 144
Terror, the, 95–96, 105–6, 108–9, 112
Theano, 28–29, 30–31
tradwife, 113, 160–62, 165
Truth, Sojourner, 121, 137, 146–55

vote, 108, 140–42, 146–47, 150

wages for housework, 163, 164, 167
Wells, Ida B, 144–45
wetnurse, 87–88, 89, 95
widowhood, 40–41, 43, 99, 104, 174
Wilder, Laura Ingalls, 140–41
Wollstonecraft, Mary, 62, 74, 82–91, 95, 118,
    133, 156–57
women's quarter, 38–40

Xanthippe, 17–19, 156–57